THE LONG SUMMER

THE LONG SUMMER

HOW CLIMATE CHANGED CIVILIZATION

BRIAN FAGAN

BASIC
BOOKS
A Member of the Perseus Books Group
New York

Published by Basic Books,
A Member of the Perseus Books Group

Hardcover edition first published in 2004
Paperback edition first published in 2005

Books published by Basic Books are available at special discounts for bulk purchases
in the United States by corporations, institutions, and other organizations. For more
information, please contact the Special Markets Department at the Perseus Books
Group, 11 Cambridge Center, Cambridge MA 02142, or call (617) 252–5298,
(800) 255–1514 or e-mail special.markets@perseusbooks.com.

The Library of Congress has cataloged the hardcover edition as follows:

Fagan, Brian M.
    The long summer : how climate changed civilization / Brian Fagan.
       p.   cm.
    Includes bibliographical references and index.
    ISBN-10 0-465-02281-2 (hardcover)
    ISBN-13 978-0-465-02281-6 (hardcover)
    1. Climatic changes—Environmental aspects.   2. Civilization—History.   I. Title.
QC981.8.C5F34 2003
551.6—dc22

                                                                          2003013917

ISBN-10 0-465-02282-0 (paperback)
ISBN-13 978-0-465-02282-3 (paperback)

        DHSB   09   10   9   8   7

To Anastasia
With love
Please—the cat's name is Copernicus, not Duane!
And archaeology? Blah . . . Bblah . . . Bblah

Seas move within the deep sea, some to sunrises, others to sunsets;
Waves on the surface aspire to noon, waves below to midnight:
Many are the streams flowing in the darkling deep
And underwater rivers rolling in the purple ocean.

Vyacheslav Ivanov, *Melampus's Dream*, 1907

Contents

PART III: THE DISTANCE BETWEEN GOOD AND BAD FORTUNE

PREFACE

With that he rammed the clouds together—both hands
clutching his trident—churned the waves into chaos, whipping
all the gales from every quarter, shrouding over in thunderheads
the earth and sea at once—and night swept down from the sky—
East and South Winds clashed and the raging West and North,
sprung from the heavens, roiled breakers heaving up.

Homer, *Odyssey*, Book V (trans. Fagles, 1996: 161)

My first introduction to ancient climate came in a freshman course on archaeology taught by a venerable lecturer who had last been in the field sometime before World War I and whose ideas had changed little since. He described the classic fieldwork of Austrian geologists Albrecht Penck and Eduard Brückner, whose 1909 masterpiece *Die Alpen im Eiszeitalter* identified at least four great glacial episodes in the Alps. Then he summarized the Great Ice Age in graphic terms, pacing backward and forward across the lecture hall floor to represent the advancing and retreating ice sheets. "Gunz," he announced as he strode forward, identifying the earliest glaciation of all. He moved back, signaling a warm interglacial period. The backward and forward movements continued, "Mindel," "Riss," and finally "Wurm": the four glaciations defined a monolithic Ice Age, the background for most human history. And after the Ice Age there was warming, a time when England, to its everlasting glory, separated from the continent as sea levels rose, and when forests spread across Europe. To a neophyte archaeologist of the late 1950s, the Ice Age seemed a remote, simple phenomenon of long-lasting climatic extremes. And when it ended, humans found themselves adapting easily to a near-modern climate.

Would that the Ice Age were that simple! Today, we know that our ancestors lived through at least nine long glacial episodes over the past
780,000 years, separated by much shorter warm intervals. For three quarters of this time, the world's climate was in transition from cold to warm
and back again. Our knowledge of this complex seesaw comes from new
generations of research using deep sea cores bored into the depths of the
Caribbean and Pacific, from cores drilled into Antarctica, into the Greenland ice sheet, and into high-altitude glaciers in the Andes. The Vostok
ice core from Antarctica tells the story for the past 420,000 years—four
glacial episodes, separated by shorter warmer periods, each about
100,000 years apart. A exceptionally fine-grained deep-sea core from the
Carioco Basin in the southeastern Caribbean off Venezuela reveals the fifteen millennia since the last Ice Age as a jagged to-and-fro of sharp
changes, of drier and warmer periods, caused in part by north and south
movements of the Intertropical Convergence Zone by the Equator. For
all these rapid shifts, the Vostok core shows that the past 15,000 years, a
time of prolonged global warming, have been the most climatically stable
of the past four hundred.

Utter the words "global warming" and you invite immediate controversy as to whether we humans have contributed to rising temperatures
on earth. Some argue that the current warm-up is part of the endless natural cycle of global climate change. But most scientists are certain that an-
thropogenic global warming is a reality. I believe that the past 150 years
of global warming, longer than any such period over the past thousand
years, have unfolded in part because of our own actions. Promiscuous
land clearance, industrial-scale agriculture, and use of coal, oil, and other
fossil fuels have raised greenhouse gas levels in the atmosphere to record
highs and contributed to the warming. In an era so warm that the sea
level has risen in Fiji an average of fifteen centimeters a year over the past
nine decades, and brush fires consumed over 500,000 hectares of
drought-plagued Mexican forest in 1998 and more in Australia in 2002,
the climatic gyrations of the past 15,000 years seem remote indeed. But
the revolution in climatology during the past quarter century provides us,
for the first time, with a historical context in which to understand the unprecedented global warming of today, as we try to anticipate an uncertain
climatic future.

Reconstructing the climate changes of the past is a difficult task, because reliable instrument records are but a few centuries old, and even these exist only in Europe and North America. Those for other parts of the world go back barely a century. While you can place limited reliance on contemporary observations of monks, country parsons, and even ancient Assyrian scribes, our knowledge of climatic changes over the past fifteen millennia comes entirely from what are called proxy records reconstructed from tree rings, minute pollen grains from ancient marshes and swamps, and deep cores from glaciers, lake beds, and ocean floors. Until recently, such records were imprecise at best, and of limited use for assessing the impact of even long-term climatic change on human life. A generation ago, the climatologist worked with a handful of tree ring sequences, a smattering of pollen diagrams recording vegetational change at widely separated locations, and a plethora of observations from glacial deposits and river gravels. Now this scattered record has become an intricate tapestry of shifts and climatic events on every time scale, woven together from an astounding variety of sources. For the first time, we have a climate record of civilization, and we can attempt an assessment of the impact of these climatic shifts on the long sweep of human history.

To what extent *did* these events shape the course of Stone Age life, early farming societies, and civilizations? Many archaeologists are suspicious of the role of climatic change in transforming human societies, and with good reason. Environmental determinism, the notion that climate change was the primary cause of major developments such as agriculture or civilization, has been a dirty word in academia for generations. You certainly cannot argue that climate *drove* history in a direct and causative way to the point of forcing major innovations or toppling entire civilizations. Nor, however, can one contend as many scholars once did that climate change is something that can be ignored. The dynamics of subsistence agriculture compel our attention. Ever since the beginnings of farming some 12,000 years ago, people have lived at the mercy of cycles of cooler and wetter, warmer and drier climate. Their survival depended on crop yields and on having enough seed to plant for the next year. Even a short drought or a series of heavy rainstorms could make the difference between hunger and plenty. The sufficiency or insufficiency of food, whether confined to a single valley or affecting an entire region, was a powerful motivator of human action, with consequences that could take decades or even centuries to unfold. In today's world, where over 200 million people cultivate and herd their animals on marginal lands, the same verities apply. Climate is, and always has been, a powerful catalyst in human history, a pebble cast in a pond whose ripples triggered all manner of economic, political, and social changes.

In this book, I argue that human relationships to the natural environment and short-term climatic change have always been in flux. To ignore climate is to neglect one of the dynamic backdrops of the human experience. The past 15,000 years provide many instances of climate change as a major historical player: the great droughts in southwestern Asia that precipitated experiments in cultivating wild grasses, the progressive drying of the Sahara that brought cattle people to the Nile Valley with their distinctive ideas of leadership, and the ripple effects of the Medieval Warm Period that had very different impacts in Europe and the Americas—to mention only a few.

I also argue that humanity has become more and more vulnerable to long- and short-term climate change, as it has become ever more difficult and expensive for us to respond to it. For tens of thousands of years, human populations were miniscule and everyone lived from hunting and the gathering of plant foods. Survival depended on mobility and opportunism, on a flexibility of daily existence that allowed people to roll with the climatic punches—by moving away, hiving off families into new territories, or falling back on a cushion of less desirable foods. Around 10,000 B.C., when farming began, anchoring permanent villages to their fields, the options afforded by mobility began to close. More people to feed, denser village populations: the risks were higher, especially when communities expanded to the limits of their land or when their herds overgrazed the landscape. The only solution was to move, which was easy enough when there was plenty of uncleared forest and fertile soil and no neighbors. In more crowded landscapes, where people had already cultivated the landscape where wild plants once grew, hunger and death were inevitable.

The stakes rose even higher when farmers came to depend on river floods and irregular rainfall, on irrigation systems that brought life-giving water to otherwise uncultivable land. The Mesopotamian solution was the city, located close to strategic irrigation canals that drew water from the Tigris or Euphrates rivers, but even that response was inadequate in the face of extreme El Niño events and southward shifts of the Intertropical Convergence Zone. At first people depended on neighbors and fellow kin; then officials reduced ration issues; soon people began dying, and law and order broke down as starving townspeople fanned out into the hinterland in search of food. Humanity had stepped over a threshold of vulnerability into a world where the costs of rolling with climatic shifts were infinitely higher.

With population growth, urbanization, and the global spread of the Industrial Revolution, this vulnerability has only increased. Over twenty million tropical farmers perished from drought-related problems during the nineteenth century. Today, in a much more heavily populated and warmer world, the potential for disaster is open-ended. Hundred-year El Niño rains inundate Peruvian coastal valleys and wash away entire urban precincts in a few hours. Cyclones and hurricanes cause billions of dollars' worth of damage as they sweep ashore in Bangladesh and Florida. A record flood of the Mississippi River, accentuated by urbanization and other environmental interference, threatens massive flood control works. The list of lurking catastrophes is far longer than in earlier times.

What's happened? Haven't modern shipping, modern agriculture, and modern industry given us a buffer of safety? Is it only that with more people and cash in the world than ever before, the losses from natural disasters will inevitably yield unprecedented numbers? No: a look at the interaction of climate and history over the past 15,000 years reveals another process at work more or less continuously over that span. In our efforts to cushion ourselves against smaller, more frequent climate stresses, we have consistently made ourselves more vulnerable to rarer but larger catastrophes. The whole course of civilization (while it is many other things, too, of course) may be seen as a process of trading up on the scale of vulnerability.

Looked at in this light, the present problem of global warming is neither proof of late capitalism's intent to commit industrial-strength sins against Mother Earth nor a hallucination imposed on the world by anti-business activists. It is simply a reflection of the scale of our vulnerability, the scale on which we must now think and act. The times require us to learn the vagaries of the global climate, to study its moods, and to keep

our skies relatively clear of excessive greenhouse gases with the same dili-
gence, and for the same reasons, that Mesopotamian farmers five millennia ago had to learn the moods of the Euphrates and keep their irrigation
canals reasonably free of silt. If they didn't, the gods grew angry. Or, to
put it in more modern terms, sooner or later they got unlucky, and their
silted-up ditches brought crop failure, humiliation, or disaster.

In fact, sooner or later they got unlucky anyway, and were forced to
adapt yet again. This book is the story of those adaptations, one built
upon another, in an spiral of climate change and human response that
continues today.

Author's Note

Some arbitrary decisions about conventions and usages were made while writing this book, as follows:

All measurements in this book are given in metric units, as this is international scientific convention.

Place names are spelled according to the most common usage. Archaeological sites and historical places are spelled as they appear most commonly in the sources used to write this book.

All radiocarbon dates have been calibrated using the tables in the journal *Radiocarbon* for 1998. More controversially, dates earlier than about 9300 B.C. are calibrated using Barbados coral growth rings, as opposed to the tree rings employed for later carbon dates. After extended discussion with more knowledgeable archaeological colleagues, I decided that it was worth adopting these calibrations—which, however, have the effect of pushing the dates of some key developments (like the origins of agriculture) a thousand years further into the past. The earlier dates used here have no effect on the central arguments of the book. It should be stressed that calibrations before 7000 B.C. are subject to future modification by new research and are, at best, provisional.

The A.D./B.C. nomenclature is used for dates later than 15,000 years ago (B.P.). "Present" is internationally accepted as A.D. 1950.

For the purposes of this book, the terms "hunter-gatherer" and "forager" are interchangeable.

THE LONG SUMMER

I

THE THRESHOLD
OF VULNERABILITY

> One who knows the Mississippi will promptly aver—not
> aloud but to himself—that ten thousand River Commis-
> sions . . . cannot tame that lawless stream, cannot curb it,
> or confine it, cannot say to it, "Go here," or "Go there";
> and cannot make it obey . . . cannot bar its path with an
> obstruction which it will not tear down, dance over, and
> laugh at.
>
> Mark Twain, *Life on the Mississippi,* 1879

A wind of Force 9 is a strong gale and it makes a sailboat's rigging
shriek unrelentingly. I huddled in the shelter of the cabin house, bracing
my feet against the cockpit seat, safety line securely fastened. We lay hove-
to in the Bay of Biscay under heavily reefed mainsail and a tiny storm jib,
and had been so for twenty-four hours, our small boat rising and falling effortlessly in the mountainous swells. Heavy rain mixed with spume drove
horizontally across the deck—the only solid feature of a gray world where
sea and sky had become one. Life was comfortable enough under the circumstances. The southwest wind was driving us away from the north
Spanish coast. We had plenty of sea room to drift and the rough seas were
not a threat as we rose and fell like a cork. There were only passing ships to
worry about. They sailed southward toward Spain in a steady stream,
pounding their way into the storm—supertankers from Rotterdam, huge

boxlike container ships, natural-gas carriers. I watched a large tanker smashing into the steep-faced waves, seemingly without effort. Cascades of spray burst high above its plunging bow. The monster rode high, barely acknowledging the storm, empty and seemingly invincible.

A howling gust thrummed through our stays and the boat heeled sharply. I ducked while spray rattled like shotgun pellets on my back. The tanker vanished momentarily in the gloom; then a sudden ray of sunlight made the long black hull glisten as the hulking ship shrugged the squall aside. For a cruising boat like ours, twelve meters long from stem to stern, the Bay of Biscay is a dangerous place: as the force of the North Atlantic rolls up onto Europe's continental shelf, sudden storms and steep-faced waves can spring up out of nowhere. We would remain hove-to, surviving easily but otherwise helpless, for another half day.

A long sea watch gives the mind plenty of time to wander. As the great ship passed effortlessly over the horizon, I mentally followed its voyage— southward past Cape Finisterre and the edge of Europe, round the bulge of Morocco and Senegal, then far southward to the southern tip of Africa. The Cape of Good Hope in midwinter is a stormy place where 25-meter waves are not unknown—walls of water so steep and powerful that they have cracked supertanker hulls like eggshells. If it suffered engine break-down or electrical failure, the enormous vessel would drift helplessly downwind, heeling sharply to the gale, great waves crashing into its cliff-like flanks. Unless deep-sea tugs could take it in tow or, miracle of mira-cles, the ship's engineer could bring the engine to life, the leviathan would crash into the rugged South African cliffs, even break asunder, its hull fa-tally weakened from flexing in the waves. In those conditions, our small boat's chances would be better than the tanker's. The massive waves that destroyed the tanker would pass beneath us with less effect than these nine-meter ones. Survival is often a matter of scale.

⚬⚬⚬

As with ships, so with civilizations.

Ur lies about halfway between Baghdad and the head of the Persian Gulf, about 24 kilometers west of the modern course of the Euphrates

River.[1] The once-great city stands amid a landscape of desolation—an assemblage of mounds. One of them, Tell el Muqayyar, the Hill of Pitch, was one of the greatest shrines in ancient Mesopotamia. Climb the restored ziggurat (temple mound) and you can see the distant palm trees lining the banks of the Euphrates to the east. Elsewhere, you gaze over a wilderness of sand that stretches to the flat horizon. (I visited the place before Saddam Hussein built an air base nearby.) To the southwest, a distant gray pinnacle is all that remains of the ziggurat that once towered over Eridu, which the Sumerians believed to be the oldest city on earth. They were not far wrong.

The British archaeologist Leonard Woolley once wrote of this landscape that "nothing relieves the monotony of the vast plain over which the shimmering heat-waves dance and the mirage spreads its mockery of placid waters."[2] It's hard to believe that this harshest of deserts supported one of the world's earliest civilizations.

In 2300 B.C., a Sumerian ruler named Ur-Nammu founded the Third Dynasty of Ur's royal house. Ur was already an ancient city, occupied for over ten centuries, a place of worship and commerce nearly as old as civilization itself. The four generations of the Third Dynasty presided over far more than a city-state. Ur-Nammu had begun his reign as a vassal of an even more ancient city, Uruk, but rebelled against his masters and set up his own kingdom by diplomacy and conquest. Soon he and his successors presided over a powerful domain whose influence extended far across the Syrian desert to eastern Mediterranean lands. They girded their city with a mud-brick fortification 23 meters thick at the base and up to 8 meters high. Inside they erected a huge ziggurat with sloping sides, what Leonard Woolley called "a mountain of God," 21 meters high with a base measuring 46 by 61 meters, a mass of solid brickwork faced with fired brick walls 2.4 meters thick set in bitumen. A small shrine to Ur's patron, the moon god Nannar, stood at the summit. Hanging greenery covered the ziggurat's terraces like shaggy mountain growth; at its base, the lavish temple complex included a sanctuary and a great paved court surrounded by offices and storerooms.

A limestone stela found in the complex commemorates Ur-Nammu's pious deeds and his conquests. One scene depicts the standing king in an attitude of prayer, while an angel-like being, flying down from above, pours water onto the ground from a vase. An inscription lists the canals near Ur dug by the orders of the king. Ur-Nammu is given credit for the irrigation ditches, but he praises the gods for the gift of water that brings fertility to the land. In Sumerian belief, the ruler was Nannar, the patron god's representative on earth, the tenant farmer as it were, and the god was the true ruler of the land. The huge farm that was Ur needed constant care and attention in a demanding environment.

The Sacred Precinct embraced the royal quarters and served as the setting for great public rituals and processions honoring the gods. Outside its walls lay the crowded city neighborhoods, accumulations of mud-brick houses built, occupied, then rebuilt in an endless palimpsest of urban renewal. By Ur-Nammu's time, the neighborhoods stood on terraced mounds of compacted debris. Separating the crowded dwellings were narrow, winding, unpaved alleyways, too constricted for carts but wide enough for pedestrians and the ubiquitous donkeys to pass. The daily traffic of Ur ebbed and flowed—a high official surrounded by guards and scribes, women with brimming water pots, donkeys laden with sacks of grain braying loudly under their master's goad. The blank walls of the houses lined the streets, their corners rounded to prevent injury to riders or cargo. Leonard Woolley excavated some of these dwellings, with their central courts and two-story chambers. Ur-Nammu's Ur was a crowded city with shaded streets and bazaars, and separate quarters for potters, metalsmiths, and other artisans. During the hot months, cloths suspended across the alleyways gave protection from the blazing sun. The air carried the scent of wood smoke and animal droppings. More than five thousand people dwelled in the shade of the ziggurat, in what at the time was one of the largest human communities the world had yet seen.

Ur's lords were the most powerful on earth, rivaled only by the Egyptian pharaohs. Their hegemony extended (at least nominally) over much of southern Mesopotamia and upstream. They presided over a place of religious pilgrimage and a mecca for donkey caravans and ships from distant lands. Canals connected Ur to the Euphrates and thence to the Persian Gulf. In its magnificent heyday, the ancient city stood amid a patchwork of canals and green fields carved out of the desert and nourished by the floodwaters of the great river. Everything and everybody depended on water and control of water, the only commodity that could nourish life in the midst of a desert where rainfall rarely exceeded 200 millimeters a year.

I am always struck by the great continuity of life at Ur. Like Eridu and other southern cities, Ur had begun as a small farming community. The first such villages appeared near Ur as early as 6000 B.C., a time of good rainfall and high floods.[3] They were little more than tiny hamlets of reed huts clustered near small irrigation canals. Each spring, bare-footed farmers would wade into the muddy silt and scoop it out to make way for the summer's floodwaters. The villages' simple irrigation worked well. Centuries of abundant river water and rainfall fostered bumper crops and growing populations. The settlements grew into rapidly expanding towns, each within its own irrigated lands. There was plenty of land and water to go around. Even a small town could easily survive a few bad years.

Then, in about 3800 B.C., the Indian Ocean monsoon track shifted southward and the rainfall pattern changed. Now the winter rains started later and ended earlier, so the farmers had to rely on river water alone for their growing crops as they reached maturity. Now the river floods arrived after the crops were harvested, which meant that agriculture depended on a much-reduced water flow.[4]

One can imagine the confusion when the rains failed and the crops dried up in the fields. The villagers harvested their stunted crops, only to watch their canals brim with floodwater a few weeks later when it was too late. Within a few years, they shifted the planting season so that their wheat and barley ripened as the Tigris and Euphrates filled their carefully prepared irrigation canals. At the same time, they made a sensible and strategic move into much larger towns and cities located close to where feeder canals could divert precious water into the surrounding desert. Growing cities like Ur became the nodal points of human life, sur-rounded by densely cultivated hinterlands and satellite communities that could extend as much as ten kilometers from the city walls. By 3100 B.C., southern Mesopotamia was a mosaic of intensely competitive city-states, each anchored to jealously guarded irrigation canals, in a world where water rights and irrigated land were the currency of peace and war. As the city became the means of survival, hyperurbanism ensued. Over 80 per-cent of all Sumerians lived in towns or cities by 2800 B.C.

The city, the hallmark of Mesopotamian civilization, cushioned people from the sharp shocks and unpredictable droughts orchestrated by angry gods. Here they propitiated the pantheon of hostile deities. Temple store-rooms burst with grain carefully inventoried against lean years, insurance against famine and the social disorder that inevitably walked in its train. Every month of the year, families worked the land, dug canals, dredged older cuttings, all against the few summer weeks when the river over-flowed. No one, whether monarch, merchant, or commoner, had any il-lusions about the threat of hunger. At least the city, with its shrines and storehouses, offered a degree of protection. During these centuries, Ur was a small ship, able to weather the commonest storms better then the tiny farming villages it had superseded.

In about 2200 B.C., a major volcanic eruption somewhere far to the north spewed enormous quantities of fine ash into the atmosphere. If historic eruptions are any yardstick, the debris veiled the sun for months on end, bringing unseasonal cold. Unfortunately for Ur's lords, the erup-tion coincided with the beginning of a 278-year drought cycle that af-fected huge areas of the eastern Mediterranean world and is clearly visible in ice cores from the Greenland ice sheet and the high Andes. With cata-strophic abruptness, the moist Mediterranean westerlies faltered. Winter rainfall plummeted. The Euphrates and Tigris floods, starved of rain and snowfall in the distant Anatolian highlands, failed as well.

The drought turned the once-fertile northern Habur plains by the Euphrates into a near desert.[5] For many centuries, Amorite herders had grazed their flocks over the open country where standing water abounded. Now they stayed close to the river and followed the water downstream into the farmlands of the south. Some nomads had always encroached on settled fields, but now their sheer numbers threatened to overwhelm the intensely cultivated hinterlands of the southern cities just as they were suffering from severe water shortages. Armies alone could not contain the intruders. Ur's ruler feverishly built a 180-kilometer mud-brick wall grandiloquently named the Repeller of Amorites. It too failed in its task. Within a few parched generations, Ur's population in-creased more than threefold. The farmers desperately straightened irriga-tion canals to increase the water flow to their fields. Cuneiform tablets tell us that the city authorities measured out grain rations in tablespoons. At first, people survived by relying on relatives for precious grain to supple-ment their measure allocations. Then they resorted to lawlessness and simply moved out into the countryside in a frantic search for sustenance. All to no avail: Ur's agricultural economy faltered, then collapsed. By 2000 B.C., fewer than 50 percent of Sumerians still lived in cities.

A century later, the rains improved, herders returned to the Habur, and new kingdoms rose from the chaos of Third Dynasty Ur. But Ur's sudden collapse was a turning point in human history: the first time an entire city disintegrated in the face of environmental catastrophe. The small but seaworthy ship had run into a storm violent enough to overwhelm it. Ur's population scattered into smaller communities, fled to higher ground, or simply perished as the apparatus of government evaporated within a few generations. When rainfall returned, it brought new cities, among them a less substantial Ur that was a shadow of itself. But humanity had crossed a threshold of environmental vulnerability. The intricate equation between urban population, readily accessible food supplies, and the economic, political, and social flexibility sufficient to roll with the climatic punches had been irrevocably altered.

Survival is often a matter of scale. A small Stone Age band could respond to a drought by moving to new hunting grounds and staying there for as long as necessary. A farming village could receive emergency grain from neighboring kin, or simply move to better-watered terrain known from trading connections. But a large city like Ur, beset with the ripple effects of a relentless drought, which brought unprecedented immigration and massive hunger, could not adjust or recover effortlessly, and collapsed. Having arisen as a successful defense against small catastrophes, the city found itself increasingly vulnerable to larger ones.

If Ur was a small trading ship, industrial civilization is a supertanker. The earliest cities were mere towns by today's standards, limited in area and with but a few thousand inhabitants. Ur was dwarfed even by later preindustrial cities: Teotihuacán, in highland Mexico, boasted some 200,000 citizens in A.D. 600. If Ur stretched the limits of vulnerability, consider just how much further Teotihuacán ventured before it too collapsed abruptly—again partly because of drought. Today, the scale of environmental vulnerability is much greater than we care to believe.

❦

French settlers founded New Orleans in 1718 on levees overlooking the Mississippi River.[6] The indigenous peoples had hunted and fished in the Mississippi delta for thousands of years, moving effortlessly to higher ground with each flood. The river meandered across the featureless silt of the delta, and people moved their dwellings with it. The French, however, made no allowance for the river and created a permanent settlement on natural levees, with no intention of moving. A great flood inundated the town's foundations within months, leading them to conclude that they would have to control the river's course. In 1724, a law required house owners to raise the foundations of their residences. The legislation had no effect, for the resulting dikes were only a meter high. Fortunately for New Orleans, there were no natural barriers on the far bank, so the Mississippi flowed outward without hindrance.

The city flooded again in 1735 and 1785, at intervals just long enough for the inhabitants to have forgotten what a high flood was like. By 1812, the artificial levees extended for more than 300 kilometers in some places and were designed mainly to protect plantation lands. The demand for sugar plantations was such that by 1828 the levees reached the head of the delta. Some plantation owners took the precaution of erecting their houses on the only available higher ground—Indian burial mounds. As the levee system became more extensive, the potential damage wrought by a breakthrough escalated sharply. A sudden break would cause what the local people called a "crevasse," a cascade like a bursting dam that swept all before it. By the mid-nineteenth century, many levees were two meters high, with every sign that future floods would be much higher.

The Mississippi feeds on water from far away—from New York, Montana, Canada, and vast regions downstream. The river basin, the third largest in the world after the Amazon and Congo basins, is shaped like a huge funnel covering all or parts of thirty-one states and two provinces, and drains 41 percent of the continental United States. In places, the stream in flood is over 160 kilometers wide and looks more like the open sea. It is as if an ocean were journeying to the Gulf of Mexico. Where the delta begins, at Old River, the water spreads out into a mosaic of bayous, marshes, and swamps that were once natural reservoirs for the rising flood. The Mississippi created most of Louisiana, not by remaining in one channel but by jumping from course to course over an arc more than 300 kilometers wide. The environmental writer John McPhee likens the river's behavior to "a pianist playing with one hand—frequently and radically changing course, surging over the left or the right bank to go off in utterly new directions."[7] The river always looks for the shortest route to the ocean, finds it, then builds up silt in the channel until, once every millennium or so, it spills to one side. This kind of shift mattered little to the mobile and semi-sedentary hunter-gatherers who camped along the Mississippi's banks. But it mattered a great deal after New Orleans rose in the delta, steamboats began to use the main channel for navigation, and the swamps were drained and turned into farmland. When levees broke, people perished—by the hundreds in the disastrous year of 1850, when thirty-two levees were breached. In 1879, the federal government formed the Mississippi River Commission, at a time when the main channel flowed higher than ever and earthen dams were shutting off major distributor channels of the river. Flood control along the Mississippi has been under the aegis of the Army Corps of Engineers ever since.

In 1882, the most destructive flood of the nineteenth century breached 280 levees. Floodwater spread out more than 110 kilometers. The main channel of the river seemed about to shift into the channel of the Atchafalaya, especially after the Corps cleared debris from the river. For generations, its leaders adhered to a policy of using levees to control the river, until the great flood of 1927 killed over 200 people and thousands of animals, and inundated 93,000 square kilometers of farms and towns.[8] By this time, the levees were six times higher than the old two-meter dikes and had succeeded only in turning the main channel into a huge aqueduct. Congress then passed the Flood Control Act of 1928, which appropriated funds for a vast, coordinated attempt to build river defenses, everything from levees to channel realignments, to spillways and gates that could be opened in times of remarkable floods. The defense work continued until the levees on either bank rivaled the Great Wall of China but were taller and thicker. Even these were insufficient, for industrial-scale modification of the landscape upstream—highway paving, parking lots, shopping centers, and housing developments—all added to the runoff and raised the height of even average floods. Above all, the Corps had to halt the inevitable shift of the Mississippi into the Atchafalaya, whose course was deepening yearly. Had they permitted the shift to occur, the state capital, Baton Rouge, would have ceased to exist, New Orleans would no longer be a port, and all the heavy industry clustered along the main channel would literally be left high and dry. Factories and refineries could not survive alongside a tidal creek. So the Corps blocked the old river meander that fed to the Atchafalaya with a huge dam and built a lock system to allow ships to descend as much as 10 meters and pass downstream at the critical point 480 kilometers upstream from the river mouth. Now the Corps controlled the river flow: it determined how much water flowed past New Orleans, how much went into the Atchafalaya, and how much flooded into the swamps.

Or did it? The battle to control the river never ceases, for a breach upstream is always possible and the awesome power of the flooding water can break out anywhere. For the moment, the Corps believes the river is contained. But given the right combination of heavy snow and much higher than average rainfall, there is a real chance that the Mississippi will follow its own will and shift course to the Atchafalaya, as it obviously wants to do. Once again, we have not erased our vulnerability but merely traded up in scale. In the case of Sumerian Ur, the largest conceivable flood would cost a few thousand lives. As soon as the waters receded, the survivors would set about replanting the fields and repairing the walls. Today, the fate of a city of a million people and many billions of dollars of infrastructure depends on our control of half a continent's worth of increasingly restless river water. New Orleans is safe against the flood that comes once every hundred years. As for the thousand-year flood or the ten-thousand-year one, we can only hope for the best.

This book is about this rising vulnerability. It is the 15,000-year story of how, time and again, humans reached a threshold in their relationship with unpredictable climate shifts and, without hesitation, crossed it.

PART ONE

PUMPS AND CONVEYOR BELTS

Each veil lifted revealed a multitude of others. They perceived a chain of interlocking and interdependent mysteries, the meteorological equivalent of DNA and the double helix.

Alexander Frater, *Chasing the Monsoon,* 1991

	Climate Events / Vegetation Zones	Human Events	Climate Triggers
9,000 B.C.	**Pre-Boreal** *(renewed warming)*	Farming spreads rapidly in southwestern Asia Abu Hureyra II and Jericho	Moister conditions *(circulation resumes)*
10,000 B.C.		Farming begins in southeastern Asia	Drought in southeastern Asia Cold in Europe
11,000 B.C.	**Younger Dryas** *(cold)* Lake Agassiz spills	Abu Hureyra I Clovis in North America	Atlantic circulation shuts down
12,000 B.C.		Monte Verde / Meadowcroft First settlement of the Americas Cave paintings at Niaux, France	Spread of forests in Europe
	Bolling / Allerod *(rapid warming)*		Rapid warming
13,000 B.C.	HEINRICH I EVENT ends	First settlement of northeastern Siberia	
14,000 B.C.		Final Ice Age cultures in Europe	Rapid sea level rise
15,000 B.C.	Some warming variable temperatures	Climatic amelioration in Eurasia	
		Cro-Magnons in Europe	Rapid retreat of ice sheets
16,000 B.C.	**Late Ice Age** *(cold)*		

Table I showing major climatological and historical events

2

THE LATE
ICE AGE ORCHESTRA
18,000 TO 13,500 B.C.

None of the dead can rise up and answer our questions. But from all that they have left behind, their imperishable or slowly dissolving gear, we may perhaps hear voices, "which are now only able to whisper, when everything else has become silent," to quote Linnaeus.

Björn Kurtén, *How to Deep-Freeze a Mammoth*, 1986

For those fortunate enough to have seen it in person, the scene is impossible to forget: on the rough walls of the Niaux cave in southern France, bison, mammoth, and reindeer swirl in the flickering light of an acetylene lantern. The paintings are a continuous palimpsest of bold images, one upon the other, with no regard for earlier paintings. In places, splayed hand impressions stand out, white fingers and palms outlined in red and black ocher blown onto the wall thousands of years ago.

The depth of time here is hard to grasp. These images were created over a span not of years or decades but of millennia. Some two hundred generations of Cro-Magnon hunters came here seeking power from the animal spirits residing within the rock.[1]

The great bestiary seems to move restlessly in the light, shimmering just as it did for the Cro-Magnons who glimpsed the paintings by the dim flickering of animal-fat lamps. Some of the paintings adorn chambers large enough to hold several dozen people. Others lurk in narrow defiles far from the open air, in places of utter darkness where shamans once lingered in solitary vision quests. Here below the earth, the worlds of the living and the dead, of humans and animals, met in a powerful symbolism never experienced aboveground.

These teeming images of animals, mysterious signs, and handprints were links to a supernatural realm of which we know almost nothing. Outside lay the harsh world of the late Ice Age, where temperatures hovered near freezing or below for much of the year. In the deep river valleys where the Cro-Magnons lived, tall pines stood motionless on the hillsides in the winter cold, the only sound the occasional thump of snow falling from a branch to the ground. On fine days, puffy clouds blew across the pale blue sky, pushed by bitterly cold north winds. But in the valleys the air was still, a light mist hovering above the valley floor where great drifts mantled the lush water meadows of summer.

If you looked closely on such a winter day, you might see a huge aurochs—the primordial wild ox—pawing the snow in search of dry grass among the dark trees. Or you might encounter two long-tusked mammoths standing motionless, their long hair resting on the snow, their breath appearing to freeze on the still air. On the coldest days, there would be little sign of humans, except perhaps for a thin tendril of white wood smoke rising from the foot of a cliff on the southern side of the valley. For all their sophisticated clothing and technology, even hunters would stay home through the bitter depths of Ice Age winters.

❧

The Cro-Magnon world of 18,000 years ago was unimaginably different from our own.[2] Each hunting band exploited the narrow compass of a well-defined territory. During the nine-month winters, the people lived in large caves and rock shelters in areas like the Vezère River valley in the Dordogne region of southwestern France, where they preyed on the animals large and small that lurked near home. Each spring, a flood of reindeer passed northward from sheltered river valleys and plains to the south. The stream of migrating beasts crowded through narrow gullies between steep slopes and by the hundreds crossed fast-running rapids. Weeks later, the herds spilled outward onto a completely different world—the vast, treeless plains that stretched from the Atlantic Ocean across Europe and into the remote vastnesses of Siberia.

This movement of reindeer—north when the warmth came, southward in the fall—was the pendulum of the seasons of the frozen European world. The steppe/tundra acted like a pump, sucking in reindeer and their predators in spring, pushing them out with the first frosts of fall. While their migration route might change considerably from year to year, the reindeer always came. And inevitably, human predators were waiting for them.

Like all successful hunters, the Cro-Magnons knew their territories intimately. They knew when berries were ripe and when wild grasses could be harvested. They could predict when the reindeer would come and how they would pass through the valleys. The hunters would track the approaching herds and lie in wait for them at river crossings and on either side of narrow defiles. They carried a light, highly efficient toolkit—wooden spears with sharp antler heads and barbed harpoon tips, also throwing sticks of antler or wood that would propel their spears with lightning accuracy.

Judging from modern-day caribou hunts, the Cro-Magnons would let the leaders of the herd pass through the water unharmed, then set upon the animals behind them, harvesting beast after beast with effortless skill. The animals would rear and whirl in panic, bellowing, their dead companions floating downstream where other members of the hunting band hauled the carcasses into the shallows. Many would escape to the far bank, to regroup and continue their inexorable march. But the hunters would cull dozens, even hundreds of beasts, butchering the carcasses with brisk efficiency on the riverbank. They would carry entire limbs or large portions of the bodies home, to be eaten or dismembered at leisure. As the men and women of the band butchered their haul, they dropped the cut and defleshed bones onto the dusty shelter floor, where they were soon buried under an accumulation of ash and occupation debris for archaeologists to find thousands of years later.

16

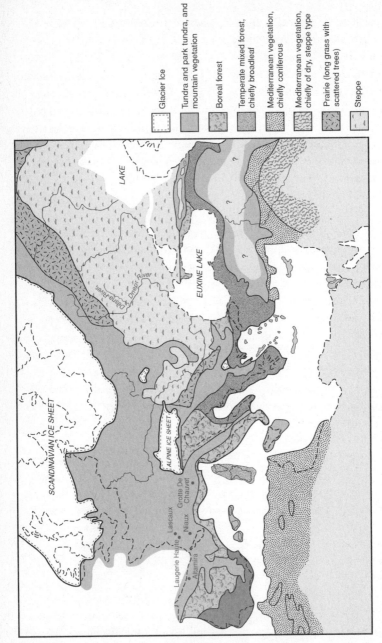

Map of late Ice Age Europe, showing sites mentioned in Chapter 1

Glacier Ice

Tundra and park tundra, and mountain vegetation

Boreal forest

Temperate mixed forest, chiefly broadleaf

Mediterranean vegetation, chiefly coniferous

Mediterranean vegetation, chiefly of dry, steppe type

Prairie (long grass with scattered trees)

Steppe

LAKE

EUXINE LAKE

Dnepr River

Danube River

SCANDINAVIAN ICE SHEET

ALPINE ICE SHEET

Laugerie Haute

Lascaux

Grotte De Chauvet

Niaux

Altamira

The reindeer were far more than quarry. They played a prominent role in the rich symbolic world in which the Cro-Magnons were immersed. The seasonal rhythm of Cro-Magnon life revolved around the reindeer migrations and the great salmon runs that choked the rapids of the Vezère and nearby streams. In spring and fall, neighboring bands would congregate to harvest reindeer and thousands of salmon, their take limited only by the ability of the hunters to process their kills and dry their flesh for later consumption. The short, warm summer brought mosquitoes, but also nuts, berries, and other edible plants. If modern hunter-gatherer societies are any guide, these were the months when bands came together to trade, hunt, and conduct major ceremonies. Marriages were arranged, disputes settled, age-old legends and myths recited. Below the earth, where the living and supernatural worlds met, animals danced and cavorted across the cave walls, painted again and again in the same places, interspersed with complex designs and sometimes human handprints.

Fall came early 18,000 years ago, a brief period in September when daytime temperatures were still warm but nighttime frosts killed the lush grass and winds drove the leaves from the few deciduous trees. Now the bands went their separate ways, living as extended families in large rock shelters, with tattered hide curtains over their openings to retain the warmth from the large hearths within. Soon temperatures plummeted and the snows came. For months, each band lived in virtual isolation, aware of others nearby, but with only sporadic contact between them.

The compass of Cro-Magnon life lay within a narrow world confined by deep river valleys and the movements of big game, with only occasional excursions farther afield. They knew of other people over the horizon, for they obtained fine tool-making stone and necklaces of exotic seashells from them. They were also aware of the seemingly endless plains to the north, where the reindeer grazed in summer.

༝༝༝

Flying over central France today, one looks down from an airliner at a patchwork landscape of green fields and woods, carefully tended hedges, and lush water meadows. Eighteen thousand years ago, this landscape was a subarctic desert—treeless, devoid of cliffs and deep river valleys, covered with low scrub.[3] Rainfall was sparse, the growing season for grasses and low plants little more than two months each year. Even in summer, the winds blew ceaselessly from the north with a cutting persistence that chilled people to the bone. Yet the winds could die down and temperatures rise dramatically within hours. Day after day, dense clouds of fine dust filled the air, turned the sky a dusky gray, and made the distant horizon obscure. Deep layers of fine glacial dust accumulated underfoot—to the benefit of farmers thousands of years later. Mammoths and other cold-loving mammals thrived on the steppe/tundra, especially in more sheltered locations like shallow river valleys. Some animals lived in these desolate landscapes year round. But many more came and went with the seasons.

One can easily think of the Ice Age steppe/tundra as a merciless, unchanging landscape. But it always breathed, sucking in animals and humans at warmer times and expelling them when conditions were too frightful to support anything but the hardiest arctic mammals. This constant cycling is the mechanism by which the great steppe/tundra helped determine when people settled in the far north.[4]

Along its northern edge, the steppe/tundra gave way to a rubble-strewn desert, then to vast ice sheets as much as four kilometers thick. The ice mantled all of Scandinavia and Scotland and spilled into northern England, the Low Countries, and northern Germany. This was the source of the ceaseless winds, which cascaded down the temperature gradients of the ice sheets. The huge glaciers absorbed so much water, and placed so much extra weight on the earth's crust, that sea levels were more than ninety meters below modern levels. The steppe/tundra extended across an exposed southern North Sea. The Baltic Sea did not exist. You could walk from England to France, and from there, if you were sufficiently hardy and well clothed, deep into Eurasia and extreme northeastern Siberia and the Americas, or southeastward to the continental shelf off Southeast Asia.

Late Ice Age Europe was a savage, unforgiving place. Some 40,000 Stone Age hunters thrived here through brilliant opportunism, social adeptness, and constant flexibility—in a world that was about to undergo a stunning transition.

❧

Eighteen thousand years ago, only one human form lived on earth—
Homo sapiens sapiens, people like you and me. We had originated in tropical Africa more than 150,000 years earlier, among a tiny primordial population, then hunted our way into the Sahara, which was better watered
100,000 years ago. Tiny bands of us camped by its shallow freshwater
lakes and hunted game on rolling, semiarid grassland. The Sahara was another giant pump. About 100,000 years ago, as the climate grew much
colder in the north, North Africa dried up and pushed its animal and human inhabitants out to the margins—north to the Mediterranean shore
and east into the Nile Valley. Soon afterward, modern humans had settled
in caves in southwestern Asia, where they lived alongside a different human species, Neanderthal people, for 50,000 years.

For reasons that are still not understood, we paused in southwestern
Asia. Some experts, like the Stanford anthropologist Richard Klein, believe this was the period when *Homo sapiens sapiens* acquired its full cog-
nitive abilities.[5] I believe they may be right. If they are, then the Cro-
Magnons who entered Europe were capable of complex reasoning,
advance planning, and fully articulate speech. Their relationship with
the world was defined as much by complex symbolism as by technological skills. The humans who pushed outward from southwest Asia were
artists and shamans, superpredators, people capable of mastering any climate on earth.

By 45,000 years ago, we had moved into much colder landscapes, perhaps during a time of somewhat warmer temperatures. Five thousand
years later, we moderns had settled in the river valleys of western Europe,
where we flourished for ten millennia alongside gradually shrinking Neanderthal populations. The Neanderthals were nimble and strong
hunters, capable of taking large, formidable beasts. But they lacked the
newcomers' intellect, their specialized, increasingly elaborate toolkits, and
their remarkable ability to adapt to ever-changing climatic conditions.[6]
The Cro-Magnons pushed the Neanderthals into ever more marginal territories until they became extinct. After about 30,000 years ago, the Cro-
Magnons were the masters of Europe.

No more than a few thousand Neanderthals had lived in the Cro-Magnon homeland. For the most part they settled in relatively sheltered environments, venturing onto the open steppe/tundra only on brief summer excursions. But the newcomers had the technology and social organization to hunt and live on the open plains in midwinter. Their sophisticated and versatile toolkit included an invisible weapon that was beyond the Neanderthals' imagining—the supernatural world.

Early scholars of Cro-Magnon art wrote of the paintings as "sympathetic hunting magic," a matter of artists carefully observing their quarry and then painting or engraving it on cave walls far from the open air. Today, many experts believe Cro-Magnon art was part of complex shamanistic rituals, that it was often drawn by shamans who had just emerged from altered states of consciousness in pitch-dark chambers far from daylight. Whatever the correct interpretation, no one doubts that the paintings reflect close spiritual relationships between the domain of the living and the forces of the supernatural cosmos. The hunter-artists treated their quarry as living beings with feelings. A supplicant could acquire spiritual power from animals painted on the rock, whose spirits lived behind the wall. Their hand imprints, outlined in paint, record their sacred acts. For the first time in human existence, the powers of the supernatural played a central role in daily life—coercing, encouraging, and defining human existence.[7]

The supernatural impinged on all members of society, young or old, male or female, healthy or infirm. Every band had its shaman, its individual of power, who mediated between the living and the dread forces that threatened or permitted survival. Shamans defined human existence in chant and song with oral traditions and familiar tales. Powerful hallucinogens allowed them to travel in trance through the supernatural realm. Shamans were respected and feared: they cured the sick and initiated the young into adult life. Above all, they defined and maintained a social order capable of both preserving life-ways and adapting them when the spirits so willed it in a profoundly changing world.

The late Ice Age is so remote from us that scientists still have only a general impression of its climatic variations. We tend to think of Europe 30,000 to 15,000 years ago as a refrigerated world that endured unchanged for many millennia. But then as now, the climate varied from year to year, from century to century, in an endless succession of colder and warmer cycles. Animal populations fluctuated with the climate, increasing in warmer millennia and declining in colder ones.

We can again envisage late Ice Age Europe as a breathing continent, drawing people and animals into itself during warmer times, then expelling them in colder ones, only to suck them in again thousands of years later. Humans never left the continent entirely, but their population, like those of the animals they depended on, ebbed and flowed.

Not that the Cro-Magnons would have been conscious of these shifts. In the days before temperatures and rainfall could be measured or recorded, everyone lived with the weather of generational memory. They would have remembered the years of deep, long-lying snow, the summers when bitterly cold winds from the northern plains never ceased to blow and edible nuts died on the trees, and the years when the reindeer changed their migration routes or came in much smaller numbers than usual. In lean times, there was a cushion of lesser game and other foods to fall back on. This safety net was part of the Cro-Magnons' flexibility in a world with a growing population where the luxury of moving into empty territory close by was becoming scarce. Only a few truly memorable years of severe cold or hunger would sear themselves into legend, to be passed from one generation to the next. But the people always knew that these were exceptional years, that the endless passage of the seasons would bring more plentiful ones. Ultimately, they believed their survival depended on the potency of the animals they hunted, on the powers of the supernatural world, and on the reliability of close kin.

∽∮∾

After about 18,000 years ago, the rhythm of the pumps became more changeable, the climatic shifts sometimes startlingly abrupt. Some years, the summers lasted long into September; the short growing season stretched from weeks into months. Trappers seeking arctic foxes for their pelts were sometimes able to work outside without their fur-lined anoraks in March; other years, the winter lasted past the summer solstice.

We know of these unpredictable shifts from the deep occupation levels of Dordogne rock shelters. Above the 18,000-year horizon, reindeer bones became less plentiful, while those of other animals such as red deer, aurochs, bison, and chamois become more important. Food could be taken literally at one's doorstep. The great rock shelter of Laugerie Haute in the Vezère Valley lay close to a river ford. Here, each fall, the reindeer crowded through the valley as the hunters watched their approach. As they crossed, the band moved in for the slaughter. The level ground in front of the shelter was a convenient killing field, now marked by reindeer skeletons found between the river and the long-occupied overhang.

As the climate warmed and the reindeer migrations ebbed, the Cro-Magnons turned effortlessly to nuts and other edible plants throughout the ever-lengthening summer. We can imagine the hunters in search of different prey, flitting from tree to tree in the valley forests where aurochs lurked, hunting them in winter when snow muffled their footsteps. They would move quietly to the edge of clearings among the trees where the fierce animals pawed the deep snow for grass, drive them into sturdy nets, or dispatch them with razor-sharp antler-tipped spears propelled by sturdy throwing sticks. In these final millennia of the Ice Age, Cro-Magnon society achieved an elaboration and sophistication unknown in colder times. Ceremonial practices flourished in dark cave chambers where bison cavorted on rocky walls.

Then, suddenly, around 15,000 years ago, the warming accelerated dramatically and the ceremonies petered out. The ancient Ice Age bestiary of mammoth and bison, arctic fox and reindeer, migrated northward with the retreating tundra. Birch and deciduous forests spread rapidly into the deep river valleys. Some of the bands moved northward, following their quarry. Others abandoned the great rock shelters and dispersed into much smaller bands, living off solitary deer and other forest animals and, more and more, off plant foods. Only occasionally did people occupy a Cro-Magnon shelter, and then only for a few days, camping on the thick layers of occupation debris left by their forgotten predecessors. No one visited the deep caves; shamans no longer penetrated the darkness in solitary vision quests.[8] The dancing bison and reindeer on the walls faded behind slowly forming stalagmites. By 12,000 years ago, the last late Ice Age Cro-Magnon hunting societies had vanished in the face of natural global warming, to be rediscovered by archaeologists only in the 1860s.

❧

Although such rapid warming was nothing new, the Cro-Magnons would not have known this. Modern science has unprecedented access to the earth's climatic archives in many forms—deep-sea and lake sediments as peat bogs, ice cores bored deep into Greenland and mountain ice caps, and tree rings, to mention only a few. From them, we know that the Ice Age began at least 1.5 million years ago with a gradual cooling of the global climate. Deep-sea cores from the Pacific document at least nine intense glacial periods over the past three-quarters-of-a-million years, each marked by gradual cooling, then rapid warming, only to be cut off again by renewed glaciation. For at least 500,000 of the past 780,000 years, the world's climate has been in transition from warm to cold and back or vice versa. Glacial periods have lasted much longer than the warmer intervals.

Deep ice cores taken from Greenland in the 1980s form the first chapter of a major revolution in our knowledge of the Ice Age. The Greenland cores took the story back some 150,000 years from the present, through two glacial and interglacial cycles. The same cores also chronicled rapid global warming between 15,000 and 10,000 years ago and numerous minor shifts since then.[9]

In 2000, an international team of scientists finished drilling the deepest ice core of all, to a depth of 3,623 meters through the Antarctic ice sheet at Russia's Vostok Station. The drillers stopped 120 meters short of the vast subglacial lake that lies under the ice, to avoid contaminating it with drilling fluid.[10]

The Vostok ice core takes us to about 420,000 years ago, through four transitions from glacial to warm periods.[11] These shifts came at about 100,000-year intervals, the first about 335,000 years before the present,

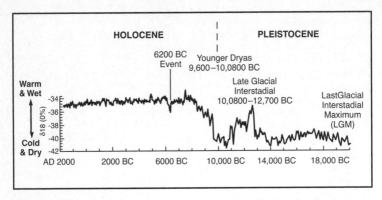

Greenland ice core climatic record extending back to the last glacial maximum (LGM)

then at 245,000, 135,000, and 18,000 years ago—a cyclical rhythm. There seem to be two periodicities involved, a primary one of about 100,000 years and another, weaker one of about 41,000 years. Together, they support the long-held theory that changes in the orbital parameters of the earth—eccentricity, obliquity, and precession of axis—cause variations in the intensity and distribution of solar radiation. These in turn trigger natural climatic changes on a grand scale. The global warming of 15,000 years ago is the most recent effect of these major gyrations, culminating in the Holocene, the millennia after the end of the Ice Age.[12]

The Greenland and Vostok cores also document major changes in atmospheric concentrations of CO_2 (carbon dioxide) and CH_4 (methane)—the most important greenhouse gases. All of the four Vostok transitions from glacial to warmer periods were accompanied by *increases* in atmospheric CO_2 from about 180 to 300 parts per million by volume. (The present level, in a world warmed by human activity, is around 365 parts per million.) At the same time, atmospheric CH_4 rose from about 320 to 350 parts per billion per volume to 650 to 770 parts per billion. Why CO_2 levels increased so rapidly during these four transitions is still unknown, but many experts believe that sea surface temperatures in the Southern Ocean played a key role in triggering changes in the atmosphere. The Greenland ice cores show clearly that shifts in CH_4 levels coincide with fast and major temperature changes in the Northern Hemisphere.

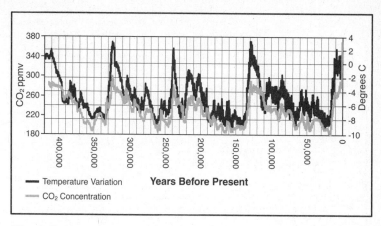

Climatic fluctuations over the past 420,000 years, as revealed in the Vostok ice core, Antarctica

If these connections are correct, we can discern a sequence of events that unfolded not only at the beginning of the Holocene but in earlier transitions as well. First, changes in orbital parameters of the earth triggered the end of a glacial period. Next, an increase in greenhouse gases amplified the weak orbital signal. As the transition progressed, the decreased albedo (solar reflection) caused by rapid melting of the vast ice sheets in the Northern Hemisphere amplified the rate of global warming.

In providing a detailed record of the beginnings and endings of all the glacial periods of the past 420,000 years, the Vostok core shows us that the world's climate has almost always been in a state of change over these 420 millennia. But until the Holocene it has always oscillated. The Holocene climate breaks through these boundaries. In duration, stability, degree of warming, and concentration of greenhouse gases, the warming of the past fifteen millennia exceeds any in the Vostok record. Civilization arose during a remarkably long summer. We still have no idea when, or how, that summer will end.

The northern steppe/tundra visited by the Cro-Magnons stretched end-
lessly in the direction of the rising sun. Dust clouds masked a featureless
landscape that undulated for thousands of kilometers, from the Atlantic
Ocean in the far west, east, and northeast into Eurasia, then into Siberia
and onto the low land bridge that joined extreme northeast Asia to Alaska.

The climate in what are now Ukraine and Russia was without modern
parallel. The Scandinavian glaciers had advanced to within a few kilometers of the present-day city of Smolensk, covering much of the vast
northwestern plain with ice. Large glacial lakes dotted the margins of the
ice sheet, surrounded by polar desert. The constant northerly winds blew
thick clouds of glacial dust far south across the plains, whose winter temperatures regularly fell below −30°C. This late Ice Age world was dry, in
many places treeless, and cold almost beyond imagining.

The steppe/tundra bordering the glaciers was a harsh place even on the
warmest days. Large dune fields dotted the plains, occasionally giving way
to lowlands and shallow river valleys where meadows and stunted willow
shrubs offered sustenance to grazing animals. Much of the vast landscape
was a near-arid wasteland of unceasing winds. Yet a few thousand humans lived here, attracted by the herds of cold-loving mammals that
flourished near the river valleys well south of the great ice sheets.[13]

The most famous of these animals was the woolly mammoth, *Mam-
muthus primigenius*, a relatively small, compact elephant, three to four
meters tall at the shoulder, compared with the four meters or more in
height of a modern African elephant. Mammoths were imposing beasts
with high, massive heads, long, curved tusks, short legs, and cushioned
feet that were well adapted to snow-covered terrain. Their thick hair covered every part of their bodies and trailed along the ground. A dense layer
of underwool insulated them against the extreme cold. There were herds
of gregarious saiga antelope, too, fast runners capable of speeds of up to
64 kilometers an hour, with large hooves for digging under snow and a
nose adapted for filtering flying dust. Steppe bison, wild horse, reindeer,
musk ox, arctic foxes—the mammalian community of the steppe/tundra
boasted twice as many species as that of the modern tundra.[14]

This inhospitable environment challenged human ingenuity to the
limit, so much so that Neanderthal bands of 50,000 years ago rarely ventured onto the plains. They lacked the clothing and technology to survive

in such savage terrain, except at the height of summer. Even then, only a handful of bands hunted there for a few short weeks before retreating southward. But where the Neanderthals rarely ventured, *Homo sapiens sapiens* thrived. The newcomers faced their environmental challenges with great ingenuity. The plains and valleys were treeless, which meant that wood was unavailable, so they dug low-profile, semi-subterranean houses into the soil and roofed them with a framework of mammoth bones, hide, and sod. Instead of brush and logs, they burned mammoth bones as fuel for their large hearths, storing the bones near their dwellings in large pits dug deep into the permafrost. Plant foods were so rare that almost all the diet came from meat, from quarry that was constantly on the move. Some groups in river valleys lived off fish and waterfowl. The hunting toolkits were light and portable, with lethal antler and bone spearheads that could inflict severe wounds at close quarters. These innovations would have been worthless, however, without a simple and little-appreciated invention that is still in use today—the needle and thread.[15]

No one knows who first made this simplest of artifacts, a small tool that revolutionized humanity's ability to thrive in environments with extremely cold temperatures. Needle and thread made it possible for humans to handle the kinds of dramatic temperature shifts characteristic of northern latitudes, where icy winds can chill the skin in minutes or sharply warmer climatic shifts can endure for years. For tens of thousands of years, humans had relied on skin cloaks and crudely sewn clothes to survive Ice Age winters. The eyed needle allowed people to fashion garments that not only fitted the individual precisely but also combined fur from several animals, so that the user could benefit from the unique properties of each kind of skin. Modern-day Eskimo use an astonishing array of furs for their traditional garments. For example, they use only wolverine fur for the opening of an anorak hood, to prevent the wearer's head from frostbite, but only caribou leg skin for knee-length boot uppers.

The needle also brought another sartorial innovation—layered clothing. Any backpacker, skier, or sailor knows the merits of layering clothes: close-fitting undergarments, a middle layer to provide additional warmth and some wind protection, and an outer windproof anorak and pants. Our ancient forebears developed layered garments at least 30,000 years ago and perhaps earlier—thanks to the humble needle.

The steppe/tundra people used such layers to remarkable effect, donning or peeling garments as temperatures changed. Thanks to tailoring, they could hunt in subzero temperatures, build house frameworks on warm summer days, and spear fish in icy rivers. Above all, they had the protection to survive rapid climatic changes, not only brief shifts but the longer-term warming and cooling that came to play a role in their highly mobile lives as the Ice Age drew to an end. Still, for all their technological ingenuity, the steppe/tundra hunters could not handle the extremes of late Ice Age climate on the plains. Generations of excavations by Russian and Ukrainian archaeologists have documented two periods of intensive human occupation, the first between about 24,000 and 20,000 years ago. Then, for two to three thousand years, extreme aridity and cold brought conditions too severe for even the best equipped Stone Age hunters. The key to survival had always been mobility and flexibility, so the obvious strategy was to move southward, into more sheltered terrain. This is what the sparse populations of the plains must have done.[16]

About 17,000 years ago, temperatures again warmed up considerably. Almost at once, hunting settlements reappeared in the shallow river valleys of the steppe/tundra. The effect was just like that of the Sahara thousands of years earlier: a giant pump. Colder conditions pushed people southward, warmer ones sucked them into hitherto uninhabitable terrain. By 16,000 years ago, this huge natural pump had repopulated the steppe/tundra.

When humans returned, the climate was still bitterly cold, the land still treeless, and the way of life virtually identical to that of earlier times. In the Dnepr and Don River valleys, people built circular or oval dwellings roofed with intricate patterns of large mammoth bones, at least four per major settlement. These elaborate structures are sometimes called the oldest ruins on earth.[17] No such finely built bone houses occur in earlier times. The archaeologist John Hoffecker speculates that the bitter cold of the previous millennia prevented humans from scavenging mammoth carcasses. As a result, bones and tusks accumulated across the landscape, piling up in small valleys and ravines, and now provided a convenient source of building material. No one knows who lived in these settlements, but most likely they were bases for extended families who may have reused the same locations again and again.

The low plant productivity of the steppe/tundra meant that the late Ice Age humans relied almost entirely on meat, which in turn dictated a mobile life-way and large hunting territories. For much of the year, each group lived in isolation, perhaps having very sporadic contact with their closest neighbors, groups as small as themselves. But we know that these people were also part of much larger social networks. Their dwellings yield dozens of bone and ivory fragments engraved or painted with abstract designs, as well as beads and pendants, sometimes made of exotic materials from afar. Fine tool-making flint traveled to the Don Valley from at least 150 kilometers away. Amber, prized in later times for its magical qualities, reached settlements in the Desna Valley from a source at least 220 kilometers distant. Fossil marine shells traveled from areas near the Black Sea (at the time a brackish lake) over 600 kilometers north to base camps in the Dnepr and Desna valleys. The distances traversed by these commodities are just about as far as those ever covered by modern-day arctic hunters. This was a world of small-scale living, of widely cast social networks, of occasional gatherings where several bands came together, but above all, of mobility, where small groups survived by ranging over enormous territories in the face of extremely harsh environmental conditions.

But the greatest challenge to late Ice Age people lay in the extreme northeastern reaches of Siberia.

During the bitter cold of the millennia before 20,000 years ago, almost nobody seems to have lived on the vast northeastern steppe/tundra that extended deep into Siberia, to Lake Baikal and beyond. There are traces of human occupation in the Baikal region as early as 35,000 years ago, with denser populations living at the southern end of the lake by 21,000 years ago, immediately before the last cold snap. So we know that hunter-gatherer communities were in the general area.[18]

To the northeast lay the rugged and diverse environments of extreme northeastern Asia, where even the most sheltered locales were excruciatingly cold. The land beyond the Verkhoyanskiy Mountains may have been so dry and cold that no humans ventured there until there was at least some degree of warming. The arid, windy steppe/tundra and shallow river valleys extended all the way to the Pacific and to a low-lying region that then joined Siberia to Alaska. This is the geologist's Beringia, a vanished continent, much of which now lies under the risen seas of the Bering Strait (see map in Chapter 3).

Northeastern Siberia is a forbidding environment even today, and it ranks with the Arctic among the most difficult areas in the world for archaeological research. The digging season is little more than two or three months. The permanently frozen soil means that the usual stratigraphic layers—the archaeologist's bread and butter—have little chance to form. Objects lie on the surface without burial for many years, they are poorly preserved, and different time periods mingle confusingly. Most of what you find is stone; everything softer tends to vanish.

Only a handful of sites document the first human settlement of this remote land. In the 1960s the Russian archaeologist Yuri Mochanov excavated Diuktai Cave in the Aldan Valley, just west of the Verkhoyanskiy Mountains, where he found traces of human occupation that were radiocarbon dated to about 16,000 B.C. The dates came from samples collected from frost-disturbed occupation layers and were processed long before the development of accelerator mass spectrometry (AMS) and tree-ring calibration made radiocarbon dating far more precise.[19] Mochanov described a transitory occupation by hunters using stone-tipped spears with small, razor-sharp stone barbs (known to archaeologists as microblades).

At the time, Diuktai appeared to contain the earliest evidence of human occupation in northeastern Siberia. A few years later, however, another archaeologist, Nikolai Dikov, excavated a small site by Ushki Lake on the Kamchatka peninsula. His radiocarbon dates, again without AMS, for this transitory encampment came out to about 15,000 B.C.

Both Diuktai Cave and Ushki Lake appeared to have been occupied between 19,000 and 15,000 B.C., during the cold of the late Ice Age. Quite apart from the scientific challenges, political conditions made it impossible for more than a handful of local archaeologists to work in the extreme northeast. So everyone assumed that Mochanov and Dikov's dates were correct and that late Ice Age people flourished, albeit in tiny numbers, in the forbidding terrain that was the gateway to the Americas.

More recently, growing numbers of overseas archaeologists have arrived to work alongside Russian scholars, using refined excavation methods and accelerator mass spectrometry to dissect both known and newly discovered sites. New excavations at Ushki Lake have produced AMS radiocarbon dates that are far later than Dikov's original chronology: the site is from 11,000 B.C., long after the Ice Age.[20] The Diuktai site remains an enigma, but Siberian archaeologists increasingly suspect that the Aldan Valley occupation is much later than Mochanov's 16,000 B.C. Why such suspicions? Simply because intensive search has failed to yield any signs of human settlement earlier than about 13,500 B.C. anywhere in northeast Siberia east of the Verkhoyanskiy Mountains.

If the latest thinking is correct, no one lived in extreme northeastern Asia during the bitterly cold millennia of the late Ice Age. Not until rapid warming began, after about 13,500 B.C., did tiny bands of hunters move into these savagely cold landscapes. Once again, the region acted as a pump. During the extreme cold of 18,000 to 15,000 B.C., human settlement was possible only at the margins of this enormous arctic near-desert. John Hoffecker believes the reason may have been that the late Ice Age Siberians were longer-limbed than cold-adapted northern people like the Eskimo and Inuit of today. They still possessed the warm-climate morphology of their African ancestors—just as the Cro-Magnons did. This militated against comfortable living in extremely cold environments, even if they had the technology to do so. Hoffecker cites research by the U.S. Army, which shows that African-American soldiers with such morphology have a high incidence of cold injury in arctic climates.[21] Perhaps the initial settlement of the extreme northeast came when modern peoples' extremities became more compact as their bodies adapted to extreme cold, something that may have started in western Europe by 20,000 years ago. (Interestingly, the Yukaghir, compactly built modern Arctic people with comparable technology to that of the late Ice Age, successfully lived in Siberia—the so-called Pole of Cold near the city of Verkhoyanskiy—where temperatures are still lower than they were in Beringia during the late Ice Age.)

Then came rapid warming, which made life easier. The pump sucked tiny numbers of people into northeastern Siberia, where they subsisted off game and a few plant foods, just as their ancestors on the periphery had done. Some of them may also have lived off fish and sea mammals along the icebound Pacific coast.

We can only extrapolate the life-ways of these early Siberians from what we know of their contemporaries around Lake Baikal and northern China. They were certainly nomadic folk, anchored to river valleys, lake shores, and other places where game congregated. They must have been consummate hunters, with lethally efficient technology that used stone barbs slotted into spear tips. They were skilled at trapping arctic foxes and other fur-bearing animals to fashion layered clothing, and at building semi-subterranean houses with dome-like roofs streamlined against the constant winds. The natural pump effect of the steppe/tundra drew them into hitherto uninhabited lands, and then inexorably into the Americas.

The warming brought more rainfall, longer growing seasons, more plentiful forage for herd animals, and tremendous fluctuations in summer and winter temperatures. Higher temperatures and greater moisture also fostered tree growth, an important consideration for people constantly needing fuel for their hearths. But for all these climatic shifts, survival was never easy and populations were never large. The keys to survival were efficient technology, both to allow life outside in subzero temperatures and to kill animals large and small, and social arrangements that allowed for both mobility and catastrophe. In a world of small hunting bands always on the move, there was always the danger that all the men in a band might perish in a hunting accident, or that the one childbearing woman in a group would die in childbirth. There was constant social tension, owing to an environment where hunger often threatened, accidents happened frequently, and people were cooped up in small dwellings during long subzero winters. Every band grew and contracted. People moved away to avoid conflict and joined other groups. Marriages could cement relationships with other bands; widows would link up with neighboring families. The ebb and flow of social life was a powerful weapon against an environment that allowed little margin for error.

Under these circumstances, the millennia of warming allowed even greater social flexibility. The age-old cross-currents of hunting life operated as they always had, though perhaps with greater intensity in a slightly warmer, climatically more unpredictable world. A son and his family would hive off from his father's band, move to a neighboring valley, or simply follow the movements of reindeer and saiga, or of mammoths, further north and east into landscapes never before visited by humans.

Thus the very first human inhabitants of outermost Asia were drawn ever forward—across the endless steppe/tundra, through shallow river valleys, northward from the arid lands and forests of northern China, across the Amur River into Kamchatka and onto the still icebound coasts of the far northeast. By at least 13,500 B.C., some of these nomadic hunter-gatherers arrived in the heart of the now-vanished land of Central Beringia.

From today's Siberian coast they would have gazed eastward across a dust-filled windy steppe covered with the same familiar shrubs that had always defined their world. At some point, without fanfare, with no sense of the momentousness of their journey, a few handfuls of hunters moved out onto a gently undulating plain, bounded to north and south by pack ice and gray ocean.

Within the compass of a few generations, a few of these bands had hunted their way across the plain onto higher ground to the east. They had crossed into a virgin continent.

3

THE VIRGIN CONTINENT

15,000 TO 11,000 B.C.

After the discovery of America, the minds of the learned
and ingenious were much exercised to account for its
habitation by men and animals.

Samuel Haven, *Archaeology of the United States,* 1856

Had you stood on what is now the extreme northeastern shore of
modern-day Siberia 15,000 years ago, you would have gazed out not over
ocean, but over a flat, scrub-covered plain stretching eastward into the
distance. On clear days you might have seen some snow-clad mountain
peaks hovering above the horizon. Most of the time, however, fine dust
borne on the endless northerly winds would have obscured any view of
higher ground. Fifteen thousand years ago, Siberia and Alaska were
joined by a wind-swept plain, featureless but for a few shallow river valleys. The desolate north and south coasts, battered by gray, heaving
swells, were masked by pack ice for most of the year.[1]

This was Central Beringia, the terrestrial bridge that linked Siberia and
a vast continent where no humans had yet set foot. The land bridge had
formed some 100,000 years ago, when the last glacial period began and
global seas fell more than 90 meters. While sea levels had fluctuated
somewhat over the last glaciation, the two continents were always joined
by dry land, which approached maximum extent during the last cold
snap of 18,000 years ago.

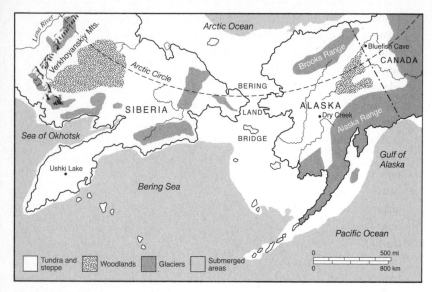

The geologists' Beringia: A map of northeastern Siberia, the Bering land bridge, and Alaska, showing major archaeological sites

As the great warming commenced, the land bridge began to shrink at the edges. Rising seas encroached on the landscape. The climbing waters rose and ebbed irregularly as the rise in sea level proceeded in fits and starts. When a scattering of humans first settled in the inhospitable reaches of northeastern Siberia, one could still hunt one's way into North America. That is probably how humans first colonized the Americas, propelled by the last spasms of the natural pump that drew animals and humans into hitherto unknown lands.

✿

The route and timing of the first settlement of the Americas is one of archaeology's great controversies.[2] The debate is remarkable more for its passions than its evidence, which can charitably be called slim. Some believe humans first arrived in the New World as much as 40,000 years ago; others argue for a date during the late Ice Age, before 20,000 years ago; and a majority feel confident that first settlement took place less than 15,000 years ago. A great deal of the debate is theoretical, all too often based on grossly inadequate data. Recently, however, new climatic data and archaeological discoveries in Siberia have provided a convincing scenario for first settlement in which the great warming at the end of the Ice Age played a major part.

Almost everyone agrees that the first Americans came from northeast Asia. Genetic, linguistic, and archaeological evidence points in that direction.[3] New research into mitochondrial DNA places the ancestry of the native Americans in Siberia. The linguistic classification of Indian languages has generated much controversy, but everyone agrees that the roots of their tongues lie in northern Asia. Archaeologists on both sides of the Bering Strait have identified cultural ties between Stone Age societies in Siberia and those in the newly inhabited continent. Even the complex morphology of native American teeth links them to Asian ancestors.

Everyone also assumes the first settlers arrived in small groups that hunted and foraged their way across from Siberia, over or along the shores of the Bering land bridge. At no point did large numbers of people travel across on a deliberate journey of colonization. First settlement was a sporadic, untidy process taking many generations, as part of the natural dynamics of hunter-gatherer life in an extremely harsh and demanding environment. The steppe/tundra supported very few animals per square kilometer, which meant that the Beringians traveled long distances in the course of their seasonal round. In this empty landscape, new bands could split off from old ones and move into neighboring valleys and promising terrain without impinging on previously claimed territories. As a result, they invaded huge tracts of landscape within each generation.

This very mobility has sadly left almost no archaeological signature. Much of what was left lies beneath the ocean. As the Canadian archaeologist Richard Morlan once remarked, looking for the ancient Beringians and their Alaskan relatives is like "looking for a needle in a haystack, and a frozen one at that."[4] We are searching for the slenderest of clues, mere scatters of stone artifacts and animal bones.

Beyond these points, universal agreement fades into the mist of speculation. No consensus exists as to a plausible scenario for first settlement.

Controversy surrounds the two fundamental questions: When did the first humans arrive and what routes did they use? I believe that the massive climate changes at the end of the Ice Age define the answers to both questions.

⚕

At first, archaeologists thought the first Americans were just big-game hunters. In 1908, a cowboy named George McJunkin unearthed some large animal bones and a sharp stone fragment in the wall of a dry gully near Folsom, New Mexico. He took them back to the ranch house, where they lay forgotten for seventeen years. In 1925, the finds landed on the desk of Jesse Figgins, director of the Colorado Museum of Natural History, who realized at once that the bones were those of large, long-extinct Plains bison. He dug into the Folsom site from 1926 to 1928. Almost immediately he found a stone spear point in direct association with the ancient bison fragments. The Folsom discovery proved once and for all that humans had lived in the Americas at the same time as long-extinct animals. Figgins estimated that the Folsom kill site was at least 10,000 years old—far earlier than the previous chronology of a mere 2,000 years.[5]

Four years later, in 1932, two amateur collectors found some quite different, finely made stone spearheads with thinned bases alongside extinct mammal bones on the shores of long-dried up lakes at Clovis, New Mexico. Some of the points lay among broken mammoth ribs, but no one knew how old they were. Further excavations after World War II showed that these early "Clovis" points lay below a later "Folsom" layer at the same location. For years, the Clovis people came to epitomize the first Americans.

At first, Clovis sites were found only on the Great Plains, with their massive herds of bison and sporadic sightings of other large animals like mammoth, mastodon, and camelids. These early finds gave birth to the idea that Clovis people were expert big-game hunters, and rapacious ones at that. In the late 1960s, the University of Arizona archaeologist Paul Martin proclaimed that Clovis people had swept through the ice-free corridor, "old hands at hunting woolly mammoths and other large Eurasian

animals." They descended on the Plains, where they found large gregarious animals and hunted them with ease. The newcomers spearheaded a
blitzkrieg of voracious hunters, armed with the newly invented Clovis
point, who killed all large animals on sight. Within five hundred years or
so, they had colonized all of the Americas, right down to the Straits of
Magellan. They had also driven most animals weighing more than 45
kilograms into extinction.[6]

Martin's overkill theory was controversial from the beginning. His
ideas ran in the face of much of what science knew about both ecology
and hunter-gatherer societies. He argued the Clovis people with so much
meat to eat would have reproduced rapidly, at an astounding rate of
about 3–4 percent annually, far above the 0.5 percent rate of historical
hunter-gatherer populations. As the archaeologist James Adovasio notes,
they "would have had to be copulating machines to accomplish this" and
have experienced a far lower infant mortality rate than is typical of
hunter-gatherers.

Archaeology also discredits the overkill theory. Clovis people did indeed hunt large animals, but archaeologists have found only twelve puta-
tive mammoth kill sites, mainly in Arizona. A further dozen locations *may*
have been mammoth kills, one as far east as Michigan. If these people
were habitual big-game hunters, they left remarkably few traces behind.
At best, such a hunt was a rare occurrence. As the Clovis researcher James
Judge once remarked, "Each Clovis generation probably killed one mammoth, then spent the rest of their lives talking about it."

The big-game hunter stereotype lingers seductively in the scientific literature despite having been discredited long ago. In fact, the Clovis people
were adept at exploiting every kind of game and plant food imaginable. Today, Clovis points are known from all the lower forty-eight states and parts
of Canada. Their densest concentration is in the southeastern United
States, a much more wooded environment than the Plains. Finds of fish,
mollusks, and seeds, as well as the bones of smaller animals, reveal people
who had adapted successfully to a wide variety of North American environments. Their contemporaries in Central and South America were equally
adept at exploiting all manner of highland and lowland environments.

For all their distinctive spear points, the Clovis people remain a shadowy
presence. In the western United States, the Clovis population colonized an

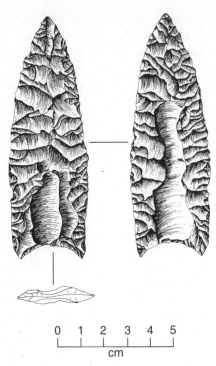

A Clovis point, from Schonchin Butte, California. *Courtesy Dr. Michael Moratto*

enormous area of highly diverse terrain, somewhat wetter than today, where the great warming had formed numerous pluvial lakes, some quite large. Most bands probably encountered few outsiders during the average lifetime and subsisted for the most part on wild grasses, nuts, and other plant foods. Small game was a staple, especially the ubiquitous rabbit. We know from historic accounts of rabbit hunts that elders would lay out fiber nets across convenient defiles. Then men, women, and children would drive scurrying rabbits by the hundred into the nets, where they were speared. Such hunts were commonplace, partly because all western bands were well aware that rabbits decimated the local vegetation, including edible plants. We can be sure that they also took place in earlier times.[7] Over much of the Clovis people's range, by contrast, a successful big-game hunt might have been the event of a lifetime.

Clovis people everywhere had to be expert hunters and gatherers who subsisted off a wide range of foods, especially edible plants. They would have needed the flexibility afforded by a broad-based diet, and the highly mobile lifeway that went with it, to survive both rapid warming and great aridity. And this flexibility must have arrived in the Americas with their very first inhabitants.

✽

Were the Clovis people the first Americans? For years, most people assumed so, and that they were descendants of arctic peoples who traveled southward from Alaska after the Ice Age. Under this scenario, first settlement took hold in about 11,200 B.C., the date of the earliest known Clovis sites. That date represents the so-called Clovis barrier, a mythic chronological fence popularized by science journalists, beyond which human settlement was a taboo subject. Talk of such a barrier is nonsense, of course, if only because first settlement was not a tidy invasion, but a process that unfolded over many centuries.

The dynamics of hunter-gatherer societies almost demanded an untidy first settlement. There was no single defining moment when humans settled south of the ice sheets. In a world where hunting bands survived by virtue of their small size, flexible social organization, and ability to adapt to rapidly changing environmental conditions, the Americas could have been settled and abandoned—or seen settlements die out—dozens of times. The rapid and irregular warming of the late Ice Age would have drawn in and expelled people from the savage landscapes of northeastern Siberia like a fibrillating heart.

Small numbers of people thus set foot in the Americas centuries, perhaps even millennia, before the Clovis people. But who were they, and what was their relationship to their successors? Unfortunately, the archaeological traces of their passing are virtually nonexistent, so we can only assemble the most general of scenarios for first settlement. This scenario unfolds in three acts, each driven by the rapid and pervasive global warming that began 18,000 years ago.

Act One begins in the primordial homeland of the ancient Americans. As we saw in the last chapter, northeastern Siberia was a truly horrible place during the late Ice Age, especially between 20,000 and 18,000 years ago, when the cold reached its height. If the region were a pump, in this era it would have been exhaling: strong winds, very dry conditions and extreme cold pushed humans southward, out to the tundra's more clement margins.

It is questionable whether any humans lived east of the Verkhoyansk Mountains in northeast Siberia before 20,000 years ago, when the Siberian climate underwent a slight warming. Certainly, no one has yet found any traces of them, even though late Ice Age people lived close to the shores of Lake Baikal to the west as early as 19,000 B.C. and probably considerably earlier. In all probability, the sheer severity of the northeastern Siberian environment, and the morphology of human bodies, precluded any human settlement until the great warming began at the end of the Ice Age, some 15,000 years ago.[8]

After that date, the climate warmed rapidly, with much higher summer temperatures, more marked seasons, and less severe winters. As in western Eurasia, a natural pump now sucked animals and people into a still forbidding land. We know this because a handful of archaeological sites in the heart of the northeast, the earliest hunter-gatherer sites in the region, date to between 13,500 and 11,000 B.C. The signature is little more than scatters of fine stone blades and a few carefully flaked spear points, but it is enough to document a human presence where people had apparently never hunted before.

No one knows where the settlers came from—perhaps from west of the Verkhoyanskiy Mountains or from the south, from the far side of the Amur River separating Manchuria from Siberia. I suspect that many of them came from the south, where late Ice Age hunter-gatherers had thrived for many thousands of years. Nor do we know whether they were terrestrial hunters or coastal groups that subsisted on fish, mollusks, and sea mammals. My guess is that they were both—people who took advantage of any food resources around.

Within a millennium, perhaps only a few centuries, some of these bands hunted their way north and east along what is now the Russian coast of the Bering Strait and onto the adjacent land bridge. Shortly after that, again within a few centuries, a few bands moved onto the higher ground of Alaska, or traversed the shores of the land bridge in skin boats or some other simple watercraft. The first settlement of the Americas followed the opening of a climatic window in northeastern Siberia around 13,500 B.C., when the great warming began. Within a generation or so, the dynamics of hunter-gatherer life must have seen some of the northeast Siberians moving eastward into Alaska.

❦

Act Two begins on the eastern side of the land bridge around 13,500 B.C., and here we are on slightly firmer archaeological ground. Alaska, unglaciated except for the Alaska and Brooks ranges, was at the time a dry oasis at the extreme edge of the Eurasian steppe/tundra. The few hunting bands that settled there occupied a diverse landscape hemmed to the east and south by vast ice sheets. A continental shelf extended outward from Central Beringia along the southeastern shore of Alaska.

Despite some relatively sheltered spots, Alaska at the height of the late Ice Age would have been a savage environment for humans. Even during the great warming it was often inhospitable, but remarkable for a local diversity that increased as dramatic warming began. There were lakes and rocky seacoasts, also sheltered valleys where game sometimes abounded and summer plant foods could be found. After a few years in Beringia, they must have seemed like paradise.

The warm-up, when it came, was dramatic. The sediments at Windmill Lake in central Alaska document the change in their populations of fossilized beetles. In 12,000 B.C., soon after the beginning of the great warming, the beetles living around the lake are those found in arctic tundra regions such as the Beringian land bridge. By 10,500 B.C., the lake bottom was catching beetles common to a much warmer climate with near-modern summer temperatures.[9] By that time, the rising sea had severed

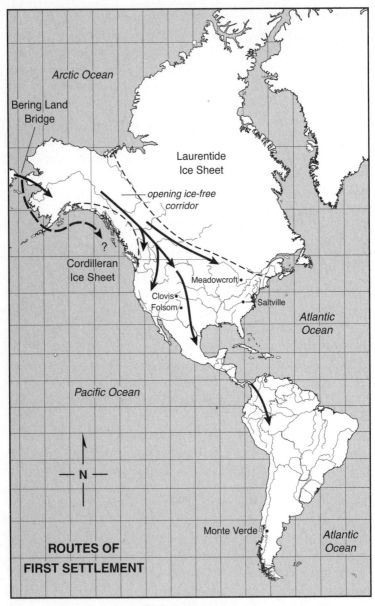

Hypothetical routes for the first human settlement of the Americas, showing the contracting ice sheets and archaeological sites mentioned in the text

the Bering land bridge, and the waters of the Pacific and Arctic oceans mingled for the first time in millennia. As the Bering land bridge vanished, its animal and human inhabitants must have moved onto higher ground on both sides of the new strait.

Even after intensive search, we still have no idea when the first humans arrived in Alaska and the Yukon. The earliest traces of them so far may come from Bluefish Caves in the Yukon, where some diminutive microblades are dated to about 13,750 B.C., when shrub tundra was spreading into a now-warmer environment. The artifact scatter is tiny and the dates uncertain, but the site is the best we have so far.[10]

By 11,500 B.C., the warming coincides with widespread human settlement. A series of temporary encampments on well-drained ridges overlooking low-lying marshlands in the Tenana River valley, 97 kilometers southeast of Fairbanks, were first occupied as early as 11,700 B.C. To the north, people lived in the Nenana River valley in the northern foothills of the Alaska Range at a site called Dry Creek as early as 11,500 B.C. Another site, some 16 kilometers north, dates to about 11,400 to 11,100 B.C.

These Paleo-Arctic, or Paleo-Indian, people subsisted for the most part on game. In the Tenana River valley they hunted swans that used an ancient flyway between Alaska and the heart of North America. Like their increasingly distant Siberian relatives, they were constantly on the move, favoring sheltered valleys with wetlands that offered plant foods as well as game. They still followed the ancient lifeways, relying for their survival on mobility, spending most of the year almost completely isolated in small bands, then coming together for a few days or weeks during the summer months. Social relationships were in constant flux. Fellow kin lived in camps dozens of kilometers apart and rarely saw one another. People married outside their bands; women would join a neighboring group if all the men in their camp were killed in a hunting accident. Such social flexibility was highly adaptive in a world where survival depended on mobility and on accurate intelligence about distant food supplies.

If no one lived in northeastern Siberia before about 13,500 B.C., those who arrived then must have passed through quickly—in two thousand years or less. If the evidence from Bluefish Caves is correct, then some of them may have walked through in just a few generations.

cあの

Act Three begins as a new player arrives on stage—the chaotic and unpredictable North Atlantic.

Though ice-free 18,000 years ago, Alaska was encircled to the east and south by glaciers that separated it from the rest of North America throughout the late Ice Age. Two enormous ice sheets mantled all of Canada and the northern reaches of what is now the United States. In the far west, the Cordilleran glacier advanced southward from source areas in British Columbia, reaching the latitude of Seattle. The Cordilleran mantled much of the Pacific Coast but left many locations uncovered—coastal refuges in a world of unrelenting ice. The Laurentide ice sheet lay over eastern and central Canada, the center of the ice mass originating near northern Quebec, Labrador, and Newfoundland, and spread out to the south and west into Pennsylvania, Ohio, Indiana, and Illinois.

The glaciers were never still. An ice sheet like the Laurentide led a life of its own, advancing and retreating in an irregular dance that reflected the volatile climatic mix in the northern Atlantic. The North Atlantic climate, in turn, was in a state of nearly continuous flux on many different time scales: hours, as fronts passed through and winds shifted; months, as the seasons changed; and years, as periods of intense cold pushed icebergs further south.

In 1988, a German paleo-oceanographer, Hartmut Heinrich, found six layers of tiny white stones from North America in sediment cores from North Atlantic sea mounts. Each layer represented a massive discharge of icebergs that occurred every seven to ten thousand years between 10,500 and 70,000 years ago. For long periods of time the sediment is mostly plankton. But on at least six brief occasions, each a matter of centuries, during the past 60,000 years, the relative portion of fine pebbly debris spiked dramatically. This dust can only have come from land—glacial debris carried far out to sea by icebergs that had broken off from ice sheets at the shore.

The paleoclimatologist Wallace Broecker and others later showed that these spikes, which they named Heinrich events, were not confined to just the few areas that Heinrich studied but were widespread in the North

Atlantic. The Heinrich layers are thickest to the north and west, toward Hudson Bay in northern Canada. Each was deposited very rapidly, at a time when the ocean was exceptionally cold. The ice in Hudson Bay built up over several cold and warm oscillations (known as Dansgaard-Oeschger oscillations after the scientists who discovered them). The oscillations grew progressively cooler as the cold-based ice sheet in the bay grew. Eventually, the ice became thick enough to trap some of the earth's heat, which thawed the base. Mud, stones, and water resulting from the thaw allowed the ice to skate, as it were, across the underlying bedrock, dumping the icebergs and their debris into the North Atlantic. In a matter of a few centuries, Hudson Bay purged itself of the accumulated ice. Eventually, the ice thinned enough for the cold surface layers to freeze again, and the ice sheet began building up for a new cycle. Ice grew slowly but dissipated rapidly, which may account for the trend toward slow cooling and rapid warming characteristic of much Ice Age climate change. Heinrich events marked the coldest point of the cycle. Why did the Hudson Bay ice behave in such a manner, while the Laurentide ice sheet cycle was much slower? Probably because Hudson Bay is at a lower elevation, resulting in thicker ice that was warmer at the base. As Richard Alley put it, "You might think of a roller coaster riding the orbital rails, with Heinrich . . . jumping off the roller coaster while playing with a Dansgard-Oeschger yo-yo."[11]

The intrusion of millions of gallons of glacial freshwater into the northern Atlantic Ocean had the effect of shutting down the circulation of warmer water in the Gulf Stream, which depends on the downwelling of salt water in the Labrador Sea. The inevitable result: a deep freeze in Europe as the prevailing warm westerly winds faltered. Cold, dry, and windy conditions settled over a broad region across North America and Europe, and extended as far south as subtropical Asia and Africa. Much of the world became drier, because the cooling reduced the amount of water vapor as storm tracks moved southward. A Heinrich event, then, is a feedback loop—a quick warming that causes its own end in a quick cooling.

The last Heinrich event, known as Heinrich 1 because it is the topmost in the sediment cores, occurred just after 15,000 years ago. The coldest part of the late Ice Age had come and gone about 5,000 years earlier, followed by an irregular warming trend. Heinrich 1 coincided with the abrupt retreat of the Laurentide ice sheet, undoubtedly in response to rapid warming. The shrinking was part of a longer-term warming cycle since the late Ice Age maximum punctuated by several abrupt warmings and coolings. Sudden discharges of fresh meltwater into the North Atlantic such as the one that caused Heinrich 1 had the effect of shutting down ocean circulation, thereby triggering sudden cooling. The youngest major cold snap was the so-called Younger Dryas event of 11,000 B.C., which endured for ten centuries. The Holocene has recorded one of the longest periods of stable climate on record. Yet subtle warmings and coolings of the North Atlantic have occurred about every fifteen hundred years, of which the Little Ice Age of A.D. 1300 to 1860 is the most recent example. How these minor changes and their effects on human history relate to the longer-term Dansgaard-Oeschger cycles is still a mystery, but we would certainly be naive to think that the current warming will not, one day, be affected by similar changes.

Climatically, the post–Ice Age warming was much like its predecessors. But there was one difference this time: there were human beings in Alaska.

৽৽

How, then, did Alaskan hunter-gatherers move south of the ice? A generation ago, scientists believed that the Cordilleran and Laurentide ice sheets barely touched. They theorized an ice-free corridor that offered a way southward even at the height of the late Ice Age. In 1979, the *National Geographic* writer Thomas Canby envisioned "an ice-walled valley of frigid winds, fierce snows, and clinging fogs . . . yet grazing animals would have entered and behind them would have come a rivulet of human hunters."[12] This was the inhospitable yet viable highway from the Canadian Arctic to the heart of North America.

But the ice-free corridor is a geological myth. Careful mapping of glacial deposits in the remote areas through which the ice sheet passed shows nothing but icebound landscape, which was exposed only when the great warming began—immediately after Heinrich 1. The ice-free corridor is a product of the great warming.

Both the Cordilleran and Laurentide ice sheets retreated with extraordinary rapidity after Heinrich 1. They had reached their maximum extent some 21,000 years ago, were in full retreat by 16,000 B.C., and split by 12,000 B.C., finally opening an ice-free corridor. The Laurentide then retreated north and east into subarctic Canada, and the Cordilleran shrank rapidly into the mountain fastnesses of the west. Today, nothing remains of the Laurentide but the Great Lakes, formed four thousand years after the retreat, and the battered and scarred landscape of the ancient Canadian shield.

A computer simulation of the melting of the Cordilleran and Laurentide ice sheets has been developed by four geography instructors at the University of Oregon. At first all we see is one solid sheet, a merger of the two ice masses. As thawing begins after 18,000 years ago, then accelerates after 11,500 B.C., a narrow corridor opens between the two sheets and gradually widens—a viable southward route through recently glaciated, rugged landscapes with only sparse vegetation and few animals. Depending on how the instructor sets the speed and degree of warming, he or she can make the corridor appear later or earlier, but it is always a relatively late event in the ice sheet's retreat. And the corridor is never hospitable. Except for a few favored locations near glacial lakes, where mammals would tend to congregate and edible plants or fish might be found, there would have been little incentive for people to linger. If they settled there, it was temporarily and in close proximity to herds of game animals.

In such biologically impoverished environments, plant foods would have been scarce outside the most sheltered locales. But the people who might have passed through this corridor were adapted to harsh extremes, with subfreezing temperatures and widely dispersed food supplies. They had developed the technology and clothing to survive comfortably even under the severest conditions.

If Paleo-Indian populations from the north did indeed pass through the widening defile, they must have moved southward not in a deliberate migration, but as a result of the annual round. The opening corridor was some 1,500 kilometers long, not a distance that people would walk in a single summer and fall, but one that might be traversed over some generations by small bands moving with the seasonal migrations of bison, caribou, and other animals. Some groups may have followed prey south of the ice sheets, then followed them back north. Generations of such movements would have extended even further southward, until some groups were living permanently south of the corridor, in much more hospitable territory.

It would be a mistake, too, to think of the corridor as steadily widening over the generations. Ice sheets are dynamic things, constantly advancing and retreating according to unpredictable atmospheric and oceanic forces. The corridor may have opened and closed again, widened and narrowed as part of this decades-long dance, before opening for good. Such movements might well have affected the rhythm of hunter-gatherer life in the barren lands, perhaps contributing to genetic and linguistic diversity in the populations south of the ice.

Paleo-Indian populations south of the ice sheets grew rapidly after 11,500 B.C., so viable breeding populations must have passed through the corridor before then—unless the first inhabitants came by sea. Advocates of a coastal route believe that late Ice Age groups traveled along the southern edge of the land bridge from the Siberian coast, then paddled southward into the Pacific Northwest along a partially ice-free shore. The retreat of the Cordilleran ice sheet may have opened a shoreline route as early as 15,000 B.C., but we have no evidence that people from southern Beringia used it. If they did indeed paddle southward, they would have had to have used skin boats, presumably some form of craft like the umiak that arctic peoples in the Bering Strait region have employed over thousands of years for load carrying and whale hunting. With driftwood or bone frames, and hulls made of sea mammal hide, skin boats are quite seaworthy and can carry heavy loads. But they are clumsy to maneuver in rough seas or against even moderate headwinds, and are at their best in more sheltered waters.

Readily built from simple materials, easily repaired and moderately portable, skin boats are an attractive prototype. Unfortunately, they do not survive in archaeological sites, and because of sea-level rise the sites where one might find traces of them are now deep under the ocean. If maritime peoples really did move into the Americas by a coastal route, they completely elude us. Nor do we have the slightest idea of their technological abilities.

The same problem arises if you argue that terrestrial Paleo-Indians adapted to coastal living in Alaska, then took to the ocean and paddled southward. Even today, these waters are a formidable undertaking for small craft, especially those propelled by paddles or oars. They would have been even more of a challenge immediately after the Ice Age, when sea surface temperatures were much colder, ice conditions more severe, and hypothermia a constant threat. If such voyages took place, they would have been planned for the short summer months, when the water was warmest and the sea calmest. Alaskan waters command great respect from those who fish them today. Summer sea surface temperatures were much colder immediately after the Ice Age, circumstances that increase the risk of dense fog and, with strong winds, intense wind chill factors.

It's hard to tell whether Paleo-Indian canoe skippers would have undertaken long journeys. Historical Indian groups like the Chumash of southern California were cautious to a fault. During Europe's Little Ice Age, most mariners avoided going to sea between November and March. Even the Norse beached their open boats in winter. Basque and English fishermen took much greater risks, but only because of the potential rewards. In February they would sail to Iceland in quest of cod, the staple of Catholic Fridays. The crews fished in doggers, open boats that offered almost no protection from storms at a time when winter temperatures and gale conditions in the Atlantic were far more severe than today. Hundreds of doggers foundered each year in the chill waters. Those who fished for cod had no illusions about the dangers of their trade and expected to die young. If people did eventually paddle down the Pacific Coast from Alaska to British Columbia, we can be sure that each voyage was a short one, undertaken in perfect weather, with potential shelter always close to hand. It may have taken many generations for any canoes to come south of the ice sheets in search of food.[13]

Those who espouse maritime colonization point out that people were voyaging from New Guinea to the Solomon Islands, a distance of some 650 kilometers, as early as 30,000 years ago.[14] Why, then, could not coastal groups in the north have taken to the ocean during the late Ice Age? I am sure that some maritime folk did indeed move south in fits and starts along the coast as conditions warmed, but whether there were voyages of settlement is another matter. There is precious little archaeological evidence to support the notion. We do know people were living along the northern continental shelf within a few thousand years of first settlement, at least in coastal valleys off the Queen Charlotte Islands of

British Columbia, where there may be signs of human occupation below modern sea level dating to at least 8,000 B.C.

Whichever route was used—I believe the terrestrial one is more credible—we can be virtually certain that neither was practicable until around 12,000 B.C., when the great warming was well under way.

We know almost nothing of these Paleo-Indian people other than that they used a wide variety of toolkits, including stone-tipped spears armed with projectile points and slotted antler spearheads fitted with microblades. Even during the great warming, the far north enjoyed but short summers and relatively limited, if vigorous, plant growth. The sparse Paleo-Indian population of Alaska would have relied on terrestrial mammals, birds, fish, and probably sea mammals for most of their diet. Except for some strategic locations near lakes, on wildlife migration routes, near sea mammal rookeries, or in places where mollusks were abundant, they spent much of each year in small encampments, perhaps wintering in semi-subterranean houses resembling the bone huts of distant Eurasia.

We can imagine a patchwork of Paleo-Indian societies dispersed over a vast, highly varied landscape. Only a few thousand people inhabited all of Alaska. In a lifetime, the average person met only a few people outside the narrow confines of his or her family band—relatives or kin based in the next valley, occasionally members of other groups when they came together for rare communal hunts. Yet these encounters were vital to survival in unforgiving environments where intelligence—about the movements of caribou, patches of plant foods, ice and snow conditions, and waterfowl migrations—was all-important. Such information passed from hunter to hunter, from old men to young, between neighbors and people encountered by chance. Modern-day San hunter-gatherers in southern Africa's Kalahari Desert spend an enormous amount of time trading information about water and food supplies. [15] Their survival depends on a constantly changing mental map of their territory and of lands some distance over the horizon. The Paleo-Indians must have done the same. To a considerable degree, this intelligence determined the seasonal rhythm of life, movements to new hunting grounds, and the ebb and flow of people from one band to another. This rhythm was like that of a small boat at sea, constantly trimming its sails to new weather conditions, sailing as fast as it could in calms and breezes, and hunkering down in storms.

The great warming saw major changes in both climate and glacial terrain. The lives of Paleo-Indians could change from season to season with a volatility once unimaginable. Constant shifts in glacial margins and in the movements of game must have played a decisive role in the lives of people who clung to ice-clad mountains and valleys. And age-old intelligence networks passed this information from band to band over long distances.

Intelligence was combined with opportunism, the most enduring characteristic of *Homo sapiens sapiens*. Hunting bands pressed their advantages where they found them—a movement of mammoth or caribou into a recently deglaciated valley where plants were sprouting for the first time, reports of plant foods for the taking along the shores of a glacial lake surrounded by retreating ice, a stopping place for geese flying southward in spring. The movements never ceased. Handfuls of people exploited newly exposed terrain where animal and plant life was thin on the ground and long distances sometimes separated food supplies. Rather than a deliberate movement southward, there would have been a constant opportunism that saw tiny bands of hunter-gatherers gradually extend their range into much warmer latitudes, perhaps within a few centuries or even decades.

Just to survive on the steppe/tundra had required a stoic toughness to overcome periods of hunger and of extreme cold and isolation. The people were conservative and cautious, but innovative as well—witness the great diversity of toolkits, which they used north of the ice sheets and carried along south, modifying them as they went. When they reached more temperate landscapes, they adapted to new circumstances with the same unconscious opportunism that had always been part of late Ice Age life.

The first settlers arrived not only with a highly flexible hunter-gather culture and portable, efficient toolkit, but with the rich symbolic life that was characteristic of all late Ice Age hunter-gatherer societies. Because they left behind no rock art or decorated artifacts, we can only guess at the existence of spiritual beliefs. Still, imagine a life where winters were protracted and intensely cold, where people spent long nights huddled close together. In those hours, stories must have been told, songs sung and legends recited, often by individuals with exceptional authority who assumed a mantle of supernatural powers. The shaman's chants and stories defined the known world and spoke of mythic animals and spirits that created and controlled existence. In a rapidly changing world of constant movement, this spiritual world must have been a pervasive and vital repository of identity, social relationships, and all that was stable in these very unpredictable lives.

We will probably never find traces of these first settlers, the few hundred Paleo-Indians who hunted and foraged their way south into completely new environments. But we can be certain that they were skilled, confident people intimately familiar with their changing surroundings.

As the great warming unfolded, plant productivity soared, both in the short growing seasons of the far north and also south of the ice sheets. For the first settlers on ice-free terrain, little was really changed. Their lives still depended on widely dispersed foodstuffs and, in not particularly well-watered landscapes, on permanent water supplies. They must have camped in sheltered valleys and by glacial lakes, where plant foods could be gathered, fish taken, and waterfowl netted. Always opportunistic, the Paleo-Indians now lived in environments where wild plant foods were far more plentiful than game. The transition to a more eclectic diet must have gone almost unnoticed. Thousands of years later, their descendants would be some of the most skilled farmers in the preindustrial world.

Within a few centuries of first settlement south of the ice, nomadic hunter-gatherer bands had settled in every corner of North America, as well as further south. We have only a few traces of them. The lower levels of the Meadowcroft Rockshelter in Pennsylvania, which lies on a small tributary of the Ohio River, have yielded fleeting traces of human occupation dating to between 11,950 and 12,550 B.C.[16] There are other transitory glimpses, too: a mastodon kill site at Saltville, Virginia, that may date to as early as 11,000 to 12,500 B.C. The earliest of these occupation levels are as much as fifteen hundred years earlier than Clovis.[17]

The southernmost footsteps of the earliest settlers come from Monte Verde, a site in a river valley in southern Chile, where the archaeologist Tom Dillehay excavated a small settlement of two rows of skin-covered dwellings that flourished by a stream between 12,000 and 11,800 B.C.[18] The Monte Verde people lived in a forest where plants were abundant year round, a very different lifeway from that available on the North American plains. Almost all the Monte Verde artifacts were made of wood.

This inchoate pattern of archaeological finds fits the scenario of ragged and irregular settlement by highly mobile hunter-gatherers who covered enormous areas within a few centuries. If their remote predecessors entered northeastern Siberia as warming began and crossed the Bering land bridge soon afterward, the movement southward must have been very rapid. There were humans in southern Chile by 12,000 B.C.

Was such a rapid movement possible? The archaeologist David Madsen made a hypothetical calculation: moving sixteen kilometers a year, people leaving Lake Baikal in Siberia 24,000 years ago would have reached the site of Denver, Colorado, by 22,900 years before present, even with a very low birth rate. [19] This is an absurdly direct and entirely theoretical migration. No one, least of all Madsen, suggests that it actually took place. But there are no compelling reasons why late Ice Age hunters and their successors, operating in a familiar environment, could not have covered large cumulative distances, simply because the carrying capacity of the land in many regions was so low and people were dispersed widely over the landscape.

By 11,000 B.C., numerous small Paleo-Indian groups were flourishing throughout the Americas. Their numbers were small and populations widely dispersed, but the initial colonization was complete. Only a few thousand people lived in the Americas, but they had adapted successfully to temperate environments of all kinds.

The great warming had provided the window of opportunity; human mobility and opportunism took advantage of it. The newcomers arrived in a land where many species of larger Ice Age animals still flourished. But mammoth, mastodon, and other big game were in serious decline. Rapid warming, major changes in ecosystems, and drought stressed large-animal populations as never before. The stress developed right after the Ice Age. By the time Clovis societies lived on the North American Plains, more than twenty large-animal species were already extinct.

Within five centuries, the last of the Ice Age megafauna had vanished, killed off by rapidly soaring temperatures and aridity in previously well-watered environments. [20] Although the Paleo-Indians may have accelerated the die-out of slow-breeding animals, human predation was at most a secondary cause of extinction.

After 11,000 B.C, only one large American mammal survived, the Plains bison. Fossil pollens from dozens of locations chronicle major vegetational changes as the Laurentide ice sheet retreated across central and eastern Canada. Now winters were shorter and warmer, summers cooler than today. Unlike other Ice Age animals, bison thrived on the short grasslands that grew in the shadow of the Rocky Mountains. They continued to flourish on the Plains until European rifles nearly brought their demise.

∞

With the first settlement of the Americas, the great diaspora of modern humans from their primordial homeland in tropical Africa was complete. Only the remote Pacific islands, and of course Antarctica, remained uninhabited, the former awaiting the development of the outrigger canoe and the domestication of easily storable foods.

The great warming propelled humanity across Beringia into a hitherto uninhabited continent and gave access to the vast, environmentally diverse world south of the great ice sheets. Within a surprisingly short time, people whose ancestry lay with the ancient Stone Age world of the north, of Alaska, Siberia, Asia, and Eurasia, had settled in the heart of the new lands. From that moment, the Old World followed a different historical trajectory from the New. Except for peoples in the far north, the two worlds did not encounter one another again until the Norse sailed westward from Greenland in the tenth century A.D. and Christopher Columbus landed in the Indies in 1492.

Two trajectories, two histories, but in the face of the same unpredictable swings of Holocene climate, in the Old and New Worlds. People reacted to them in remarkably similar ways. The first Americans brought with them ancient cultural traditions from the late Ice Age, of hunting and plant gathering, perhaps of fishing and sea mammal hunting. They also carried with them rich spiritual beliefs, chants and myths, complex worldviews passed from generation to generation from time immemorial. Like their ancestors across the land bridge, they were brilliant opportunists, stoical, tough, and capable of quick improvisation. Perhaps these qualities explain the close similarities in how societies in both worlds reacted to long- and short-term climatic change.

For thousands of years, the flexibility and small scale of hunter-gatherer life allowed people everywhere to adjust effortlessly to drought and flood, to warmer and colder temperatures, or to rising seas by simply moving or making adjustments in their diet. Their vulnerability increased as some groups settled in permanent villages in those rare places where abundant food was at hand. By 10,000 B.C., some groups in southwestern Asia had taken to growing cereal grains as a way of coping with drought. Experiments in growing native plants in North and Central America began with the intensive harvesting of often hard-to-process native grasses and nuts as early as six thousand years ago. Soon after, people were deliberately growing them. By 3,000 B.C., many people in Egypt and Mesopotamia lived in towns and cities, settlements born in part from a need to manage increasingly dry conditions and to produce more food. Towns and cities first appear in the Americas in the first millennium B.C., again in response to a need to organize society more closely to produce more food in drought-prone environments. Almost simultaneously, great civilizations flourished in the Old World and in the Americas, societies increasingly vulnerable to short-term climatic events by virtue of their ever-greater complexity and inability to swing with the climatic punches.

In both Old World and New, human societies reacted to climatic traumas with social and political changes that are startling in their similarities. As the Harvard biologist Stephen J. Gould once remarked, we are all products of the same African twig. We share vast reservoirs of human potential and reaction, which caused us, whether native American or European, Australian or Eurasian, to create similar responses to the vagaries of climate change during the long summer.

4

EUROPE DURING
THE GREAT WARMING
15,000 TO 11,000 B.C.

> It's a warm wind, the west wind, full of bird's cries.
>
> John Masefield, *The West Wind*, 1902

Sailing the Gulf Stream off the Florida coast can be a memorable experience, especially during a winter northerly, when the northbound current meets strong winds blowing in the opposite direction. I remember crossing to the Bahamas in thirty knots of wind, slamming our way with well-reefed sails into unbelievably steep seas, ducking constantly as our boat crashed into the waves. We were rash to cross on such a day, but on the other side the calm anchorages of the Abacos Islands beckoned.

At anchor that evening, we reflected on the mighty power of the unseen current pushing us northward, which had caused us to steer as much as twenty degrees off the direct course to Nassau to allow for it. The Gulf Stream is part of a vast global conveyor belt of moving water that has the power to change climate and alter human lives. We imagined throwing a bottle into the turbulent waves, then following it as it passed north, then east, deep into the North Atlantic, skirting the southern edge of the Grand Banks. Months later, the weathered container would be floating far off the west coast of Ireland, before being carried on the wings of the west-flowing Irminger Current across to the South Labrador Sea.

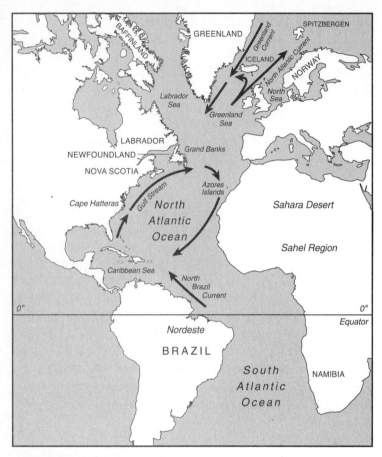

North Atlantic circulation

Now arctic air cools the water surrounding the bottle as it floats in the South Labrador Sea. The heavier, salt-laden surface water sinks deep into the ocean; let it carry our imaginary bottle with it. The bottle and the salt water continue their journey at great depth, drawn along by a fast-moving southward conveyor belt, past the Caribbean to South America and the northern coast of Antarctica. In the far south, the bottle has two options, either to travel northeast into the eastern Indian Ocean or a much longer distance into the heart of the northern Pacific. Eventually, our container is cast nearer the surface, into warmer water, where the circulation causes a massive flow of upper ocean water from the tropical Pacific to the Indian Ocean through the Indonesian archipelago. The conveyor belt flows back round the Cape of Good Hope northward into the Atlantic, where the entire cycle begins anew.

The water battering our heavily reefed boat off Florida had been propelled there by two counteracting forces in the North Atlantic. High-latitude cooling and low-latitude heating—thermal forcing—drive the flow to the north. High-latitude freshwater gain and low-latitude evaporation cause haline forcing, which moves water in the opposite direction. These days, thermal forcing dominates. The downwelling of salt water in the north nourishes the great ocean conveyor belt, which in turn sucks along the northward counterflow that brings warmer temperatures to Europe.

The Atlantic conveyor system has power equivalent to one hundred Amazon Rivers and is one of the great drivers of global climate.[1] Vast amounts of heat flow northward and rise into the arctic air masses over the North Atlantic. This heat transfer accounts for Europe's relatively warm oceanic climate with its moist westerly winds, which has persisted, with vicissitudes, through the Holocene.

Why didn't the cold return after the last warming? Changes in the earth's orbit have increased solar insulation and surface temperatures on a long-term orbital time scale. The answer also lies in the pace of ocean circulation. The invisible circulation of the oceans has accelerated and slowed dramatically over the past 100,000 years. At the height of the late Ice Age, the conveyor flowed at only two-thirds its present velocity. We know this because the oceanographer Jean Lynch-Stieglitz has used tiny ocean foraminifera to measure changing ratios of oxygen isotopes in deep-sea cores across the Florida Straits during the height of the late Ice Age.[2] These ratios change with the temperature of the water in which these creatures live. At the same time, the water becomes much denser as the ratios change, temperatures fall, and the water becomes saltier. Lynch-Stieglitz used a commonly employed mathematical model to calculate the current flow driven by the changing density of the water. She was able to demonstrate that during the late Ice Age, the downwelling of salt water in the Labrador Sea had slowed dramatically while ocean temperatures off Europe plunged. One definitely would not have gone swimming off Long Island or the Spanish coast!

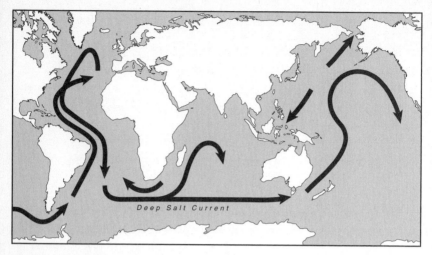

Deep Salt Current

The Great Ocean Conveyor belt

The circulation slowed because meltwater from the Laurentide ice sheet mantling Hudson Bay and eastern Canada had flowed into what is now the Labrador Sea for thousands of years. Heinrich events, with their sudden release of icebergs, contributed significantly. The constant influx of freshwater shut off the downwelling of denser salt water from the surface of the ocean in the North Atlantic. This, in turn, closed off the counterclockwise circulation of warmer water from the Gulf Stream northeastward toward Europe, and then to the west below Iceland. Deep-sea cores and Greenland ice borings from the late Ice Age contain high levels of fine dust carried into the atmosphere by cold glacial winds from the north and east.

Then came rapid warming. The dust levels dropped suddenly as the Laurentide beat a rapid retreat. The Hudson Bay meltwater stream slowed, then ceased. Downwelling resumed in the Labrador Sea. The Gulf Stream switched on and the North Atlantic circulation resumed its flow. Moist westerly winds now prevailed over the ocean, bringing much warmer temperatures to northwestern Europe.

One day, computer simulations of the intricate relationships between changing sea surface temperatures and atmospheric conditions will give us a better understanding of the complicated dynamics that set off this dramatic climatic change. Perhaps slow cyclical changes in the eccentricity of the earth's orbit and in the tilt and orientation of its spin axis triggered the shift, thereby altering patterns of evaporation and rainfall and the intensity of passing seasons. The geochemist Wallace Broecker believes these seasonal changes caused the entire atmosphere-ocean system to flip suddenly from one mode during glacial episodes to an entirely different one during warmer periods. Each flip of the "switch" changed ocean circulation profoundly, so that the great conveyor belt carried heat around the world in different ways.[3] From what little we know of the cycles of cold and warm climate, we would be naive indeed to assume that another cold oscillation will not descend on earth some time in the future.

⚬⚬⚬

Fifteen thousand years ago, perhaps 40,000 Cro-Magnons lived in central and western Europe, well under half the number of people who pass through London's Heathrow Airport in a day. The largest bands spent much of the year in the sheltered valleys and lowlands south of the steppe/tundra. Their lives revolved around the seasonal migrations of reindeer, spring and fall salmon runs, and the hunting of cold-loving mammals. The men trapped hundreds of arctic foxes, beavers, and other furry animals for their pelts, as efficient, layered clothing was an important weapon against the pervasive cold and the abrupt twists and turns of late Ice Age climate. Women gathered plant foods in season and were responsible for the time-consuming work of making and repairing tailored, layered clothing.

The Cro-Magnons were experts at assessing the condition of their prey, especially the fatness of the animals.[4] This is why the main reindeer drives were probably in autumn, after the animals had gorged on rich plant food during the warm months. Many historic hunter-gatherer societies were selective in seeking out fatter animals and marrow. The meat from fatter animals tastes better and provides a feeling of satiety that leaner flesh does not. Fat is a major source of energy, is more efficiently metabolized than protein, and stores important vitamins and essential acids. Obviously, ancient hunters were unaware of these nutritional niceties, but they would have been well aware of what kinds of meat were better for their health and well-being.

The amount of animal protein that a human can safely consume without serious long-term health consequences is about 50 percent of the daily caloric intake. This is why many hunter-gatherer societies severely restrict the amount of meat that pregnant women can eat, for excessive protein levels can endanger the health of their fetuses. The need to broaden the diet may explain why many historic arctic societies habitually ate the partially digested stomach contents of caribou and reindeer, as well as the digestive tracts of some birds and sea mammals. Some coastal Eskimo groups even harvested kelp through the ice in winter. We can be sure that the Cro-Magnons did all they could to diversify their diet.

These hunting societies relied heavily on large and medium-sized mammals—aurochs, bison, mammoth, reindeer, wild horses, and other prey. Human life was connected to these beasts through powerful symbolism. The magnificent cave paintings of Altamira, Grotte de Chauvet, Lascaux, Niaux, and many other sites bear testimony to the power of the Ice Age bestiary. There, people placed their hands against the rocky walls, apparently to acquire power from the animal spirits that lurked within.[5]

Europe was still bitterly cold. Fifteen millennia ago, a huge ice sheet mantled all of Scandinavia, northern Germany, and part of the Low Countries, as well as much of Britain, which was part of the Continent.[6] Sea levels were over 90 meters lower than today. As you sail on a moonlit night across the southern North Sea, admiring the silvery path of the moon on the gently rippling waves, it may be hard to believe that you are sailing a few meters above what was dry land as recently as ten thousand years ago. Fishermen trawling the Dogger Bank have dredged up antler spear points and other artifacts from the ocean floor.[7]

Then the warming came, and the landscape changed beyond recognition within a mere two thousand years.

By 12,700 B.C., summer temperatures at some locations were warmer than today. The humble beetle once again serves as our barometer of change. These tiny creatures are extremely sensitive to temperature changes, especially in northern latitudes, and British beetles are especially

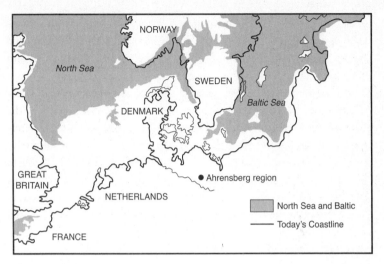

Northern Europe in 9000 B.C.

obliging. Before 13,000 B.C., Britain's cold-loving beetle species tell us that the mean July temperature was about 10°C. Then the beetle population changed drastically. Summer temperatures rose rapidly, to an average of about 20°C in about 12,500 B.C., then gradually cooled to around 14°C in 11,000 B.C.[8] The warming coincided with a dramatic shrinking of the Scandinavian and Alpine ice sheets. The melting released billions of liters of freshwater into the ocean. By 12,000 B.C., sea levels were rising in some places as much as 40 millimeters a year.

In the first decades of the twentieth century, the Swedish botanist Lennart von Post developed the science of palynology, the study of minute pollen grains preserved in waterlogged deposits like Scandinavian bogs. Post realized that these tiny pollens were highly diagnostic of the trees once growing in the vicinity. He collected them in column samples, which provided a chronicle of changes in tree cover in northern Europe throughout the Holocene. Thanks to the work of Post and his successors, we know that the steppe vegetation that covered much of the European landscape during the late Ice Age slowly became denser and more productive, with invasions by junipers, willows, and other shrubs. Then the tree cover thickened.

By 12,000 B.C., birch forests covered much of England and many parts of western and northern Europe. The only check for trees spreading across Europe was their rate of natural dispersal. Some trees, like birch and elm, disperse their seeds by wind. These clearly advanced more rapidly than oaks, whose seeds are dispersed by birds and other agencies such as streams and are also much slower growing. Experts believe that trees such as birch, pine, alder, and hazel could advance at a rate of 1–2 kilometers a year over periods of five hundred to two thousand years. A tree's eventual range also depended on the location of the glacial refuges from which it dispersed. Pine, for example, spread from refuges on the continental shelf off western Ireland, whereas beech spread from Italy and the Balkans.[9] To this day, stands of birch predominate in eastern and central Europe in environments that further west support pine. In the absence of soil or distance constraints, plants can respond remarkably quickly to climatic changes. For example, in New Zealand, the southern beech (*Nothofagus*) was confined to a few sheltered locations during the late Ice Age, when grassland and scrub covered most of the land. But the rapid warming at the end of the Ice Age had beeches completely replacing the open vegetation of earlier times within a mere three hundred years.

During the ecologically unstable period between 13,000 and 8,000 B.C., many factors affected the spread of trees, among them patterns of animal browsing, disease, and fires started by lightning and other causes. Humans, too, may have affected tree distribution by deliberately firing dry grass to foster new growth and to encourage game to feed on fresh green offshoots. The fire stick was a powerful instrument of environmental change.[10]

After two turbulent millennia of rapid vegetational change, Europe looked fundamentally different. The birch forest that had spread first across the north was now pushed far northward into Scandinavia and northern Russia. Tundra and steppe effectively vanished. These environmental changes created unique challenges for people adapted to a deep-frozen world.

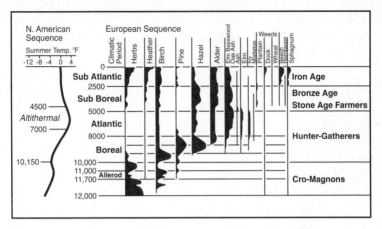

Changing vegetation patterns in Europe as revealed by pollen analysis

For a start, big-game hunting became problematic. Between 14,000 and 9,500 B.C., a wave of extinctions affected the Cro-Magnon's favorite quarry, especially animals with body weights of over 44 kilograms.[11] The familiar Ice Age creatures that vanished in this period included the mammoth, woolly rhinoceros, giant deer, and numerous smaller mammals. Quite why this epidemic of extinctions swept across the Americas, Europe, and northern Eurasia is somewhat of a mystery. Many larger animals may have been unable to adapt to rapidly warming temperatures. For instance, a recently discovered family of mammoths perished at Condover in England at a time when the familiar steppe/tundra landscape was shifting northward and giving way to tree cover. In many places, rising sea levels, mountain ranges, and other natural barriers may have prevented such animals from following the more open terrain.

A variety of complex and still little-understood environmental stresses led to the extinction of the more specialized and less adaptable Ice Age species. Some eighty genera vanished from northern Eurasia alone. Mammoths survived only on the bitterly cold and isolated Wrangel Island in the Siberian Arctic, where steppe/tundra conditions persisted on an island cut off from mainland Beringia by rising sea levels. Here the arctic elephant continued to thrive in an Ice Age time capsule, where isolation caused them to become dwarf mammoths. Eventually, this remote population died from natural causes, the last of them in about 2,500 B.C. as the pyramids of Giza rose alongside the Nile and plows were coming into use in central and western Europe.

What role did human hunters play in this extinction? Almost certainly a very minor one, for their ancestors had lived alongside and preyed on the same large mammals for tens of thousands of years. For this reason, it seems unlikely that they overkilled large mammal populations, even if they eventually contributed to their demise by hunting weakened, hungry, and slow-breeding animals when they came across them.

By the time the megafauna had vanished, the people had adapted successfully to a new world.

∞

Opportunism, flexibility, and mobility—once again, these essential qualities of late Ice Age societies had come into play. Just like the hunter-gatherers of Siberia and Alaska, the Cro-Magnons were unfazed by climatic change. They had two options—move northward following their ancient quarry, the reindeer, which migrated with the north-moving tundra, or stay where they were and adapt to entirely new environments. As far as we can tell from very inadequate archaeological evidence, they did both.

As extinctions took hold in the more wooded south, woodland animals became more commonplace, among them red deer, wild boar, and aurochs, a formidable prey even for well-armed hunters. Animal resources became less accessible and harder to hunt with spears. Late Ice Age Cro-Magnon bands had been able to exploit fall reindeer migrations where thousands of animals passed through narrow river valleys and crossed streams on their way to and from summer pastures. They harvested hundreds of animals every year. Now the game was more dispersed, generally solitary and harder to pursue over dense forest, woodland, and occasional clearings. To hunt a red deer required infinite patience, superb stalking abilities, and accurate weapons.

As the game dispersed and grew scarcer, plant foods became more abundant and the obvious key to survival. The mixed deciduous woodland that colonized much of western Europe was a highly productive, if seasonal, environment in terms of edible plants, especially in spring and fall. In fall, there were rich nut harvests from hazel and other trees. There were fruit and fungi, grass seeds and edible tubers, as well as the ubiquitous bracken rhizome, easy pickings for people who knew their environments intimately. With much longer growing seasons, even a child could collect enough food to satisfy its hunger for much of the year. In southern Europe, for example, Mediterranean stone pine forests yielded kernels that had a protein value two-thirds that of lean steak and could feed entire families for months on end.[12]

The changeover to plant foods required no technological innovations, for the artifacts used to gather and process wild grasses, nuts, or tubers were simplicity itself—wooden digging sticks, hides, trays or baskets made from vegetable fibers, and a variety of stone grinders and pestles carefully shaped from convenient boulders. Flat-topped stones had ground red ocher and painting materials, as well as seeds and roots, for thousands of years. They merely became a more prominent feature of the local toolkit.

Though earlier Cro-Magnons had, above all, been meat eaters, they were well aware of the need to broaden their diet. Like hunter-gatherers everywhere, they always lived in edible landscapes, however harsh. They knew the seasons of even the most inconspicuous plants, when nuts could be harvested, and when reindeer shed their antlers. The environment was a living entity that provided both staple foods and a cushion of other animals and plants that could be consumed when reindeer migrations were unpredictable or salmon runs poor. When the great warming came, Cro-Magnon groups adapted to changed circumstances by becoming omnivorous. As relatively open birch, hazel, and pine woodland gave way to closed canopy forest, open habitats became increasingly scarce. Most forest clearings lay near lakes and river banks, or by marshes and swamps. After 9000 B.C., a mere four thousand years after the beginning of the great warming, most hunter-gatherer groups in Europe lived in such open environments or, increasingly, by seacoasts.

Estuaries and sheltered bays provided a bounty of birds, fish, mollusks, and sea mammals. A reliable food supply, one would think, but one has only to look at coastal Inuit communities in the Canadian Arctic to realize that there were many complications—severe storms and early ice breakup, which could disrupt fisheries and sea mammal hunting, and the failure of salmon runs, to mention only a few. Furthermore, many fish and mollusk species have little fat, which makes them of little nutritional value to those who live off them. Fattier fish like salmon are notoriously difficult to preserve, even in environments with long, subzero winters that allow one to freeze the catch for later use. Dried and smoked fish have a relatively short shelf life and certainly would not keep more than a few months—too short a time to alleviate food shortages lasting several seasons or years.

Inevitably, then, the Europeans of the great warming turned to plant foods, especially starchy seeds and nuts, which could usually be stored for years and provided a much more reliable staple than grease or small mammals. Not that plant foods would have been a universal panacea. Exceptionally heavy rains, drought cycles, or great storms would have brought people to periodic food shortages and social instability. In times of stress, they would have fallen back on their safety net of less desirable plant foods and relied on exchange with neighbors to tide them through the lean months. The much greater productivity of carbohydrate and oil-rich plant foods, and social links with neighbors, were the savior during this long period of rapid warming.

The shift from hunting to gathering plant foods had other, more subtle consequences. During the summer months, people may have cut back on hunting so that they could gather easily stored plant foods.[13] They would either consume the resulting food surplus immediately, storing it as additional body fat, or hoard it in underground pits or aboveground containers, in which case they could expect to lose as much as a third to decay, rodents, and theft. Storage on one's person has the advantage of mobility, but in all probability one would have lost most of the extra fat long before the hungry months of late winter and early spring. Storage in a pit or aboveground means that food can be rationed out through the lean months, but at the price of drastically reduced mobility.

Many nuts and seeds are very high in protein, and consumed in large quantities they were as harmful to pregnant women as animal flesh. One solution might have been to pulverize nuts, shells and all, and then boil them, skimming off the oil that floated to the surface. Alternatively, one could drink this broth-like liquid and discard the solids—a practice followed by the historic Indians of southeastern North America. Some nuts, such as certain acorns, contain high levels of tannins, which have to be leached out by boiling or soaking, while other compounds make certain grasses and nuts either mildly toxic or less easily digestible, again requiring extended processing. Parching, grinding, or boiling starchy plant foods required great investments of labor daily before they could be eaten or stored. Such activities tied bands down to one location for longer periods of time.

The climates of the great warming became more sharply seasonal, so that animals were forced to accumulate larger body fat reserves to tide them through the scarce months of late fall through early spring. At the same time, hunters would have cut back on their hunting of larger animals in the winter and spring. Instead they would have relied on stored meat, obtained from carefully selected prey such as well-nourished females killed in summer and fall. They would also have pursued fatter males in late winter and spring, but not hunted animals during the annual rutting season. In really bad years, the hunters may have butchered their prey for only the fat-rich parts, such as the brain, kidneys, and marrow in the limbs.

Another fat-yielding strategy involved extracting grease from porous tissue in the extremities of limb bones and vertebrae. The bones would be smashed up, then boiled in hide, bark, or basketry containers using heated stones—a laborious process. John Speth believes that both stone boiling and the extraction of grease may have first appeared during the great warming. The boiling would produce nonprotein calories, but probably not enough for an adequate diet.[14]

The warming climate and greater seasonality almost certainly caused periods of nutritional stress for which people tried to compensate by hunting smaller animals that retained higher fat levels during spring. These prey included waterfowl, beaver (valued for their fat tails), wild pigs, insect larvae, sea mammals, and some fish species. Much of the well-documented shift from larger to small animals during these millennia may reflect not only the increasing scarcity of large terrestrial mammals but also these nutritional needs.

What saved the Cro-Magnons was their environmental knowledge, and above all their mobility. They now lived almost entirely in the open, abandoning the caves and rock shelters that offered sanctuary during long Ice Age winters. Solitary, unpredictable game, forest hunts during the winter months when snow underfoot made stalking easier, and the seasons of widely scattered clumps of plant foods made mobility imperative and hunting territories much larger than they had been in earlier times. This is why only transitory occupation layers appear in great shelters like Laugerie Haute, and why the magnificent cave art of earlier times was forgotten. The people moved their spiritual life aboveground and carried their symbols of belief with them.

In the absence of rock art, we can only speculate about these beliefs, for any symbols of them were painted or carved on perishable wood, or on bark or hides. But we can be sure that there still were respected elders, men and women of power who interceded between the realm of the living and the supernatural world, who explained the world order in song, chant, and trance. We can also be certain that the hunter still enjoyed an intimate spiritual relationship with the aurochs, deer, and other prey that lurked in clearing and forest. Shamans may even have preserved folk memories of long-ago hunts, of mythic beasts that no longer cavorted on earth, and of frigid winters that lasted into summer. Certain essentials of daily human existence remained unchanged. If living hunter-gatherer societies are any guide, spiritual life during the great warming was as powerful and sophisticated as it was in the heyday of the cave artists. Everywhere, men and women went about their daily lives surrounded by the unseen forces of the supernatural realm, which provided guidance and precedence, gave shape to human existence, and ordered a world that changed little from one short generation to the next.

The Cro-Magnons had always hunted with the spear and spear-thrower, which are excellent weapons when used at close quarters to harvest migrating reindeer. Such implements can inflict fatal wounds when wielded by an expert stalker but are cumbersome in thick forest, where the long shaft catches on branches and undergrowth. At some point either very late in the Ice Age or during the early stages of the great warming, when forests were beginning to displace hitherto scrub-covered tundra, some European hunters developed a new and much more lethal hunting weapon—the bow and arrow.[15]

The bow was a tremendous advance over the spear and spear-thrower. It allowed the shooting of a projectile at a speed of 100 kilometers an hour, far faster than the most aggressive of spear casts. Furthermore, one could shoot up to 200 meters and achieve a remarkable accuracy between 20 and 50 meters. This is the optimum range, for beyond this distance the force of penetration diminishes rapidly.

The earliest bows were simple but powerful weapons. A few early bows found in Scandinavian bogs have a fiber or thong string and are as much as 1.6 meters long, capable of propelling an arrow through tough bear skin at a range of 50 meters. The arrows for such weapons, preserved in waterlogged marshes and swamps in Scandinavia, are about 90 centimeters long and about a centimeter in diameter. Armed with a razor-sharp stone point, the arrow, binding, feathers and all would weigh about a gram. Such weapons were lethal in the hands of a hunter and stalker expert enough to come within range of a bear, deer, or other medium-sized game.

The bow was a precise weapon that could be used to kill or wound animals where obstacles like trees hampered a close approach. It could also be used to shoot birds on the water and on the wing. But this precision depended on tiny, delicately fabricated stone points, with tips so sharp they could penetrate fur and a tough hide. In the early years of the twentieth century, the University of California researcher Saxon Pope went hunting with the famous Yahi Indian Ishi, using only traditional weaponry.[16] Pope noticed that stone points are more effective than steel arrows against deer and birds. They are much sharper. A stone point enters the quarry obliquely, cuts the skin and does serious damage to the organs it encounters. Add a second armature, like a barb, and the arrow inflicts a much larger wound. The most effective barbs formed lateral cutting edges, especially effective when several of them were mounted on the same shaft.

The bow and arrow developed out of earlier, increasingly refined hunting technologies that could be used against animals large and small. But the new weaponry required much smaller stone blades and large numbers of tiny barbs and points. The technology itself was simple enough—a matter of creating small, often cylindrical "cores," carefully shaped lumps of flint and other fine-grained rock from which dozens of small bladelets of more of less standardized size could be struck.

The technology developed over many centuries. By 10,000 B.C., many groups made arrow tips of different forms, among them triangle and trapeze shapes, for use alongside spears armed with stone points. Soon everyone began to use small, sharp arrow points. Two thousand years later, tiny stone blades were snapped twice to form trapeze-like arrowheads mounted transversely at the tip of the shaft.

Bows and arrows had other important advantages. The hunter was no longer dependent on just one missile but carried an entire quiver of arrows that weighed less than a single spear and spear-thrower. A bow and arrow was effective against a wide range of animals and was a far more versatile weapon. Spears and spear-throwers are highly effective for close-range hunting, for stabbing reindeer or wild horses during mass drives. They are far less efficient against solitary animals and smaller creatures, many of which are fast-moving targets that offer the hunter only a fraction of a second to aim and fire.

Think of a hunter with a bow stalking red deer in dense forest or hunting chattering squirrels high above him in the trees. He can stand off a short distance, hide among the tree trunks and undergrowth, then aim and fire with much greater ease. An expert bowman can pick off a squirrel many meters up and drop it to the ground. Above all, the bow and arrow allowed hunters to pursue birds on the wing for the first time. Nets and drives were still useful against rabbits, walking birds, and waterfowl, but a bowman could crouch downwind in the reeds by a small lake, perhaps use realistic decoys to lure his prey, then shoot unsuspecting birds as they came close. If the shoot was well planned, the carcass would float gently to within reach. No spear could bag a flying bird, but any archer of reasonable skill could shoot one, or at least stun it with a fast-moving arrow, then kill it when it fell wounded to the ground.

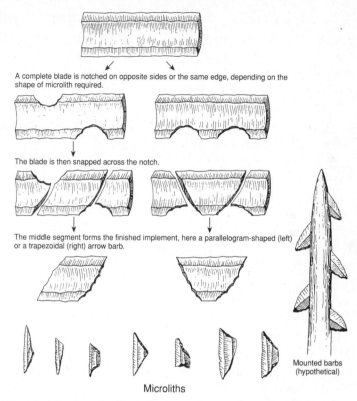

A complete blade is notched on opposite sides or the same edge, depending on the shape of microlith required.

The blade is then snapped across the notch.

The middle segment forms the finished implement, here a parallelogram-shaped (left) or a trapezoidal (right) arrow barb.

Microliths

Mounted barbs (hypothetical)

Microlith technology. A variety of lethally sharp arrow barbs were made from tiny flint blades that were notched or snapped. They were mounted in slots in wooden arrows and spears. Full size

Only in the north, at the margins of the tundra, did the old lifeway persist, but with the benefit of the new hunting technology. Here reindeer were still an important staple, preyed on by hunters as they moved between winter and summer pastures. The Ahrensburg tunnel valley in Schleswig-Holstein, northern Germany, was a long glacial valley through which rivers flowed into the Elbe to the southwest.[17] A shallow glacial lake and numerous waterholes covered the valley floor, places where reindeer congregated in fall and spring. The valley lay just inside the southernmost boundary of the late Ice Age ice sheet and was soon uncovered by retreating ice. When the first hunters arrived there, in about 12,000 B.C., the landscape was open tundra, with only a few birch trees. The tundra extended as far north as modern-day Copenhagen, but seasonal temperatures were quite warm, rising to as high as 13°C in July, with winter lows in the −5°C range. During the ensuing thousand-year cold period, temperatures fell rapidly and subarctic conditions returned. By that time the tunnel valley lay at the northern limits of the forest, which reached the area from the Elbe Valley to the south.

The reindeer hunters thrived throughout the great warming, through the ten centuries of bitter cold, and into the ensuing warm-up. Between about 10,100 and 9900 B.C., groups of hunters gathered by the lake, where they killed large numbers of reindeer. The hunters lived in the valley year round, but large-scale hunting took place in fall, when the reindeer were fat from summer grazing. For most of the year, the people preyed on isolated beasts. In autumn, they harvested migrating animals as they approached the lakeside.

Before World War II, the German archaeologist Alfred Rust, who learned his craft on Stone Age caves in the Near East, excavated sites at Stellmoor and Meiendorf on the southern side of the valley lake on a shoestring budget, having bicycled from Syria to Germany when his funds ran out. At Meiendorf he uncovered reindeer hunters, who used spear-throwers and stone-tipped spears armed with shouldered stone points to kill their quarry. But some centuries later, their successors turned to bows and arrows.

As the mass of reindeer approached the valley, the hunters headed them off at the proverbial pass and stampeded them down a narrow, grassy stretch between the lake and the surrounding higher ground using light stone-tipped arrows. The reindeer were moving to the north-northeast and would have come to the lakeshore at a sharp angle. Here they would either have to cross the narrow lake or move up to higher ground. The hunters lay in wait, killing as many beasts as possible on dry land, then shooting at the confused survivors as they tried to cross the lake to safety. Crouched bowmen fired volley after volley of arrows. Rust and his excavators recovered no less than 105 finely made pinewood arrows from the lake deposits, as well as reindeer bones bearing the telltale wounds from razor-sharp arrows. The archaeologist Bodil Bratlund has studied the lesions on the bones and established that the hunters shot at their prey from about the same level, waiting to fire until the animals were alongside them and presented the best target.[18] They loosed their final volleys as the animals passed out of range, wounding a few stragglers in the rear flanks.

Farther south in the forest, the hunter worked alone. During the height of the late Ice Age, many Cro-Magnon groups had congregated in larger bands, living off relatively predictable reindeer migrations and salmon runs. But the fundamental social unit was always the family and fellow kin, the ancient ties that bound people living far apart with intricate obligations that passed from one generation to the next. With the great warming, the bands scattered, for the forested landscape could never support large, long-term settlements except where fish abounded, and even then sedentary living required a great diversity of predictable foods. There were no great social changes as the Ice Age ended, just a general dispersal and a reliance on the eternal verities of hunter-gather society: constant mobility, sudden hunting accidents, and the need to acquire intelligence about food supplies from afar.

5

THE THOUSAND-YEAR DROUGHT

11,000 TO 10,000 B.C.

> The rudest savage, skilled as he is in the habits of the food-plants he gathers, must know well enough that if seeds or roots are put in a proper place in the ground they will grow.
>
> Sir Edward Tylor, *Anthropology*, 1881

Fifteen thousand years ago, the effects of Ice Age chill extended into the heart of southwestern Asia. From Greece to Egypt, the eastern Mediterranean lay under the influence of northeasterly anticyclonic winds that blew from the high-pressure masses over the Scandinavian and Siberian ice sheets. There was seasonal rainfall then, as there is today, but conditions were considerably drier: semiarid at best in many areas between Turkey and the Nile valley. The Nile, itself nourished by floods from East Africa and the Ethiopian highlands, flowed at least six meters above its modern level, and was narrower and shallower than the present river. Only a few thousand people lived along its banks, camping at water's edge, fishing in shallow pools, and foraging narrow strips of territory along the patches of oasis in a hyperarid landscape. A sparse population of mobile hunter-gatherers adapted to semiarid living flourished throughout southwestern Asia—along the eastern Mediterranean coast, in the Jordan valley and the arid interior, by the Tigris and Euphrates rivers, and on the Anatolian plateau—wherever there were water and plant foods. Few bands numbered more than a dozen people, each anchored to such permanent water supplies as existed.[1]

Most late Ice Age bands lived in the Levant. This westernmost part of southwestern Asia comprises many landscapes, from the southern slopes of the Tauros Mountains in Turkey to the Jordan rift valley and rugged terrain of the Sinai peninsula in the south. Environments here are divided into long north-south strips, starting with the coastal zone in the west and ending with the deserts in the east. The hunters lived through cold, wet winters and hot, dry summers that were drier in the south, from the Jordan valley down, as they are in modern times. The richest biomass was in the coastal zone, and the carrying capacity of the landscape dwindled rapidly as one went inland.

These were seasonal landscapes. Seeds were abundant from April to June and fruits between September and November. The gazelle, a small desert antelope, flourished everywhere. There were other animals, too, including aurochs, deer, and wild boar. Here, as in Europe, plant foods were less important than they became later, simply because the climate was too dry.

❦

When the great warming began, the northeasterlies subsided. Moister air flows from the Atlantic and Mediterranean brought higher rainfall. Warmer conditions after 13,000 B.C. saw a rapid increase in acorn-rich oak forests, documented in pollen samples from ancient lake beds in eastern Iran, the Jordan valley, and other locations. For the first time in millennia, surface water was abundant; freshwater springs provided ample drinking supplies over much of the area. Hunting bands moved eastward into hitherto uninhabitable lands.

The Cambridge University archaeologist Dorothy Garrod was the first to identify these folk in an excavation on Mount Carmel in the late 1920s, in what is now Israel. She named them Kebarans after Kebara Cave, where she found their tiny arrow barbs and the stone scrapers they

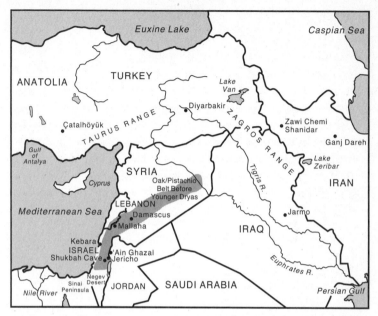

Map of southwestern Asia before and during the Younger Dryas, showing major archaeological sites

used for processing skins.[2] Like the European Cro-Magnons, the Kebarans during the late Ice Age had lived mainly off game, in areas with reliable water supplies. With the great warming, they ranged over a vast area from the Levant deep into the Negev desert and the Sinai, to the Euphrates and into Anatolia. They were highly mobile people who lived in small bands and exploited large hunting territories. Like ancient Californians of later times, they exploited an extremely diverse landscape of well-watered valleys, oak-mantled hills, and semiarid plains. In some areas, the people may have dispersed into the uplands in summer, moving into caves and rock shelters near lowland lakes in the winter. Their summer camps would have been little more than temporary brush shelters, abandoned as the band moved on. The Kebaran toolkit was correspondingly portable, probably no more than a couple of dozen artifacts, many of them in perishable wood. All that survive are thousands of tiny geometric microliths, which once served as arrowheads or razor-sharp barbs. Most

Kebaran bands preyed on gazelle and ate few plant foods except at lower elevations, where some wild cereal grasses grew.[3]

As temperatures warmed, the Kebarans turned to nuts and seeds, just as the descendants of the Cro-Magnons did in Europe, especially in the better-watered oak and pistachio forest zone that now extended from the middle of the Euphrates River basin through the Damascus region and then into the Jordan River. Kebaran sites at these higher elevations now contain pestles and mortars, the tools for processing seed and nut harvests for later storage—an essential in a land of seasonal rainfall and periodic drought. By 11,000 B.C., when Europeans had adjusted to a world bereft of large Ice Age animals, the Kebarans had embraced plant foods as a major part of their diet.

❧

The oak and pistachio belt was perhaps the inspiration for the biblical land of milk and honey, where an astounding range of edible plant foods could be harvested. The people who lived there favored territories that lay on ecotones, the boundaries between contiguous ecological zones, where they could exploit different foods at different times of year. Unlike their predecessors, many groups now used caves year round, presumably because they offered shelter from the rain, and places where plant foods could be kept dry. Plant foods—the wild grasses of spring and early summer, and the acorn and pistachio nuts of fall—were now so abundant that many groups lived not in temporary camps but in much larger permanent communities, where they built substantial round dwellings with thatched roofs. Archaeologists call these descendants of the Kebarans the Natufians, after a wadi near Shukbah Cave in Israel where their artifacts were first discovered by Dorothy Garrod in 1928.[4]

There's nothing particularly distinctive about the Natufian toolkit: the people relied on the same simple hunting weapons as their neighbors and predecessors. But a glance at their artifacts highlights the importance of plant foods in their lives—bone-handled sickles with sharp flint blades for reaping wild grain, and numerous mortars and pestles employed for pounding nuts.

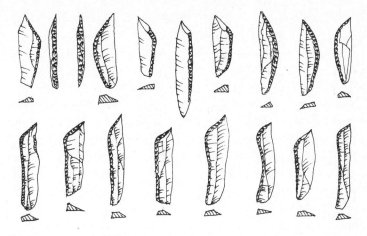

Kebaran stone tools. Full size

Every fall, the Natufians harvested millions of acorns and pistachios. Both nuts have the advantage that they are easily stored and can keep for two years or more if secured away from insects and rodents. Harvesting is straightforward—a matter of shaking the branches or climbing into trees to collect the ripe fruit.

The brownish pistachio nut is a member of the cashew family and is easily processed, for the fruit tends to split on one side when ripe without discharging the nut inside. A small pounder, or even one's fingers, is sufficient for extracting the ready-to-eat kernel. Acorns are another matter. The productivity of oak groves can be astounding, although the yield of individual trees varies sharply from year to year and from one species to another. Acorn meal was an important staple in many parts of the world in ancient times, and was still important in nineteenth-century Europe. Unfortunately, data on harvest yields is hard to come by, but in California's North Coast ranges, yields as high as 590 to 800 kilograms per hectare were not uncommon. Such yields could have supported 50 to 60 times *more* people than were in the area at European contact. Acorns are nutritious, containing as much as 70 percent carbohydrates, about 5 percent protein, and between 4.5 and 18 percent fat. They have one major drawback: they are a labor-intensive crop to process. Shelling and pounding them takes hours, far longer than milling grass seeds. Even then, the meat is inedible, for acorns contain bitter-tasting tannic acid, which has to be leached away by soaking them with time-consuming care before cooking.[5]

Acorns and pistachios produced food surpluses more than large enough to permit Natufian communities to remain for long periods at one location. But the surplus came at a price—a vast expenditure of daily labor. In California, the anthropologist Walter Goldschmidt once observed a woman pound three kilograms of acorns in three hours. It took her another four hours to leach the meal by flushing it through water. After seven hours, she ended up with 2.6 kilograms of edible meal, enough to feed her family for several days. A hunter can skin and butcher a deer, on the other hand, in a few minutes. The hunt may take longer than acorn harvesting, but food preparation is much simpler and more cost effective. When acorns became a staple, life in a community changed profoundly.[6]

While both men and women must have harvested the nuts, the labor of storing and processing them fell entirely to women. For thousands of years, men had hunted while women gathered and processed grasses and other plant foods. This processing took time, but nothing compared to that needed for acorns. To pound and leach acorns for regular daily consumption involved a quantum jump in women's work, to the point that they were tied to their mortars and pestles, as well as their storage bins. After tens of thousands of years of unfettered mobility, the Natufians were now anchored by their acorn harvests to long-term base camps. But with relatively predictable harvests and good storage bins, such more-or-less permanent settlement was entirely feasible.

The dull pounding of pestles and mortars would have sounded through Natufian settlements most days of the year, both from within the village and from nearby outcrops, where hollows in the rock served the same purpose. With abundant, storable food supplies, Natufian communities grew rapidly. The Mallaha site in Israel's Hula valley covered more than 1,000 square meters, a far larger area than any earlier hunter-gatherer camp elsewhere.[7] The inhabitants invested enormous labor in building level terraces for their houses on the hillside, mixing fine plaster for the walls, and digging storage pits. Places like Mallaha were permanent villages, occupied over many generations.

How do we know this? Because a humble animal, a rodent, steps out of the background to provide definitive proof of more permanent settlement. The house mouse, *Mus musculus*, appears in Mallaha refuse heaps in large numbers, together with rats and the remains of house sparrows, all animals intimately associated with prolonged human habitation and well-established households.

At times, the people would move out into seasonal camps to harvest grasses or nuts or engage in mass gazelle hunts. Interestingly, Mallaha and other large Natufian settlements abound with immature gazelle bones, such as one would expect when hunters took antelope that breed year round, as gazelles do under favorable environmental circumstances. But the anchor of Natufian life was the acorn and pistachio harvest, nourished by the balmier conditions of the great warming. Combine the nut harvest with systematic burning of brush and grasses to stimulate new growth and attract game and you have the elements of a carefully managed landscape.

The Natufians' intensive exploitation of plant foods anchored them to groves of nut-bearing trees and grass stands in a way unimaginable during the Ice Age. Their permanent villages were a far cry from the highly flexible and mobile bands of earlier times, or of the desert groups that were their neighbors. At first, the experiment was successful. The new, larger settlements flourished and expanded over many generations. Populations throughout the oak and pistachio belt grew rapidly. Soon neighbors hedged in each group's territory as the landscape filled in, creating potential for conflict over nut groves and other foods, especially in dry years.

Inevitably, a rapidly growing population overexploited what was, ecologically speaking, still a marginal environment exceptionally vulnerable to even minor climatic shifts. Some bands expanded into drier, even more marginal lands. The stage was set for a serious crisis. In about 11,000 B.C., the crisis came in a series of intense droughts that endured for many generations.

⁊᠙᠙᠙᠙

We have a remarkably complete record of the onset of this crisis from a long-lived settlement by the Euphrates River in Syria.

In the 1970s, the Syrian government undertook an ambitious hydro-electric scheme to harness the waters of the Euphrates, a project that involved the building of the Tabqa Dam across the river and the creation of Lake Assad. The flooding threatened many archaeological sites, among them an 11.5 hectare occupation mound called Abu Hureyra.[8] Fortunately for science, the British archaeologist Andrew Moore was able to probe the depths of the ancient village before it was inundated. His meticulous excavations chronicle the vicious troubles that overtook the Natufians and their contemporaries during the Younger Dryas.

Abu Hureyra began in about 11,500 B.C. as a small village of simple dwellings dug partially into the ground, then roofed with branches and patches of reeds supported by wooden posts. Moore excavated the houses with the greatest care, distinguishing the harder undisturbed soil from the softer fill inside the hut depressions. Thick ash and sandy earth deposits represented generations of domestic occupation, which Moore and his colleagues passed through fine screens. Then they ran large soil samples through water in a flotation machine, which separated thousands of tiny seeds and other plant remains, as well as fish bones and tiny beads, from their surrounding matrix.

Thanks to the flotation machine, Moore acquired 712 seed samples, each with as many as 500 seeds from over 150 different edible plants. This enabled the botanist Gordon Hillman to reconstruct the plant-gathering habits of a village of 13,000 years ago, which stood in a strategic location. Below it was the well-watered Euphrates floodplain, while above it a grassland steppe stretched away from the settlement just as it does today. Open forests of oak, pistachio, and other nut-bearing trees lay within easy walking distance. Today, you would have to walk at least 120 kilometers west to reach the nearest forest.

We know the forest was much closer in 11,500 B.C., because Hillman found fruit stones and seeds from hackberry, plum, and medlar in the botanical samples from the settlement, as well as white-flowered asphodel, another plant that flourishes in the same forests. No one could have exploited these forest fruits on any scale unless they were close at hand. Pistachio nuts abounded in the village. Today, the nearest pistachios are in the highlands 90 kilometers away. Hillman believes that pistachio trees once grew in long lines on low wadi terraces a short distance from the village.

During the spring and summer, the inhabitants had easy access to wheat and two forms of rye, wild cereals that grew at the boundaries between oak forest and served as important staples. Today, under undisturbed conditions, such grasses would grow no closer than 100 kilometers from the site.

For five centuries, the Abu Hureyra people had not only a wealth of easily exploitable plant foods close at hand, but also a reliable meat supply. Eighty percent of their meat came from desert gazelles. The hunters did not bother to harvest individual animals. Rather, they culled herds en masse, killing animals of all ages, including the youngest beasts, over a few weeks in early summer, when the gazelle moved north to the river valley in search of lush pasture. Sometimes they slaughtered entire herds.

All these food sources—gazelle migrations, spring grass harvests, and the bounty of nuts in fall—gave the Abu Hureyra people a relatively predictable diet, an interlocking set of easily storable foods that allowed them to inhabit the same location for generations. Rainfall fluctuated from year to year, but in general, climatic conditions were highly favorable. In bountiful years, their storage rooms contained enough food to carry them through the occasional short-lived drought or failure of the nut harvest. But their dependence on labor-intensive foods made it nearly impossible for anyone except a hunting party or a family collecting plant foods to leave the village for any length of time. The Kebarans' mobility long forgotten, the Abu Hureyra peoples' ability to adjust to much drier conditions was severely restricted. They had crossed a threshold of environmental vulnerability.

After 11,000 B.C., the classic strategies of social flexibility and mobility no longer sufficed, not only for the Abu Hureyrans, but also for thousands of people living elsewhere in southwestern Asia. No longer could people simply move away to better-watered locations, or fall back on less-favored ones. In many parts of the Fertile Crescent, they lived in crowded, if edible, landscapes, in settlements occupied over many generations, within territories where others crowded close and where boundaries were strictly defined—perhaps by a streambed or the edge of a valley, a grove of oaks, or a dry wadi. The very permanence of these communities, their close roots to wild grass stands or oak trees, was created not so much by population growth but by women and their processing activities. Their work fed many more people, but at a price—the loss of mobility, of a social flexibility that was as old as humanity itself. The new, permanent base camps were extremely vulnerable to sudden climatic shifts, especially to major drought cycles.

This loss of mobility came not as a result of agriculture, as is commonly believed, but as a consequence of two thousand years of improved rainfall after 13,000 B.C. A constellation of unique circumstances brought a relatively small number of hunter-gatherer bands like that at Abu Hureyra to an entirely new relationship with their environment and with one another. We humans are like spiders, acting within invisible webs that we have woven: webs of interaction among themselves and worlds of meaning whose horizons define action, experience, and memory. The web had remained much the same for tens of thousands of years. Now it was different. For the first time, people lived cheek-by-jowl in crowded settlements, not for a few weeks but generation after generation. Even if they wanted to, they could not move away. Relationships between families, between kin, between young and old, became infinitely more complex. So did the spiritual relationships of people with their land, and with the oak groves, pistachio trees, and grass stands that their ancestors had exploited before them and which their descendants would inherit in turn. These earliest of villages developed societies that foreshadowed the farming communities that would spread rapidly across southwestern Asia a few generations later.

Then, around 11,000 B.C., a prolonged and increasingly severe drought descended on Abu Hureyra, triggered by a dramatic geological event thousands of kilometers away, in North America.

∽

A thousand years earlier, the heaving waters of Lake Agassiz lapped the retreating Laurentide ice sheet for 1,100 kilometers. At its maximum extent, the lake covered parts of Manitoba, Ontario, and Saskatchewan in Canada, Minnesota and North Dakota in the United States. A southward bulge of the Laurentide known as the Superior Lobe formed its eastern margin. This ice peninsula blocked the lake waters from draining east down what is now the Saint Lawrence River valley.[9]

Lake Agassiz

Lake Agassiz was the largest of the many meltwater lakes that lay along the Laurentide ice sheet's southern margins in 11,500 B.C. It supported cold-loving mollusks that flourish in water temperatures of about 5 degrees Centigrade and was such a large body of open water that it exercised a profound influence on the climate of the surrounding ice sheet. The cold surface of the lake caused a stronger southward flow from the perennial high-pressure centers over the ice to the north. This flow, in turn, blocked warmer winds and rainfall from the southwest. As a consequence, the Laurentide received minimal rainfall. The combination of global warming and scant snow accumulation meant that the margins of the ice sheet, and the Superior Lobe, retreated inexorably. Lake Agassiz grew and grew, swollen by glacial meltwater. By 11,000 B.C. the lake waters extended so far eastward they almost completely flanked the lobe's southern edge.

The rise continued. A tiny rivulet of freshwater crept across the deflated lobe and its moraines into what is now Lake Superior. The rivulet soon became a narrow stream, cutting rapidly into the soft ground. Soon the outflow became a rushing torrent, then a deluge. A vast inundation of glacial meltwater burst into the Saint Lawrence River. Within months, perhaps weeks, Lake Agassiz ceased to exist, except as a few remnants, like modern-day Lake Winnipeg.

For months, the huge outburst of freshwater flowed into the Labrador Sea. The Agassiz meltwater floated atop the dense, salty Gulf Stream, forming a temporary lid that effectively prevented warm water from cooling and sinking. Like an electric switch, Lake Agassiz's fugitive waters turned off the Atlantic conveyor belt. Recent research also suggests that meltwater from the Antarctic may have played an important role, but exactly what remains controversial.[10]

For two thousand years, since the end of Heinrich 1, salt water downwelling in the southern Labrador Sea and off Iceland had propelled warm water from the Gulf Stream north and eastward, keeping Europe several degrees warmer than equivalent latitudes elsewhere. Now the Atlantic circulation came to a sudden halt. Within a few generations, temperatures fell rapidly, and once more the Scandinavian ice sheets advanced. A sea ice cap formed within short order, preventing the Gulf Stream from starting up again, helping trigger an intensely cold climatic regimen in Europe.

Climatologists call this thousand-year event the Younger Dryas, after a small polar flower that was then commonplace, whose pollen abounds in waterlogged deposits of the time. Hundreds of carefully calibrated radiocarbon dates place the event between about 11,500 and 10,600 B.C.

Breathtaking climatic changes rippled across Europe. The Netherlands saw winter temperatures plunge regularly below –20 degrees Centigrade. Snow might fall any time from September to May, while summers were cool, averaging between 13 and 14 degrees. Throughout much of Europe, tree cover retreated, to be replaced by *Artemisia* and other shrubs typical of severe, cold conditions. Dramatic temperature fluctuations, wide annual climatic swings, and severe winter storms pummeled Europe.[11] Lake cores from southern Sweden show rapid cooling at the onset of the Younger Dryas in about 11,000 B.C., followed by very gradual warming.

The cold endured for ten centuries. Then, just as abruptly, the Gulf Stream started up again. Computer simulations performed on environmental changes in the Netherlands hint that warming resumed within a mere fifty years. Perhaps a series of unusually warm summers melted the ice over the now-thinning freshwater. Or conceivably an evaporation of water vapor in the tropical Atlantic far from the ice sheets caused such a build up of salt water that downwelling began once again at the edges of the ice zone. The resumed circulation would have quietly eaten into the sea ice.

Far to the west in Canada, the waters of Lake Agassiz had evaporated into some smaller lakes, taking with them the barrier to rainfall flowing northward onto the remnants of the Laurentide ice sheet. After a thousand years or so, another ice advance into the Superior Basin once again blocked off the Saint Lawrence Basin and a new lake formed.

The renewed glacial conditions in the north and the shutdown of the Atlantic circulation had an immediate climatic effect far to the southwest, in Anatolia and the Levant. The colder anticyclonic conditions of the late Ice Age returned, albeit in a somewhat less severe form. A harsh and prolonged drought sank over southwestern Asia for ten centuries.

The drought affected Abu Hureyra almost immediately.[12] In about 11,000 B.C., people stopped gathering tree fruit and nuts from the forest fringe, perhaps because the groves were no longer close to the settlement. At the same time, they increasingly focused on wild cereals, including feather grass and asphodel seeds. Gordon Hillman, who studied the Abu Hureyra flora, points out that such seeds and plants would prosper as the forest margin retreated in the face of prolonged drought. As the forest canopy thinned, the low-lying grasses would receive more sunlight.

Four hundred years later, in 10,600 B.C., asphodel and wild cereal grains vanish from Abu Hureyra. Even pistachio fruitlets are less common.

Clearly, the surrounding landscape could no longer support such dense village populations. The botanical samples show that people turned in desperation to less palatable foods, to drought-resistant clovers and medics that were far from nutritious and required much more processing to detoxify before consumption. Everyone had to work much harder for basic food staples and to eat a much broader range of plant foods. Even valley-bottom plants become scarcer, as if the Euphrates overflowed its banks only rarely now.

Like many other southwest Asian settlements, Abu Hureyra lay in a region where even minor shifts in rainfall patterns could trigger major vegetational changes. As time passed, the landscape became drier and drier and the forests retreated far beyond walking distance, even past the range of economic harvest by outlying camps. The nut groves may also have lain in neighboring territories that were off-limits in a time of intense competition for food. There are no signs of warfare, such as war casualties in local cemeteries, apparently just a quiet acceptance that food was scarce and a greater reliance on kin to help stave off hunger.

At first, the people adjusted to drier conditions by turning to small-seeded grasses and other standby foods. In about 10,000 B.C., they took the next logical step—attempting to grow grasses to expand the wild harvest. The first domesticated seeds appear in the village—rye, einkorn (a variety of coarse-grained wheat), and lentils—but they were not enough to feed everyone. After years of good living, the village had swelled to perhaps three or four hundred inhabitants, a population density far beyond the constraints imposed by a mobile existence. A permanent settlement like Abu Hureyra was no longer viable in the absence of the nut harvests and in the face of a severe drought that made even less desirable foods ever scarcer. We can imagine the cold months of winter, hungry families huddled in their dwellings, with even firewood in short supply in an arid landscape no longer forested. Despite the experiments with cereal grasses, Abu Hureyra was a community under stress from protracted drought. A few generations after the experiments began, the village was abandoned. Whether the abandonment was deliberate or gradual we have no means of knowing. But with fellow kin unable to help, food supplies faltering, and no end to the drought in sight, the ancient strategy of mobility was the only option, whatever the cost.

Abu Hureyra has one of the earliest records of cereal cultivation in the world, but it was not the site of the first such experiments, which occurred some distance away. Back in the 1920s, the University of Chicago Egyptologist Henry Breasted coined the memorable term Fertile Crescent for the great arc of southwestern Asia where agriculture and civilization first began. One end lies in the Nile valley, the other in southern Mesopotamia, beyond the Tigris and Euphrates rivers. In between, the crescent arches through the Levant and the Jordan valley, through southeastern Turkey and across the Iranian highlands and northern Iraq. Breasted's perceptive characterization has stood the test of time.

Wild plant species ancestral to some of the world's most useful crops flourished within the Fertile Crescent and still do today. So did aurochs and boar, wild goats and sheep. Once domesticated, this remarkable diversity of useful plants and animals provided foragers-turned-farmers with a balanced source of raw materials like vegetable and animal fiber, oil, and milk, and, ultimately, with the means to build transportation.

But where in this huge area were the first cereals domesticated? More than a quarter century ago, the agronomist Jack Harlan of the University of Illinois studied stands of wild einkorn in the Karacadag Mountains of eastern Turkey. He harvested einkorn by hand with such success that he was able to show that a small family group could gather enough wild grain in three weeks to sustain themselves for a year.[13] While the Natufians to the south were harvesting both grasses and nuts, the still-unknown hunter-gatherers of the Karacadag were subsisting off wild einkorn, the ancestor of modern domesticated wheat. Within a few generations of carefully selecting the most productive plants, they unwittingly modified einkorn's genes. We know this because of DNA research by the Norwegian geneticist Manfred Heun and his colleagues. Analyzing the DNA from 68 cultivated einkorn wheat strains (*Triticum monococcum monococcum*) and from 261 wild einkorn lines (*Triticum monococcum boeoticum*) that still grow in southwestern Asia and elsewhere, they were able to identify a genetically distinct group of 11 wild varieties that were most similar to domesticated einkorn.[14] These, presumably, are the distant ancestors of modern wheat. This particular wild group flourishes near the modern city of Diyabakir, near the Karacadag Mountains in eastern Turkey. This geography does not prove, of course, that people living there were the first farmers, but archaeological sites nearby do contain the seeds of both wild and domesticated einkorn.

Domesticated einkorn is genetically similar to the wild version. The ancestral line is even closer to the wild type: differences in genetic loci distinguished the two varieties. These few changes, resulting from repeated cycles of sowing, growing, and harvesting wild einkorn with stone-bladed sickles, were of enormous value to farmers. Heavier seeds and denser seed masses made for a more productive domesticated crop. A tougher rachis, the hinge that joins seed and stem, allowed farmers to harvest the ripe crop when they chose, instead of having to time their harvesting for that brief moment when the seeds fell to the ground or could be tapped off into a waiting basket. It is likely that early farmers exerted strong selection pressure on the wheat genome. Gordon Hillman and Stuart Davis developed a mathematical model by harvesting wild einkorn plots in eastern Turkey by hand and other methods, then using the yield and loss figures to calculate the amount of time it would take for the entire crop to achieve the tough rachis of domesticated wheat.[15] They found that if the crop was harvested in a near-ripe state with stone-bladed sickles (widely found in early farming sites) or by simply uprooting the stalks, then full domestication would have been achieved within just twenty to thirty years. But if the crops were reaped when less ripe, the process would have taken longer, perhaps two or three centuries.

Einkorn was domesticated very rapidly in eastern Turkey, as were chickpeas and bitter vetch. Barley, emmer wheat, peas, lentils, and flax were tamed within a very short time elsewhere in the Fertile Crescent. Another wild grass, *Aegilops squarrosa*, grows on the shores of the Caspian Sea. When this grass hybridized with domesticated emmer wheat spreading east from the Fertile Crescent, the result was bread wheat, the most valuable of all ancient crops. Like einkorn, these crops needed few genetic changes to become domesticated, a process that occurred almost as a by-product of a local strategy to deal with long, severe droughts.

Every hunter-gatherer knew that seeds germinated when buried or cast onto damp ground. Thus it was a logical step to scatter seeds to expand natural stands of wild grasses in the hope of acquiring more grain. It is, of course, futile to search for the first domesticated grain or the first stone-bladed sickle. But we know enough to be sure that the transition was rapid. Within a few generations, the habit of repeated planting and harvesting changed the genetic makeup of wild grasses and altered the course of history. The savage droughts of the Younger Dryas were almost certainly the trigger for the change.

∽

We left Abu Hureyra in about 10,000 B.C., abandoned by its inhabitants at a time of intensifying drought. We do not know their fate, but can only surmise that they dispersed into smaller settlements close to reliable water supplies—at natural oases—where food could be found. Here they may have continued to plant grasses to supplement their wild plant diet. Within a few generations, as cultivated gardens began to produce greater yields than stands of wild grasses, this occasional strategy turned into full-fledged farming. When warming resumed at the end of the Younger Dryas, agriculture was the staple of life. Around 9,500 B.C., a new and very different settlement rose on the abandoned mound.

This new Abu Hureyra was a much larger village, a closely knit community of rectangular one-story mud-brick houses separated by narrow lanes and courtyards. The people were almost completely dependent on cereal agriculture. Just how dependent is dramatized by the condition detected of the women's bones.[16] Day after day, the women of the community spent hours on their knees bent over grinders, their toes tucked under their feet. The weight of the body was used to grind the grain, the toes being the base for applying the motion. Hours of grinding pestle on quern placed severe stress on the knees, wrists, and lower back. Inevitably, many women developed arthritis in the back, deformed toe bones, and other conditions from repetitive labor, while the men did not. But the skeletons of both men and women show enlarged upper vertebrae, the result of habitually carrying heavy leads on the head.

There was nothing new in women gathering and processing plant foods. Judging from modern hunter-gatherer societies, the women foraged for plant foods and processed them, while the men hunted and fished. Life in the new Abu Hureyra maintained this basic division of labor. The men hunted gazelle, tended herds, and fished. Perhaps they helped clear farming land. But planting, weeding, and harvesting were in the hands of the women, just as the laborious task of processing grain and nut harvests had been in the old village. The now much more onerous task of food preparation anchored women to permanent settlements and put a brake on the continual mobility that had characterized hunter-gatherer societies for thousands of years.

For the first seven hundred years of the second Abu Hureyra settlement, the men still harvested gazelle by the hundred each spring, as their predecessors had done. In about 9000 B.C., the community abruptly switched over to herding goats and sheep. Why this change occurred we do not know. Perhaps it was the result of overhunting. But the needs of expanding herds added a new dynamic to the rhythm of daily life. For another two to three thousand years, the people of Abu Hureyra lived atop their ancient and growing village mound, fettered to fields and grazing grounds that their ancestors had farmed before them. Here, and elsewhere in southwestern Asia, the ties between the living and the dead were strengthened. Life revolved as always around the unchanging cycle of the seasons, but now planting and harvest, life and death, occurred in a world where one's ancestors were the guardians of the land and the intermediaries between the present generation and the feared supernatural forces that brought rain or drought, life or death.

Abu Hureyra was far from unique. The same experiments took place at dozens of villages large and small, no doubt helped by the old habit of trading information among travelers about food resources and gossip about who was doing what. Individual households and entire communities tried cultivating wild plants to increase harvest yields. Inevitably, the cultivators triggered genetic changes in emmer, rye, and other plants that turned the foragers into farmers within a few generations. And when the distant Atlantic switch flipped open once again, in about 9500 B.C., and the Gulf Stream resumed its flow, the new economies spread rapidly far beyond a few hundred communities in southwestern Asia and revolutionized human life—all, ultimately, because Lake Agassiz broke its banks.

PART TWO

THE CENTURIES OF SUMMER

Sometime too hot the eye of heaven shines,
And often is his gold complexion dimm'd;
And every fair from fair sometime declines,
By chance, or nature's changing course untrimm'd;
But thy eternal summer shall not fade . . .

William Shakespeare, Sonnet 18

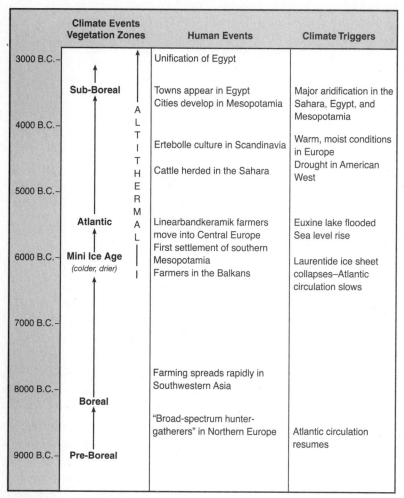

Climate Events Vegetation Zones	Human Events	Climate Triggers
3000 B.C. —	Unification of Egypt	
Sub-Boreal	Towns appear in Egypt	Major aridification in the Sahara, Egypt, and Mesopotamia
	Cities develop in Mesopotamia	
4000 B.C. — A L		
T	Ertebolle culture in Scandinavia	Warm, moist conditions in Europe
I T H	Cattle herded in the Sahara	Drought in American West
5000 B.C. — E R M		
Atlantic A L	Linearbandkeramik farmers move into Central Europe	Euxine lake flooded Sea level rise
6000 B.C. — **Mini Ice Age**	First settlement of southern Mesopotamia	Laurentide ice sheet collapses–Atlantic circulation slows
(colder, drier) I	Farmers in the Balkans	
7000 B.C. —		
	Farming spreads rapidly in Southwestern Asia	
8000 B.C. — **Boreal**		
	"Broad-spectrum hunter-gatherers" in Northern Europe	Atlantic circulation resumes
9000 B.C. — **Pre-Boreal**		

Table 2 showing major climatological and historical events.

6

THE CATACLYSM
10,000 TO 4000 B.C.

There's not a sea the passenger e'er pukes in,
Turns up more dangerous breakers than the Euxine.

Lord Byron, Don Juan, V.5

Each fall, the farmers at Abu Hureyra and at dozens of other communities throughout the Jordan Valley would watch the western skies for the first signs of clouds. They would clear their small gardens, sited close to places where wild grasses grew. Men and women alike would turn over the soil with simple wooden digging sticks to make the land ready for seed. The clouds would build each afternoon, promising a shower, but would evaporate toward sunset. Then the day would come when the heavens darkened and the first drops fell. Rain would pelt the dry earth into the night. Next morning, they would awaken to the glorious scent of newly wetted earth. Every household was out in the fields, scattering precious seeds, then covering them with a layer of newly turned soil. In a good year, the shoots would soon burst green from the ground, moistened by well-spaced rains. But sometimes the first rain came, then no more for weeks, and the crop took, then died.

It was always so with subsistence farming. Even in good times, the farmer lived from harvest to harvest, rain to rain.

The end of the Younger Dryas brought much warmer temperatures and increased rainfall to eastern Mediterranean lands. The chill, dry northeasterly winds of the cold centuries gave way to moist westerlies from the Atlantic and Mediterranean. Well-watered forests soon flourished again from Anatolia to the Jordan Valley, as bountiful with pistachios and acorns as those of a thousand years earlier. But human society had less interest. The hunters and gatherers had become farmers.

Over a large area, from the Jordan Valley in the south to southeastern Turkey in the north, and east in the Iranian highlands, numerous small communities now subsisted not on wild grasses and other plant foods, but on domesticated emmer, rye, and barley. Hunting and wild plants were still important, especially gazelle and deer, but humans were now food producers.

They had also domesticated animals.

The story of domestication comes from fragmentary wild goat and sheep bones, from a prey harvested by the hundreds by hunters on the southern shores of the Caspian Sea and on the Iranian highlands of the Fertile Crescent. Thousands of broken animal bones from a summer encampment at Zawi Chemi Shanidar in the mountains of Kurdistan tell us that the inhabitants killed large numbers of immature wild sheep in 10,500 B.C.[1] This implies careful selection. Perhaps the hunters penned in the animals' grazing grounds so they could readily harvest particular beasts. By 8000 B.C., the inhabitants of a nearby mountain valley settlement, Ganj Dareh, were herding domesticated goats. We know this because of the large numbers of subadult males and mostly older females among the bones. Such a killing pattern comes from slaughtering surplus rams as they reach maturity. The females are kept for breeding purposes until they are old and barren.

How did domestication take place? We can only speculate. The arid conditions between 11,000 and 9500 B.C. concentrated human settlement around permanent water sources such as lakes, perennial rivers, and springs. Here the most diverse wild plant foods are to be found. Here, too, game congregates, both for water and to graze on the lusher vegetation. Inevitably, animals and humans were thrown together, so much so that the hunters would know individual herds intimately and could perhaps identify specific animals.[2]

Wild goats and sheep were the earliest animals to be tamed. Both are gregarious, highly social animals that will follow a dominant leader or

Map showing sites mentioned in Chapter 6 and the spread of farmers into Europe

move together. They also tolerate feeding and breeding in a confined environment. In time, they would have become accustomed to hunters walking in full sight of them. Selective hunting would have focused on males and older animals, sparing the young to preserve the herd. It was surely a matter of ancient knowledge that one could gain control of herd movements by controlling the movements of a few key members. At some point, the hunters learned that the herd might be constrained within a large pen. Or perhaps they captured groups of young and penned them for later consumption. The animals matured and bred. Soon there were surplus males, so the people culled them, keeping the females to breed more young. The same genetic processes that produced domesticated wheat here selected for docility, productivity, and captive breeding. When the hunters isolated wild herds from a larger gene pool for selective breeding under human care, they produced domestic goats that yielded regular milk supplies, which soon became a village staple, and sheep with woolly coats.

Animal domestication developed simultaneously at several locations right around the time warming resumed, in about 9000 B.C., just as farming was taking hold over a far larger area than it had during the Younger Dryas. Agriculture and animal husbandry are not necessarily compatible activities, nor did cultivation lead to domestic animals. Herders, with their insatiable demands for grazing and water, are always on the move, while farmers stay close to their lands. Tension between nomads and settled villagers developed as soon as people domesticated animals, as droughts drove herders and their animals onto settled lands. Both plant cultivation and animal domestication resulted from the need to ensure reliable food supplies at a time of intense drought. And as village populations rose, the pressure on gazelle and other game increased, to the point that many communities acquired domesticated animals to ensure a dependable source of meat and other products.

Once people became farmers, village communities became anchored to their land. These small, crowded villages were far larger and more enduring than the Natufian base camps of a millennium earlier. Within a short time, some of these settlements achieved an impressive size.

⌘

Most early farming villages covered a hectare or so at most. In dramatic contrast, the growing agricultural settlement at Jericho in the Jordan Valley straddled at least four hectares. A temporary Natufian camp had flourished near the bubbling Jericho springs by at least 10,000 B.C., a natural oasis during the drought of the Younger Dryas.[3] Soon a much larger farming community rose close to the springs, a dense cluster of beehive-shaped houses separated by courtyards and narrow alleyways. The large village huddled behind a massive stone wall, complete with a masonry tower, bordered by a rock-cut ditch nearly three meters deep and over three meters across. Just the building of the wall would have required a huge investment of communal labor, an impressive political and social task to pull off. Whether the walls were built as a defense against neighbors or as flood works is a matter of controversy, but it is worth noting that Jericho lay at a strategic point in later centuries, where trade routes from the desert to the east met coastal trading networks. Perhaps this strategic position gave Jericho an unusual importance. But even if the community grew prosperous off long-distance trade, it must have generated large local food surpluses to support the building of defensive works. That implies ample crops, plenty of rainfall to sustain them, and a carefully fostered relationship with the land.

Behind this relationship lay a new preoccupation with ancestors and with the fertility of animal and human life. New spiritual beliefs flowered at Jericho, where people buried their dead under the floors of their houses. Often the survivors decapitated the deceased and buried their skulls in pits in their dwellings, either alone or in caches. Mourners sometimes modeled the features of the dead person on his or her skull in painted plaster before burial, perhaps as formal commemoration of ancestors. Here and elsewhere, ancestor worship came in many forms. At 'Ain Ghazal, in the suburbs of Amman, Jordan, a cache of haunting clay figures survives—their bodies partially decorated, necks elongated, eyes staring intently at the viewer. The archaeologist Gary Rollefson believes that the figures once stood in some form of shrine, adorned with regalia and clothing, perhaps as symbolic representations of ancestors.[4]

The relationship with the land probably changed profoundly, before agriculture began, in societies where permanent settlement replaced temporary hunting camps and well-defined territories nurtured human life through harvests of wild cereals and nuts. These territories became tribal lands vested with a historical continuity. The ancestors became guardians of the land and intercessors between the capricious forces of the environment, the supernatural realm, and the world of the living. The power of the ancestors came from the soil, which was dormant, came to life, produced harvests, seemed to die, and then repeated the same cycle, as did human life. When people became farmers, these relationships became one of the profound focuses of society and spiritual belief.

❦

We see the same concern with ancestors and with the fertility of the soil to the north and west, where farming spread rapidly as warming began. Even quite early, agricultural methods achieved considerable sophistication, involving the rotation of cereals and pulses to ensure higher yields and sustain the soil's fertility.

By 8300 B.C., farming villages flourished on the Anatolian plateau in central Turkey, some of them close to sources of lustrous obsidian, fine-grained volcanic glass much prized for toolmaking and ornaments.[5]

Obsidian has been famous since the days of Pliny the Elder. He recounted its discovery by one Opsius in Ethiopia—a miracle rock that "reflects shadows instead of images." Its sensuous texture comes from a violent past. Obsidian forms when molten lava flows into a lake or ocean and cools rapidly, producing a glassy rock. Iron and magnesium color the stone dark green to black. Sometimes ancient air bubbles created distinctive gold, green, or yellow sheens in the molten rock. Obsidian outcrops are rare; their cobbles were highly prized for their brilliance and the sharp, thin flakes that could be struck from them.

Villages close to the volcanic flows traded large quantities of obsidian to communities near and far in the form of prepared blade cores. Small quantities of Anatolian obsidian traveled hundreds of kilometers along the eastern Mediterranean coast and as far south as the Persian Gulf. Fortunately, each obsidian source produces glass with highly distinctive trace elements. Using spectrometers, experts can source even tiny obsidian fragments to specific outcrops and reconstruct the complex exchange networks that linked villages hundreds of kilometers apart. Inevitably, the leaders of some settlements gained control over the local obsidian trade. Their communities achieved a greater complexity than the simple farming villages that were now common throughout Anatolia.

The great mound of Çatalhöyük in central Turkey covers 13 hectares.[6] The settlement's sun-dried brick houses with flat roofs rose in terraces one above another, the bare walls forming the settlement's outer wall. People entered their houses by ladders from the roofs, emerging into a well-plastered main room with benches, a hearth, and a wall oven. Çatalhöyük

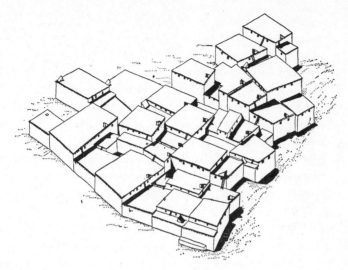

Flat-roofed houses at Çatalhöyük. *Courtesy Grace Huxtable*

was no ordinary settlement. It was larger than Jericho, and its inhabitants prospered off cereal agriculture, stock keeping, and above all, the long-distance trade in black obsidian obtained from the peaked cone of Hasan Dag and other volcanoes about 130 kilometers to the east. The community was carefully planned and very compact. All the houses had the same general floor plan. Even the doorways and bricks were standardized.

The original excavations at Çatalhöyük in 1967 exposed 139 rooms, of which 40 appeared to be some form of shrine—elaborately decorated spaces adorned with exotic figurines that tended to blend into residential areas. The archaeologist James Mellaart found that the wall paintings in the shrines were not permanent decorations but were erased periodically with a layer of white paint, to be painted over soon afterward. The artists drew plain and geometric patterns, flowers, plants, and other symbols, as well as human hands framing geometric and naturalistic designs. Goddesses, human figures, bulls, birds, leopards, and deer appear on the walls. Three shrines have walls decorated with vultures attacking human bodies, as if they are cleansing the newly exposed corpses of the dead. In one case, the vulture's legs are human, suggesting a ritual performed in vulture garb. Skeletons from the houses come from defleshed bodies, as if the dead were exposed on mortuary enclosures away from the community. Later, the relatives collected the bones and interred them in cloth or skins below the platforms of houses or shrines.

One wall painting depicts the huddled rectangular buildings of Çatalhöyük in the foreground while the twin-peaked Hasan Dag spews lava in the distance. Fire spouts from the summit. Hasan Dag was the source of the magical obsidian that brought prosperity to the town. Obsidian's volcanic origin may have linked it to the realm of deities and the defleshed ancestors revered in the village shrines.

Bulls' heads and goddesses adorn Çatalhöyük's shrines, the former perhaps a male deity, the latter a fertility figure. One of the shrines contained a painted relief of a pregnant goddess wearing a dress like a veil. Mellaart believes that the people thought of their deities in human forms, endowed with supernatural attributes from a familiar animal world. Bulls or rams symbolized male fertility, leopards the power of animal and human life. In many paintings leopards support the goddess as she gives birth.

Life and death lay at the center of the Çatalhöyük goddess cult. She is pregnant or gives birth, is accompanied by animals, even by the vulture as a symbol of death. In farming, women's activities of planting, harvest, and the preparation of food acquired a symbolic association with fertility and abundance, with life and death. Perhaps the goddess was a creation deity, a symbol of the endless cycles of the new farming life and the passage through the seasons. The earth was the mother, the womb of existence, the place where the ancestors lived.

Perhaps, then, the greatest legacy of the great drought and the warming that followed was not food production but a completely new way of living, closely bound to the soil. People were thus exposed as never before to the harsh realities of short-term climatic changes—the floods and drought cycles that are part and parcel of the hazards of a subsistence farmer's life.

The same concerns with endless, cyclical human existence, with fertility and ancestors grounded in the soil, spread widely as farming villages took root throughout southwestern Asia. By 6000 B.C, farmers were living on the fertile shores of the vast, brackish Euxine Lake to the north of the Anatolian plateau. Many of them had moved north and west, across a

Drawing of a vulture devouring ancestors from Çatalhöyük. *Courtesy Grace Huxtable*

narrow plain that separated the Euxine from the rising waters of the Aegean Sea, where they settled along the western shores of the lake and on the rich soils of the Danube basin. Beyond their villages stretched the boundless reaches of the primordial European forest, which had colonized the rolling terrain once occupied by the late Ice Age tundra.

Even as farming villages rose along the Euxine shore, events on the other side of the world were signing their death warrant.

❦

In about 6200 B.C., huge meltwater accumulations undermined the retreating Laurentide ice in northern Canada.[7] At a certain point, the huge ice sheet imploded, sending a massive outflow of meltwater cascading southward to the Gulf of Mexico. Another freshwater pulse rushed into the North Atlantic, perhaps as strong as that produced by the draining of Lake Agassiz at the onset of the Younger Dryas. Almost immediately, the ocean conveyor belt slowed perceptibly, and even stopped for as long as four centuries. Much colder, drier conditions, similar to those of the Younger Dryas, descended on Europe. The moist westerly air masses that brought rainfall to the eastern Mediterranean gave way to cold northerly flows. The Balkans and eastern Mediterranean suffered severe droughts, just as they had four thousand years earlier. The 400-year Mini Ice Age was a global event, visible in the Carioco deep-sea core in the southeastern Caribbean, in North African lake beds, and even in the heart of the Western Pacific Warm Pool, which at present has the highest mean sea surface temperatures in the world. Cores drilled into an ancient coral reef in Indonesia show an abrupt sea surface cooling of about 3 degrees Centigrade.

Most important of all, the Laurentide collapse triggered a rapid rise in the world's oceans. By 6200 B.C., the waters of the North Sea were rising about 46 millimeters annually. Huge tracts of southern Scandinavia had vanished under water. Britain was finally severed from the continent. To the south, the Sea of Marmara came ever closer to bursting its banks.

For four centuries, southeastern Europe, Anatolia, and the eastern Mediterranean suffered under prolonged drought. Lake levels fell dramatically; some lakes dried up completely. Rivers and streams withered in the face of the wave of aridity that swept down from the north. Oak and pistachio forests again retreated across the parched landscape as temperatures sank rapidly.

History repeated itself, but with a difference. During the Younger Dryas, many communities in the forest belt had turned to cultivating wild grasses. Within a few generations they had become full-time farmers, growing cereals on such carefully selected and well-watered soils as they could find. When the Atlantic conveyor switched on again, farming spread rapidly throughout the Levant and into the far corners of Anatolia. Now, with renewed drought, hundreds of farming villages saw their crops wither in their gardens, among them obsidian-rich Çatalhöyük. Some settlements dwindled to a mere handful of inhabitants or turned to sheep herding as a means of survival. Others were simply abandoned. Hungry farmers retreated to the few rivers and streams that still flowed and to the shores of much-shrunken lakes.

Many of them may have settled by the western and southern shores of the Euxine Lake, 900 meters or so below the now-arid plateau around the abandoned Çatalhöyük settlement.[8] Here, temperatures were considerably warmer; sheltered river valleys still offered fertile, well-watered soils. Pollen samples from deep-sea cores show that grassland and steppe covered the lake's coastal plains. For the four centuries of the Mini Ice Age, the Euxine was a giant oasis for farmers adapted to growing crops only on damp, arable land where little or no forest clearance was needed.

No one knows what these lakeside communities were like. Their villages and small towns lie too far below the waters of the Black Sea for us to do more than extrapolate from what we know about their contemporaries elsewhere. They herded cattle, goats, and sheep; cultivated emmer, barley, and pulses; and lived in close-knit settlements of mud-brick houses linked by narrow alleyways, each with its own ovens, storage bins, and courtyards. None of them was self-sufficient. Every cluster of villages was linked to neighbors down the coast, up- or downriver, or on higher ground far from the lake. They must have traded foodstuffs and volcanic rock for stone tools, sea shells, and other ornaments, perhaps jewelry, clay vessels, and baskets. Like their forebears in Asia, they must have had profound spiritual ties to the landscape that provided their crops, under the protection of revered ancestors, just as it had done since the beginnings of village life far to the south and east four thousand years before.

Little had changed over the centuries. The farmers still used the simplest of artifacts to turn carefully selected soils. They possessed no heavy axes, no complex woodworking tools, no plows or hoes to work the soil. Their implements of tillage were digging sticks and flint-bladed sickles. Men still habitually carried bows and arrows or spears. Women still laboriously ground domesticated and wild grains day after day with the most elementary grinders, pestles, and mortars. And since people were still dispersed on patches of easily cultivable soil, they had space to pursue game, catch fish with traps and nets, and forage for grasses, fruit, tubers, and nuts in grassland and forest. Sedentary the farmers might be, but their simple agricultural economy and regular dependence on game and wild plant foods gave them a flexibility unheard of in later agricultural societies.

The Euxine villages had neighbors inland. Before 6000 B.C., farmers had moved northwest from the Aegean region onto the Hungarian Plain.

The newcomers lacked the heavy ax technology to clear dense forest but instead cultivated carefully selected arable land, usually near rivers or lakes where good grazing was close to hand, just as their predecessors in southwestern Asia had done for many centuries. In southern Bulgaria, the farmers built their villages a few kilometers apart, each with its own patches of different cultivable soils.[9] The fertile plain supported ribbons of settlement along river floodplains and on nearby terraces, strategic locations where both grazing and fishing or hunting grounds lay nearby. One has the sense of people living a rather generalized farming life, where they were very careful to exploit a wide range of wild foods as well. In many respects, they were still hunter-gatherers, but with subsistence farming and herding grafted onto the ancient practices. This gave them a flexibility that accommodated crop failures and even prolonged drier periods. A similar hybrid lifeway was now dominant over an enormous area of southwestern Asia and into southeast Europe. The Mini Ice Age cemented these early agricultural adaptations in place.

In 5800 B.C., the Atlantic circulation kicked in anew, and the warm years abruptly resumed. Once again, moist westerly air flows reached the eastern Mediterranean and the Balkans. The seesaw of the North Atlantic Oscillation remained firmly in a "high" mode, with low pressure over Iceland and a high over the Azores. Persistent westerly winds brought heat from the Atlantic's surface to the heart of Europe, keeping winter temperatures mild and summer rainfall plentiful. Temperate Europe entered a "climatic optimum" that would last for another two thousand years.

The farmers prospered in the newly mild climate. In the most fertile areas of northern Greece and southern Bulgaria, people used the same locations again and again for many centuries. The great Karanovo mound in Bulgaria ultimately reached a height of 12 meters and covered an area of some 300 square meters.[10] Generations of farmers lived in these long-established settlements.

Then, in 5600 B.C., the Euxine Lake began to change.

⚬❦⚬

Imagine a lake whose waters suddenly rise 15 centimeters a day. Envisage living in a village on a river terrace a short distance inland, watching an inexorable flood moving upstream as much as 1.6 kilometers daily. The inundation never pauses, just rises and rises, drowning crops, leaving only treetops emerging from the still, rising water. A red-brown muck from the water coats the green leaves, which soon vanish beneath the rising deluge. Canoes drawn up on the river bank float away. Within days, the flat river valley forms part of a growing, increasingly brackish sea.

All you can do is flee to higher ground.

One of the greatest natural disasters to affect humanity came in about 5600 B.C., when the rising waters of the Mediterranean flooded the deep basin of the Euxine Lake, 150 meters below the Sea of Marmara, to form the Black Sea.

Until about fifteen years ago, everyone assumed that there had always been an outflow linking the Black Sea and the Sea of Marmara. Discovery of the Euxine cataclysm came as a complete surprise to both geologists and archaeologists, even to the oceanographers Walter Pitman and William Ryan and the small international group of scientists involved with them in Euxine research.[11] They pieced together an elaborate mosaic of clues from deep-sea cores, sonic reflection probes of the ancient shoreline, pollen samples, and ancient mollusk shells. The cores and probes mapped parts of the extensive submerged shoreline of a huge freshwater lake 150 meters below the Mediterranean. The team identified gravel deposits formed by a falling sea level, as well as a pristine ribbon of sand dunes that had been submerged by rapidly rising water. There was a moment when tiny marine shells suddenly appeared in the core samples. Using accelerator mass spectrometry radiocarbon dating, Pitman and Ryan were able to date the sudden changeover from fresh to salt water to close to 5600 B.C.

The Euxine was the progeny of retreating glaciers in the far north. The huge weight of the ice sheets depressed the earth's surface, leaving higher ground on the edges—the effect somewhat akin to the impression left by a body on a mattress. As the ice retreated northward, a moat of higher ground trapped meltwater, chunks of ice, and rocky debris. The same ice sheet moat retreated north with the ice, diverting water flow to the south,

The Euxine Lake and its drainages

into a vast depression that is now the Black Sea. For two thousand years, so much meltwater flowed south that it passed from the Euxine Lake into the Mediterranean through a narrow outlet where the Bosporus now lies—to the tune of about 300 cubic kilometers a year.

When the Younger Dryas came, the inflow virtually ceased. Soon more water evaporated from the surface of the lake than entered it. The outlet channel collected mud and debris, which gradually formed an earthen berm. The Euxine, now a slightly brackish lake, slowly drew down to a level 150 meters below Mediterranean sea level. As the waters shrank, river valleys and deltas formed. Fertile coastal soils supported native wheats and other grasses. Fish abounded in the shallows. The Euxine sediments display a very low salinity level, so the water was palatable to both animals and humans.

During the Mini Ice Age, the surface of the Mediterranean was about 15 meters below modern shorelines. But the collapse of the Laurentide ice sheet added to ocean waters that had been rising since the end of the Ice Age. By

5600 B.C., the Sea of Marmara was lapping at the edges of a shrinking berm. Driven by wind and tide, sea water ebbed and flowed onto the earthen barrier, then retreated once more. Then, inevitably, perhaps driven by the coincidence of a storm and a higher-than-normal wind-driven water level, some water began to trickle over the far side. It cascaded downslope, down erosion gullies and into the lake far below. Within days, the stream became a torrent, then a roiling waterfall flowing at over 90 kilometers an hour. The deeper the water cut into the berm, the faster it flowed, gouging out a flume between 85 and 144 meters deep. Enough water passed through the defile each day to flood Manhattan Island to a depth of almost a kilometer. Soon the fertile deltas and river valleys vanished under water. The largest freshwater lake in the world rose at an average rate of 15 centimeters *a day*.

In two short years, what was once the Euxine Lake was filled to the same level as the inflowing Mediterranean; it was now the Black Sea. The largest freshwater lake in the world had become a brackish ocean, an environmental catastrophe of truly monumental proportions. Pitman and Ryan were moved to wonder whether the Euxine cataclysm survived in folk memory to become the biblical Flood, but such attributions are, at best, pure speculation.

Still, the people living by the lake must surely have thought the forces of the supernatural world were angry, and that ancestors were powerless to appease them. Muddy water rose above sandy beaches, flooded river deltas in hours, and drowned fish traps laboriously planted in shallow water. The rising lake drowned out marshes, washed away sheltered canoe landings, and killed carefully tended gardens. Thousands of fish floated dead in the newly salt water. Helpless villagers watched as their thatched houses and storage bins vanished under the brackish tide. At some points, the shoreline advanced up river valleys as fast as an active young man could walk. Communities near the former lake had varying amounts of warning, but sooner or later everyone had to grab a few possessions and drive their cattle, sheep, and goats to higher ground.

We do not know what time of year the flood began, but the effects would have been devastating on people tied to their lands, who relied on stored food, hunting, and fishing to see them through the winter. Whether caught with growing crops in their gardens or, even worse, at harvest time, or with only stored food to hand, the farmers were left with only their herd animals and whatever they could take from the forest. Nor do we know how many people died in the cataclysm. People or communities unlucky enough to be directly in the path of the torrent below the berm undoubtedly perished quickly. Most likely, many communities suffered from hunger or famine-related disease.

The water stabilized after about two years. Hundreds of villages lay deep below the now-saltwater sea. Settlements far inland now lay at the head of sheltered bays or exposed to the fury of cold winter storms blowing onshore. But life went on as it always had, in a landscape dissected by countless rivers that led inland into an unknown terrain of endless forests. Many farmers moved upstream, tending the old, carrying young children, driving their cattle and smaller stock with them. The refugees dispersed in many directions. Many of them appeared abruptly on the Bulgarian plains and then made their way up the Danube Valley onto the northern Hungarian Plain. Still others traveled up the Dneiper River, then westward into the heart of a continent where farmers had never ventured before. Whichever valley they traversed, they searched for the same kinds of soils that farmers had always favored, where there was moisture to nurture crops during the growing season.[12]

The communities that emerged onto the Hungarian Plain found themselves in the heart of a fertile landscape already occupied by well-entrenched farming societies. They seem to have settled in the western parts of the plain, where their settlements lay in ribbons along rivers, avoiding heavier soils and the dense forest that pressed in on every side. Within a few centuries, the newcomers had taken up the lighter soils in a landscape that was insufficient to support a high density of farming villages.

Perhaps even before 5600 B.C., some now-crowded communities leapfrogged from the plain into unexplored river valleys to the north and west. We can trace their movements across central and western Europe by tracking their highly distinctive clay vessels decorated with swirling impressions and incisions, and by the foundations of the timber longhouses where they lived. Archaeologists call this culture the Linearband-keramik complex. In one of the most significant population movements of human history, farmers jumped first to the upper Danube, next to the upper Rhine and Nekkar rivers, then down the Rhine into Poland and finally to southern Belgium and northern France. Within a few centuries, clusters of farming villages had settled a band of easily cultivable loess soils and river valleys from western Hungary to the Low Countries.[13]

❦

The pioneers entered a world where dense forest stood like a dark green phalanx mantling hillside and valley alike. Within the deep shadows, the trunks and roots of fallen trees rotted on the forest floor, pathless except for the occasional game trail. Carpets of bright green moss lay underfoot surrounding ponds and deep bogs of waterlogged vegetation. An occasional clearing let sunlight between the serried trees, where bison, deer, and elk grazed, only to vanish silently when a hunter approached. The forest spread with the great warming, from the Balkans to the Atlantic Ocean, from Italy to the Baltic Sea.

Little of the ancient growth remains today, except for some isolated patches in western Europe and in the menacing darkness of Poland's Bialowieza Forest, where bison, elk, and other game survive to this day.[14] The great oaks fell victim to insatiable demands for arable land, and for firewood and charcoal for iron smelting. But eight thousand years ago, the forest stretched to the far horizon, pristine and undisturbed except where hunters fired the undergrowth to attract game to feed on new shoots.[15] Only a few thousand forest hunters dwelt among the trees. They were elusive, cautious people, armed with bows and arrows and an intimate knowledge of myriad woodland plants—bog cranberries, mushrooms, wild garlic. They knew how to stalk deer and elk in the depths of winter when the hunter could tread lightly among the trees. Aromatic wild honey came from hollow trees, from bee's nests known only to people who knew the shady landscape intimately. They defined their hunting territories in terms of inconspicuous signposts—rotten trees where bees nested, tree roots, inconspicuous streams and seemingly featureless bogs. Then, as in Roman and medieval times, the forest was a dark, mysterious place. Some experts believe the farmers stuck to the lighter, less forested loess soils because no Stone Age hunters lived there. We do not know.

The agriculturalists settled the new lands just as their ancestors had done, carefully selecting easily cultivable soils, leapfrogging over neighboring village communities to find unoccupied fertile land. Within a few generations, a lattice of isolated homesteads, hamlets, and villages extended up the river valleys and along the forest edge.[16] Each community took up land that was essentially empty. No one had cultivated these soils before; crop yields were high, and harvests were easily amplified with game and plant foods like acorns. Not that the newcomers were moving into an empty landscape: as they settled near water meadows and river banks, they encroached on the ancient territories of indigenous hunter-gatherers. We can imagine a cautious encounter between several farming families setting up camp on a low ridge overlooking a river. As they level a site for their dwelling, some bow-carrying hunters appear as if from nowhere. The two parties confront one another, weapons at the ready, each unable to understand what the other is saying. Perhaps the farmers make gestures of friendship, of greeting. After a few minutes, the hunters vanish into the nearby forest.

As the seasons pass, the indigenes watch from the shade, studying men and women clearing the land, staying carefully upwind of the acrid smoke as the newcomers fire dry grass and undergrowth in the fall. They track cattle and pigs browsing at forest's edge and deeper among the trees, melt quietly away as the entire community harvests ripe acorns from the great oaks on the edge of the valley. After a time, the two groups meet again. The hunters bring honey and elk hides, which they lay on the ground outside the village; the farmers display emmer meal and seashells. These bartering transactions become routine in a few years. We can only speculate as to what happened over the generations. Some of the hunters must have been drawn even closer into the farming orbit. Perhaps they served as cattle herders or captured some beasts that strayed into the forests. Eventually, some groups became farmers, at least part time, and the ancient foraging lifeway passed gradually into history. But for centuries, there were hunters at the periphery and sporadic interaction between two quite different worlds. Sometimes, there must have been violence over cattle thefts and disputed hunting territories. The landscape soon became more crowded. Conflicts must have erupted between people with quite different attitudes to the land. Inevitably, however, the farmers prevailed.

Flomborn and Schwetzingen, two Linearbandkeramik cemeteries west of Heidelberg in the upper Rhine Valley of southwestern Germany, have thrown unexpected light on interactions between hunter and farmer in about 5300 B.C. and over the following century and a half.[17] By comparing the strontium isotope values in the bones and teeth of individuals from the cemeteries, American and German archaeologists were able to study their immigration patterns. Strontium enters the human body through the food chain as nutrients pass from bedrock through soil and water to plants and animals. Tooth enamel forms during gestation and childhood, so the ratio of two strontium isotopes, 87 Sr and 86 Sr, does not change through life. In contrast, the strontium ratio of bone changes constantly through reabsorption and deposition. Thus, people who move from one geological region to another can be identified from differences in the strontium isotope ratios of their bone and tooth enamel. Sixty-four percent of the men and women sampled from the Flomborn cemetery had ratios that placed them in geological regions to the east, as if they were immigrants. The Schwetzingen cemetery, 45 kilometers away, dating to about the same time, contained many fewer migrants, nearly all of them women. The archaeologists believe this was the result of intermarriage with people living on the highlands on ether side of the Rhine Valley, to which their strontium ratios are identical. The immigrants may have come from hunter-gatherer groups at the periphery of the settled lands.

Almost invariably, the earliest Linearbandkeramik settlements lie at the edges of river valleys and on fertile, well-drained loess soils. The natural humidity of river valley gardens, their high productivity, and the ease of working them by hand without heavy tools meant that one could use the same plot of land many times without even fertilizing it. But eventually the soil would become exhausted and the village would move to a new site, again contributing to the spread of the new economies. As each community cleared land and established itself, so the next generation moved off, along river valleys and through more open country, to establish another village some distance away in virgin land.

A visitor would have approached a Bandkeramik village along tortuous paths, which skirted water meadows and dense forest, passing by marshes and through willow groves by the river. Suddenly, the newcomer would emerge on a patch of cleared land, where charred tree stumps stood out among the growing wheat. The gardens lap to within a few meters of a weathered, thatched longhouse framed with stout posts. The wattle and daub walls show signs of constant repair, using clay and cattle dung from the nearby livestock pens, where some girls are milking the cows. A hundred meters away, six men work on the timber frame for a new dwelling. The uprights are in place, enclosing an area 20 meters long by 7 meters wide. Several generations of one family live in such a dwelling, one end of which houses their livestock during the winter.

A long-established settlement like this one would have several tracts of cultivated land belonging to different families. Wattle fences kept voracious goats and sheep away from the growing crops. Postholes preserved in the sandy soils have allowed modern investigators to trace the foundations of longhouses and field boundaries. Unfortunately, the house floors have been plowed out or have eroded without trace. From such excavations, we know that some Linearbandkeramik settlements contained such a single house, others no more than a handful of dwellings. A few reached a considerable size—as many as a dozen houses. But whether these were all occupied at the same time is a matter for debate.

Linearbandkeramik communities revolved around households or extended families, each with its own longhouse. Each was a self-governing entity; but for all their separateness, families tended to build their houses in informal clusters, perhaps to facilitate communal tasks like land clearance and house construction. People tended, also, to settle in the best farming areas, then cluster close to kin and other neighbors. Sometimes the clusters formed long lines. For example, to the west of modern-day Cologne, Germany, farming communities settled along the banks of large rivers in a ribbonlike pattern, each longhouse between 50 and 100 meters from its neighbors.

Bandkeramik folk clustered where groundwater lay near the surface, for damp soil was as important as rainfall. Each fall, after the dry days

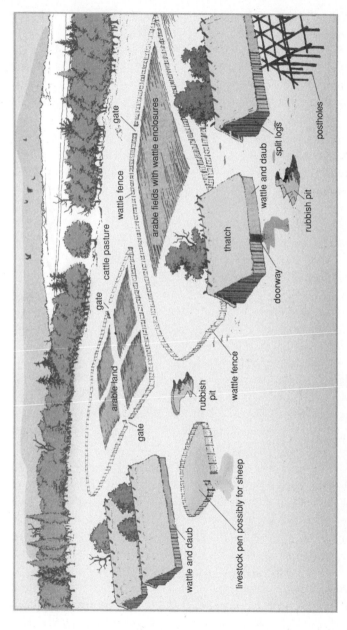

Reconstruction of a Linearbandkeramik farmstead

of summer, the villagers would clear the brush from their fields. The sky would be black with ash and smoke percolating into the forest canopy and carried by the warm westerly winds. The clearance would be over by the time entire communities fanned out into the forest to harvest acorns and hazelnuts. Basket after basket of nuts would be carried back to the village, where the women would store them in carefully prepared granaries.

The long months of winter were the quiet time of year but the best season for hunting, when a skilled stalker could move silently through the trees on a carpet of snow. The hunters would track bison, deer, and elk, looking for them in open clearings, using massive tree trunks as cover until they could get a clear shot.

By March, every family was in the fields, weeding the gardens and turning the soil with digging sticks and simple hoes. Then they scattered seed over the cleared ground. By April, spring wheat and other cereals had been sown, planted clear of flooding rivers and watered by the best rains of the year. The harvest came in early summer, as wild grasses and other edible plants came into season. By the time the hot weather dried out the soil, the crop was safely in storage. The higher temperatures of July, August, and September cracked the ground and aerated the soil naturally before the winter rains came. By then, it was time to prepare the fields.

The simple forms of cultivation used by the Bandkeramik folk were virtually identical to those used in the Levant during the Younger Dryas three thousand years earlier. The Europeans made but minimal changes in the farming cycle, notably adjusting planting times to reflect a cooler climate. Like their remote predecessors, they did not rely entirely on unpredictable rainfall. The amount of labor involved was miniscule compared with what would come later, when people began to settle in drier environments where agriculture depended on the vagaries of rainfall alone and on much larger-scale forest clearance.

This was not a life without hunger. Every household was tied to its cultivated land, at the mercy of unpredictable droughts or unusually heavy rains, which could wipe out a crop in short order. Undoubtedly there were months, even years, of food shortages and hunger, but the people could fall back on their herds, and on deer and other game that grazed and browsed by the river or in the forest. They also minimized the risk of crop failure by choosing their farm sites with great care, clustering their dwellings fairly close to kin, and by eating a diversity of alternate foods, including animals and plants from the forest at their doorstep. In settling in their new homeland, the Linearbandkeramik folk merely followed the ancient strategies of all simple farming societies—diversified crops combined with animal husbandry and a safety net of game and wild plant foods.

Such a lifeway, with its built-in flexibilities, worked well at a time when people lacked heavy stone tools to clear even moderate-sized trees. But the farmers were capable of burning off fields, of clearing young trees and undergrowth, all techniques of managing the environment that been in use from time immemorial. Their life enabled them to weather the vagaries of short-term climatic change.

⚬⚬⚬

Until 4000 B.C., farmers occupied only a tiny part of the European continent. Newcomers in an ancient world of hunting and gathering, they shared much the same forms of simple agriculture over long distances. In many respects, they enjoyed the flexibilities of hunter-gatherer life, with the addition of cereal crops and domesticated animals. They lived in a far from crowded world, where, initially at any rate, there was enough land to go round on the most fertile and easily turned arable soils. Life and its rituals still centered around the household.

But by 3500 B.C., Europe was a changed landscape. It was a land of timber architecture, of free-standing dwellings clustered in hamlets and villages—still a forested continent, but one gradually being altered to accommodate new ways of living off the land. As simple farming became more established and interactions with indigenous hunter-gatherers increased, especially in the more densely populated west, so the new economies came into wider use. The broad standardization of Linearbandkeramik society gave way to a series of regional cultures as farmers slowly filled the landscape and territorial boundaries grew more closely established.

Warm temperatures and plentiful rainfall led to greater agricultural productivity, to a new political and social arena where farmers competed for the best soils and increasingly moved onto heavier soils. Forest clearance accelerated gradually, but the proportion of cultivated land was miniscule and did not approach that of modern Europe until the first millennium B.C. The process of infilling continued well into the Middle Ages.[18]

For thousands of years, most life and ritual had revolved around the age-old link between the living and the dead, the ancestors and the land. During the fifth millennium B.C., a change rippled through farming. Ritual suddenly went public. We know this because earthen enclosures appear, covering a few hectares, often with multiple ditches. At one such enclosure, at Tesetice-Kyovice in southern Moravia, a circular ditch about 60 meters in diameter surrounded two palisades with four opposed entrances. Many broken clay figurines came from the ditch fillings, while all the dwellings lay outside the enclosure.[19] These may be the first public arenas for elaborate rituals of a type unknown in earlier times. Why the change took place we do not know. It may have been connected to a need to mark territorial boundaries, to invest tribal lands with the authority of revered ancestors.

Especially in the west, emphasis shifted from the household and the village to burials as a symbol of community, defined not by individual interments with elaborate adornment but by communal graves.[20] The new traditions came from a melding of ancient hunter-gatherer and farming beliefs, reflected in the building of timber or stone mortuary houses buried under earthen mounds. These tumuli were monuments to the ancestors, built in the midst of landscapes full of symbolic places and imbued with powerful supernatural meaning. Now people built their own monuments in the landscape, sometimes using rocky outcrops as the part of the burial chamber. Sometimes the mounds stood on recently cultivated land, often on conspicuous ridges where they may have served as territorial markers. Whatever their placement, they were integral parts of a cosmos where the supernatural and the material worlds came together in the power of the ancestors.

Such monuments abound in western Europe. For instance, the long earthen mounds at Avebury in southern England form a dense group on the rolling chalkland.[21] In 4000 B.C., sixteen hundred years after the Euxine flood, Avebury was still sparsely inhabited. Then the inhabitants began building tombs for their ancestors. By 3400 B.C., just as cities were growing in Mesopotamia, a dense cluster of long barrows lay around Avebury, some with stone internal burial chambers, others with now-decayed timber compartments. Some were little more than piles of stones with flimsy rows of hurdles, identified today by soil discolorations subdividing the interior.

The first long barrows were modest structures, but the builders soon became more ambitious. Most famous is the West Kennet long barrow, a much eroded tumulus 100 meters long and about 2 meters high that lies on a low ridge against the skyline.[22] As you climb the ridge, the mound suddenly rises up before you as if ascending from the underworld. In its heyday, the fresh white chalk of the steep-sided mound would have glittered brilliantly in the sun, even from afar on a gloomy day. At the western end, a passage with four side chambers and a single end room, formed from great natural sandstone blocks, opens into a crescent-shaped forecourt. The remains of at least forty-six people of both sexes, including children and infants, lay in the chambers, the young and the old placed in spatial opposition. Judging from several incomplete skeletons, the mourners left the bodies to decay, then removed some of them for burial elsewhere. Each generation laid its burials in the same chambers, sometimes moving older bodies aside and piling up the bones in confusion. With only forty-six people buried over five hundred years, it is clear that only prominent individuals, perhaps important kin leaders, were interred in the burial chambers.

At the end of five centuries, West Kennet was sealed with large sandstone boulders. Like the other Avebury barrows, it had stood on or near cultivated land, every one of these burial places linked to individual communities or clusters of villages protected by the ancestors. Soon afterward, communal burial gave way to the burial customs of new societies, where individual power and prestige shaped human life. The ancestors receded into the background.

❦

Until now, we have described the ripple effects of long-term climatic shifts—the initial warming, the Younger Dryas, and the rapid warming of the early Holocene, culminating in the Mini Ice Age of 6200 B.C. triggered by the collapse of the Laurentide ice sheet. We have seen how the Cro-Magnons and their successors, and the hunter-gatherers of southwestern Asia, adapted effortlessly to major climatic shifts by virtue of their mobility and effortless opportunism. The vulnerability equation began to change when mobility gave way to sedentism in the oak and pistachio forests of the Levant; but even then, people adjusted to the severe droughts of the Younger Dryas by the simple expedient of deliberately cultivating wild cereals. Within a few generations, the foragers became farmers, anchored to their lands by high-yield cereals and then by their herds.

With the renewed warming, farming spread rapidly, but not universally. The earliest cereal cultivation depended on light, well-watered, preferably damp soils near rivers and lakes, in places that required minimal forest clearance. The old ways of subsistence remained central to human existence and offered a lifeline when crops failed or herds were decimated by drought or disease. Hunting and wild plant gathering, fishing and fowling, were a safety net, offering a flexibility as potent as mobility in a farming environment where neighbors were widely spaced, there was plenty of cultivable land, and wild foods abounded nearby.

When the Mediterranean Sea inundated the Euxine Lake, hundreds of sedentary farming communities along the lakeshore moved rapidly inland, up the Danube and other rivers, bringing with them their simple farming methods and cushioning the disaster by relying heavily on the wild foods that were always there for the taking. They surely suffered hunger and death, but the sheer flexibility of the early farming adaptation permitted rapid movement, whether on the shores of the new Black Sea or inland. During the two millennia of warm climate that followed, their descendants leapfrogged north and west into the heart of temperate Europe with its dark forests and great rivers.

But inevitably, populations grew on the fertile soils, the larger communities swelled, and the best arable land was taken up. During the fifth millennium B.C., the process of filling in began. People moved onto drier, heavier soils and adopted heavier implements of tillage, such as the simple scratch plow, to turn over thick sod so that it could aerate and drain. The edible landscape had been eaten; people would now have to work harder for their bread.

Many centuries later, in Medieval times, almost every European community lived at the subsistence level from harvest to harvest, with only enough surplus to plant the next year's crop. An exceptionally dry year, heavy rains, or a late frost brought the specter of hunger and death. And when a heavy rain cycle came, like that of A.D. 1315 to 1321, people died by the thousand from famine-related epidemics and hunger. Centuries before, farmers with simpler technology had effectively cleared the landscape of its natural cover, of its game and wild plant foods, thereby removing the safety net that made the difference between temporary food shortage and famine, between the survival of a small farming community and its demise.

By 5000 B.C., the major climatic shifts that affected humanity were largely over. Sea levels had stabilized at near-modern levels, the great ice sheets were almost gone, and global vegetation was effectively that of today except when modified by human activities. The Holocene is the longest period of stable, warmer climate to have descended on earth since 15,000 years ago. But this does not necessarily mean that the climate was always benign, or that there was plenty of rain in every part of the world.

7

DROUGHTS AND CITIES
6200 TO 1900 B.C.

I am the fecund seed, engendered by the great wild ox, I
am the first born son of An,
I am the "great storm" who goes forth out of the "great
below," I am the lord of the Land . . .
I am the *gugal* of the chieftains, I am the father of all
the lands.

The god Enki, in the Sumerian epic
"Enki and the World Order"

The Mini Ice Age of 6200 to 5800 B.C. was a catastrophe for many farming communities between the Euxine Lake and the Euphrates River. Month
after month, a harsh sun baked soils that were no longer fertile. Dust cascaded out of a cloudless sky, lakes and rivers dried up, and the Dead Sea
sank to record low levels. Farming societies shrank or evaporated in the face
of unrelenting drought. Many turned to sheep farming as they resorted to
the classic famine strategy of habitat tracking: moving to areas less affected
by drying and cooling, where they could eke out a living off their herds.

Then, in 5800 B.C., the good times returned. The Atlantic circulation
switched on; the moisture-laden Mediterranean westerlies abruptly resumed. Within a few generations the farmers expanded from their places
of refuge into a warmer and better-watered landscape throughout the
Fertile Crescent, to the banks of the Tigris and Euphrates rivers.[1]

Some farmers founded settlements far downstream, where the two great rivers entered a floodplain of sluggish channels and innumerable streams. Here was abundant water, easily diverted into storage basins and onto fields. All the farmers needed to do was to build simple levees and canals. By 5800 B.C., small agricultural communities dotted the landscape of southern Mesopotamia.

❦

Southern Mesopotamia, "the land between the rivers"—now southern Iraq—is a world of cultivated fields, marshes, and sand dunes, much of it a desolate wilderness of salt-encrusted desert. Almost no rainfall nourishes this terrain. The extreme forces of nature confront you on every side—some of the hottest summer temperatures on earth, bitter winter winds, and tumultuous storms, river floods that can sweep away a village in moments. Mesopotamia has always been a place where even the gods were often malevolent, and rulers were given to violent reaction. Yet farmers thrived here.[2]

Within three thousand years, the tiny hamlets of 5800 B.C. had become some of the earliest cities on earth. Urban centers like Eridu, Nippur, Ur, and Uruk were surrounded by green patchworks of heavily irrigated fields and labyrinths of narrow canals. Cities arose here because farmers were tied to places where they could water their lands, and unfettered movement was impossible because so much of the landscape was completely dry. A city was a different entity from a village, not just larger in size but requiring both economic specialization and much more centralized social organization than smaller-scale societies. This scale of operation led almost inevitably to still larger political entities, to city-states, and eventually empires, loose alliances that linked cities and their rulers over large areas.

During the 1920s and 1930s, the charismatic archaeologist Leonard Woolley unearthed the ziggurat (temple mound), royal cemeteries, and residential precincts of the Sumerian city of Ur.[3] Woolley excavated, and imagined, on a grand scale. Ur was not a dead city to him but a thronged settlement with busy streets. He would lead visitors to the excavations

Sites and cultures mentioned in Chapter 7

down winding alleys and into abandoned 4,000-year old brick houses. He actually knew the names of many of the individual owners from cuneiform tablets found inside their dwellings. He would point out details of the roof design, drainage contrivances, even the height of the steps. In his hands, Ur came to life, its narrow streets and bazaars teeming with artisans and merchants, with heavily laden donkeys bearing copper ingots or timber from far upriver.

Five thousand years ago, Ur was one of the great cities of the ancient world, flourishing in a land where the god Enlil, king of the lands, "made the people lie down in peaceful pastures like cattle and supplied Sumer with water bringing joyful abundance."[4]

Then the river changed course and Ur died.

I came to the place years ago, long before an air base rose nearby, expecting city walls and spectacular buildings, but there was little to see.

The reconstructed ziggurat still towers over the dusty mounds of the once-vibrant city. I climbed to the summit and gazed out at salt-encrusted desert that extended to the horizon on every side. The relentless forces of climate change, of shifting rivers and rising soil salinity, had doomed Ur and its contemporaries.

Ironically, Ur and its ancient neighbors were born of human responses to earlier climatic changes. They were, to some degree, a product of climatic stress, but because of the their scale they were themselves vulnerable to larger-scale environmental stresses.

The story begins in the late Ice Age, when the Persian Gulf was still dry land; global sea levels were 90 meters lower than today. The Tigris and Euphrates rivers flowed through deep valleys into the Gulf of Oman, 800 kilometers south of their present estuaries. As sea levels rose during the great warming, the newly formed Persian Gulf caused massive alluvial buildup in the Mesopotamian plain, where the gradient was extremely low. With a mere 30-meter drop over 700 kilometers, the rivers moved sluggishly, marshes and swamps abounded, and even major waterways changed course from year to year.

By the time of the Mini Ice Age, the Persian Gulf was just 20 meters below modern levels. As the final surge from the collapsing Laurentide ice sheet raised sea levels again, the Gulf peaked at about 2 meters above modern levels between 4000 and 3000 B.C.[5]

Some of the most extreme environments on earth surround Mesopotamia—the Sahara Desert, arid northwestern Pakistan, and the cold reaches of Central Asia. Three different weather regimes collide here. The winters bring some rainfall from moist Mediterranean westerlies, but most snow and rain come from southward penetration of arctic circulation from central and eastern Europe. Monsoon circulation from the Indian Ocean brings humidity during the hot season, but no rainfall. This intersection of atmospheric flows means that Mesopotamia's climate can change rapidly in response to such phenomena as a shutdown in North Atlantic circulation or a major El Niño event that affects monsoon patterns in the Indian Ocean. Some of these rapid shifts were brief; others lasted centuries and changed history.

We still lack definitive information on ancient climate changes in southern Mesopotamia, where alluvial buildup and shifting rivers prevent pollen analysis.[6] But we do have proxy records from lake beds elsewhere and deep-sea cores from the Arabian Sea. These tell us that summer temperatures were higher and rainfall greater between 10,000 and 4000 B.C., thanks to changes in the earth's orbital parameters. These shifts exposed the northern hemisphere to between 7 and 8 percent more solar radiation than previously. Mesopotamian rainfall may have been as much as 25 to 30 percent higher than today, much of it derived from summer monsoons, which resulted in a sevenfold increase in overall moisture because of a higher ratio of rainfall to evaporation. Both the westerlies and the monsoon systems operated with greater intensity. Except during the Younger Dryas and the four centuries of the Mini Ice Age, the plains of northern Mesopotamia and the southern delta were well watered for six thousand years.

When the warming resumed abruptly after the Mini Ice Age, farming communities fanned out over northern Mesopotamia with their flocks and herds. The northern plains, like those of Assyria north of Mosul in modern-day Iraq and the Habur Plains west of the Euphrates in Syria, were soon dotted with small farming villages, each with its own mosaic of fields.[7] In winter, herders grazed their animals along the great rivers, dispersing over the plains in spring and early summer in a pattern of seasonal movement that was to endure for many centuries. With a quarter to a third more rainfall than today, the farmers could rely on fields nourished by winter and spring rains, as well as on irrigated lands.

Within a few centuries, both farmers and herders had settled far to the south, in a landscape where cultivation, even on damper soils, was essentially impossible without irrigation. Here the longer rainy season was even more beneficial. Winter temperatures were lower, which meant that plants remained dormant for a longer period. The rains lasted well into spring and early summer, providing an extended growing season, helped by the timing of the summer inundation. Today, the Euphrates River flood, controlled by rain and snowfall in Anatolia, arrives too late in the parched southern summer to be of any use for watering crops. Before 4000 B.C., the growing season was later and longer, so the arrival of the inundation often coincided with the time when water was most needed—if levees and storage basins were up to the task of containing the flood.

So long as spring and summer rainfall remained plentiful, small farming villages and nomadic herders could support themselves comfortably, with plenty of food surpluses, grazing tracts, and irrigable land to go round.

❦

We will never know when the first farmers settled in southern Mesopotamia. Layer after layer of silt masks the ancient landscape. The earliest known settlements appear in about 5800 B.C., at the end of the Mini Ice Age, tiny hamlets of mud-brick and reed huts covering no more than a hectare or so. These farmers melded inconspicuously into the flat, sandy landscape. Once abandoned, their collapsing houses reverted into the alluvium from which they were created, along with the abandoned remnants of their simple irrigation works—small canals to divert river water into natural storage basins, and low levees that steered floodwater in the right direction. Archaeologists identify these folk by their distinctive black painted pottery fashioned from a fine greenish clay, and call them 'Ubaid people, after a site of that name where they were first identified in the 1920s.[8]

The 'Ubaid farmers found that they could extend their supply of arable land by digging ditches and letting water run through them. Every farmer knew that crops thrived when watered and was careful to select fertile soils with high water tables. The idea of irrigation was nothing new, but southern Mesopotamia was one of the first places where such farming methods came into widespread use as a necessity. Just as the Egyptians would soon do along the Nile, 'Ubaid villagers simply extended ancient farming methods by bringing water to their fields. They were more concerned with subtle contours in the flat topography than with fertility, for they knew full well that carefully watered fields would produce bountiful crops. Over many generations, the elders became expert at judging when to plant their emmer and barley, the moment when frosts would no longer decimate seedlings. Judging from farmer's almanacs preserved on clay tablets, they also learned the telltale signs of potentially catastrophic floods and of low-water years—arcane knowledge passed from father to son as part of the fabric of survival.

Simple irrigation works and plentiful rainfall served the 'Ubaid farmers well. As the centuries passed, the inconspicuous hamlets became clusters of small rural communities located around a single larger settlement. By 5200 B.C., six centuries after the first known colonization, the largest of these towns covered about ten hectares and housed between 2,500 and 4,000 people, many of them living on food produced by others.

These larger communities and the food surpluses that supported them came at a high price in backbreaking work. Every fall and winter, gangs of men and women clustered along small canals and cleared them of silt and weeds with hoes and digging sticks. Some of the channels extended as much as five kilometers from the river into the dry landscape. Other work parties, meanwhile, would add clay and silt to levee banks and to the edges of the natural storage basins that trapped water during the summer flood. No household could farm the alluvium alone. Everything depended on carefully deployed and well-organized work parties that labored for the common welfare.

For more than a millennium, life revolved around the small, dispersed community, around the household and ties of kin, which brought people together for irrigation work and other communal tasks, just as it had done since the earliest days of farming. But a second layer of organization was needed as well. From the very beginning, each community in the south depended on communal labor pulled together by village leaders.

The hard work paid off. Within a few centuries, the larger 'Ubaid communities could boast of substantial buildings and small temples, even if most people still lived in mud-brick and reed huts with roofs formed of bent sticks. If much later cuneiform tablets are to be believed, this was the time when the roots of ancient Mesopotamian religious beliefs were put down, when enduring chants and myths enshrined a pantheon of gods and goddesses who presided over the destiny of humanity, bringing rain, nourishing fertile soils, and ensuring plentiful harvests. Those who interceded with the spiritual world, who presided over the rituals that renewed human life, had always carried authority. The shaman and spirit medium of earlier times now became a full-time priest or priestess supported by rapidly growing food surpluses.[9]

By 4800 B.C., some of these settlements were of impressive size. Uruk, by the Euphrates River, grew rapidly and absorbed the villages within sight of its ziggurat. Life revolved around the temple and the marketplace, for Uruk maintained trading connections with people far from the delta.

❧

For the next thousand years, life was good. Everyone lived in small, dispersed communities, close to strategic watercourses or natural storage basins, where they could fish as well as farm, and could irrigate the land without excessive labor. Then, about 3800 B.C., the climate became suddenly drier, a trend that affected southwestern Asia and the eastern Mediterranean region for well over a thousand years.[10] Solar insolation, the rate of incoming light at the earth's surface, declined throughout the world, a phenomenon well documented by radiocarbon-dated tree rings and lake bed cores from southwestern Asia and as far away as southern California. Such changes are due to alterations in the earth's angle to the sun, which determines the amount of radiation that reaches the surface. Almost immediately, the southwestern monsoon with its summer rainfall weakened and shifted to the south. The rains faltered, began later and ended much earlier. Now the summer flood arrived *after* the harvest, reducing the amount of water available for the near-ripe crops. The summer inundations were far smaller than earlier floods, reflecting sharply lower rain- and snowfall in the Anatolian highlands.

The climate grew increasingly unstable. Drought cycles descended on the southern villages. Repeated environmental shocks devastated small settlements anchored to capricious river channels and a constantly changing landscape. For generations, people had relied at least partially on rainfall to nourish growing crops. Now they were dependent on irrigation alone. Food surpluses vanished and gave way to shortages.

The hungry villagers had few options. Their fate was tied to their carefully irrigated lands, now parched and cracking in the harsh sun. Archaeological surveys tell us that many people simply abandoned their villages. We can imagine them destitute, desperate, wandering aimlessly across the landscape in search of food. This was the classic response to famine, and remains so today. Ancient Egyptian farmers abandoned their fields en masse in a frenzied search for food when droughts strangled the Nile River flood in 2100 B.C. When the monsoon failed in late–nineteenth-century India, thousands of villagers took to the road, turning the Punjab into a giant charnel house.[11] The 'Ubaid catastrophe was not on such a scale, but the long-term effects of a shorter rainy season rippled through southern Mesopotamian society for generations.

Some survivors were lucky. Their communities lay near large tracts of semiarid grassland, and they could turn to cattle, goat, and sheep herding to survive. Some of them became full-time herders, moving constantly with their flocks. Others managed to move east to higher ground that was less affected by drought, and adequate water made it unnecessary to depend on irrigation agriculture. Still others remained where they were, eking out a living by combining irrigation farming with the classic subsistence farmer's safety net. They hunted diminishing game stocks, ate fish, and foraged for plant foods.

The safety net, however, could not possibly support the dense populations living in sedentary settlements occupied over many generations. These people were victims of their own success, living in a landscape with minimal carrying capacity unless ample rainfall and irrigation fertilized the soil. For many centuries, Mesopotamian farmers had taken their irrigation water from the Euphrates through large feeder canals that extended into the surrounding plains.[12] The feeders were like growing trees—branching into progressively smaller boughs, as small canals diverted water from the main course onto the fields. Obviously, the strategic points were those where the main canals branched off the river, for it was there that people could control what water reached whom, especially in a climatic regimen where rainfall varied dramatically from one year to the next and flood levels were declining. As solar insolation declined, these vital nodal points were where the densest populations congregated and the first much larger settlements formed.

By 3500 B.C., when the droughts intensified, Uruk was far more than a large town. Satellite villages, each with its own irrigation system, extended ten kilometers in all directions. These lesser settlements provided food and goods for the city, but each depended on the others for survival.

Some communities specialized in pottery, others in metallurgy or fishing, each bringing their wares to Uruk's markets. Increasingly, defense was a consideration, for everyone needed protection from neighbors who craved their water supplies and material goods. At the same time, landowners began double-cropping, using plows and draught animals, and shortening fallow periods, while making a much greater labor investment in canals.

Irrigation work now continued year round, supervised carefully by kin leaders. A new breed of official attached to temple storehouses to keep careful record of crop yields and grain stocks—the first bureaucrats. Each fall, gangs of men from extended families would labor under the hot sun, digging out silted up canals, clearing reeds and undergrowth from blocked watercourses. Other workers would dig in lines, excavating new canals and creating new fields. Once the canals were ready, each plot was wetted thoroughly, to soften the sun-hardened soil. Each household would plow its own land, but large teams would work together to break up the hard clods and level the fields before seeding.

Throughout the winter, every family would water its fields from the irrigation canals once a month or so, depending on the rainfall, and weed the growing crops. In these early days, water supplies were a household and community concern, rather than that of the central government, but this would change as the city became ever more powerful. When harvest came, every able-bodied person worked in the fields from dawn to dusk until the crop was gathered. This "family farm" model persisted for centuries, but eventually gave way to far more centralized irrigation works that were part and parcel of city government.[13] Ubiquitous officials collected most of the harvest as taxation for the state's granaries. More and more, people depended on the state for food, on rations paid out for services rendered.

There was no respite after the frantic work of the harvest. In anticipation of the summer floods, hundreds of men worked feverishly to divert water away from the growing towns and cities into natural flood basins. At the same time, officials supervised the moving of grain supplies into large granaries situated high above the floodwaters on temple mounds, where a growing priesthood administered them.

All of this required many human hands. Yale University archaeologist Frank Hole believes that these hands came from "the landless and destitute," those who had fled their traditional villages when the rains failed.[14] He believes that they became a labor pool that could be mobilized to transform the village-based agricultural system of the 'Ubaid farmer into a much more productive system under the aegis of growing cities. The same laborers, fed on public rations, could also build temples, city walls, and other public works. All this labor was carried out in the name of the gods, who controlled the fate of humankind and the malevolent forces of the cosmos. The villages had coalesced into cities, each surrounded by brilliant green tracts of densely cultivated farmland in a brown and yellow landscape.

The climatic crisis deepened. Between 3200 and 3000 B.C., two centuries of rapid drying and cooling, perhaps triggered by an Atlantic circulation shutdown, created further political disruption. Uruk had controlled trade routes with the north for many centuries, even establishing trading colonies in northern Mesopotamia and on the Anatolian plateau. As the drought intensified, many of the colonies collapsed. In northern Mesopotamia, more villagers flocked into larger settlements, while Uruk itself and other southern cities received even more refugees. As the population rose, new cities formed in the hitherto uninhabited buffer zones between the original larger settlements.

By 3100 B.C., the southern cities had become the world's first civilization.[15] Sumerian civilization was a mosaic of intensely competitive city-states, each presiding over a highly organized hinterland, ruling over territories that butted up against those of their equally competitive neighbors. Each city-state had its own secular and religious leaders, its own patron deity, and thousands of people under its sway. Each city's ziggurat towered over the flat landscape, the successor of the much humbler shrines of earlier millennia. Here the state propitiated the forces of a violent, unpredictable natural world and interceded with its divine patron. At Eridu, Enki served as the god of water and of all things vegetable and animal. The bull god and moon god Nanna presided over Ur in the south. Nippur was the realm of Enlil, the wind god and deity of the hoe. His son

Ninurta controlled thunderstorms and the plow. Everywhere, the gods symbolized the yield of earth and water.

The ideology of Sumerian life reflected a land of violent, erratic forces, where rain could come at the wrong time and floods after the harvest could inundate whole villages. No ruler could relax in a land that could become desert in a moment or lose its water supplies in a matter of days, as it sometimes did when the flood-swollen Tigris or Euphrates altered course without warning. The Sumerians themselves marveled at the abundant crops their ancestors reclaimed from the desert. In one Sumerian creation legend the god Ninurta dammed up the primeval waters of the underworld, which always flooded the land. Then he guided the floodwaters of the Tigris over the fields:

> Behold, now, everything on earth,
> Rejoiced afar at Ninurta, the king of the land,
> The fields produced abundant grain . . .
> The harvest was heaped up in granaries and hills.[16]

In the 1920s, Leonard Woolley unearthed a farmer's almanac in the archives at Sumerian Ur. A farmer instructs his son to keep "a sharp eye on the opening of the dikes, ditches, and mounds [so that] when you flood the field the water will not rise too high in it." The young man was adjured to propitiate the gods at every turn, for river waters could rise without warning, or life-giving water could be prevented from reaching the fields. The Sumerians dreaded years of poor rainfall: "The famine was severe, nothing was produced," recalls an ancient myth. "The fields are not watered. . . . In all the lands there was no vegetation, / Only weeds grew."[17]

One cannot blame them. The lessons of history were all around them in dry streambeds and abandoned villages. Their temple records contained detailed accounts of past experience—the first such written records anywhere that went back further than the short span of generational memory. It seemed that there was safety in numbers. The city, originally an adaptation to much drier climatic conditions, became the hallmark of Mesopotamian civilization. The archaeologist Robert Adams, in his widespread settlement surveys of southern Mesopotamia in the 1960s, discovered that by 2800 B.C., over 80 percent of the Sumerian population lived in settlements covering at least ten hectares, a form of "hyperurbanism" that lasted only a few centuries.[18] By 2000 B.C., the figure had declined to under 50 percent, as people moved away from cities that were again suffering through catastrophic drought.

❦

Sumerian cities bickered constantly with one another over land, water rights, trade, and raw power. Clay tablets and cuneiform inscriptions boast of diplomatic triumphs, wars, and dirty dealings, in idioms that seem startlingly familiar today. The founding of new cities had infringed on ancient territorial boundaries and raised the political stakes at a time of declining water supplies. Some rivalries endured for centuries and inspired stirring rhetoric on both sides. "Be it known that your city will be completely destroyed! Surrender!" proclaimed the city of Lagash in 2600 B.C., at the height of a dispute with neighboring Umma over a strip of land known as "Edge of the Plain," the "beloved field" of the god Ningirsu, chief deity of Lagash.[19] Mesalim, the powerful ruler of Kish to the north, mediated the dispute, dividing the strip between the two cities. With impeccable religious protocol he negotiated the deal between Shara, the supreme deity of Umma, and Ningirsu of Lagash. None other than Enlil himself supervised the king's careful survey of the land and the erection of a monument to validate it. Under the agreement, Lagash leased the land to Umma for "grain-rent," a portion of the annual yield.

Inevitably, given a volatile political environment where a city's power swung like a pendulum according to the ability of its ruler, the deal fell apart. The dispute festered for generations over agriculture, payments for land, and the proper use of irrigation canals. Both cities looked for excuses to go to war. Armies would descend, set fire to shrines and villages, divert irrigation canals, and depart laden with loot. The routine of flamboyant rhetoric, sudden attack, and bloody conflict was part of the backdrop of Sumerian life, where standing armies were now routine, for, in truth, many such conflicts were impossible to resolve in a fractured political world. Every Sumerian ruler lived in a maelstrom of shifting alliances, border disputes, diplomacy, and wars. The center of political power seesawed from city to city, fed by the egos of grandiloquent, sometimes megalomaniacal leaders. They were known as *ensik*, earthly representatives of the city-god, the stewards of royal estates. The organization of Sumer into city-states worked well as far as organizing local agricultural production was concerned, but it tended to prevent any larger entity from coalescing. With such a jigsaw of small polities, without a common power to hold them all in awe, there was no hope of resolving conflicts.

The city-state was a product of a long-term problem triggered by increasing aridity. It provided the best way of feeding one's own people and protecting local interests. In its earliest iterations, the Mesopotamian city was a unique way of responding to environmental crisis.

For all their provincialism, the Sumerians inhabited a much larger world than that of their 'Ubaid predecessors, whose universe rarely extended beyond a few neighboring villages and some communities farther upstream. Uruk had broken the mold and forged a network of trading contacts so extensive that some archaeologists refer to it as a nascent "world system."[20] Sumer was without timber, metals, or semiprecious stones, but it had grain and other basics to offer. Trade expanded, much of it via pack ass caravans that traversed the semiarid landscape with ease, the animals feeding off grassland and field stubble along the way. Each summer, large wooden rafts supported by inflated goatskins floated down the Tigris, heavily laden with semiprecious stones, copper ingots, and other commodities. The raft skippers drifted and paddled their heavily laden craft downstream, delivered their loads, then sold the precious raft timber before returning with the deflated skins on the backs of pack asses. Five thousand years later, the Victorian archaeologist Austen Henry Layard used the same kinds of rafts to ship tons of Assyrian sculptures from ancient Nineveh to Basra on the Persian Gulf.[21]

People moved from the south to the north over many centuries. 'Ubaid communities colonized northern lands as early as the fifth millennium B.C. Uruk established trade outposts in Assyria and Anatolia. Herders were always on the move from the arid lands or up and down the rivers. The Sumerian lords competed with growing cities north of the delta and as far away as northwestern Syria. They attacked trade routes and annexed competitors, but were often distracted by the constant internecine strife and petty rivalries closer to home. No one succeeded in patching together a single state until 2300 B.C., when King Lugal-zagesi of Umma crafted a unified south by adding Ur, Uruk, and later Lagash to his domains. He then gained the endorsement of the priests of ancient Nippur, which gave him effective, if loose, mastery over the south.

There had long been rivalry between the southern cities and those in the north, where there had been larger territorial states for some time. One of them was headed by the city of Kish, whose king had mediated between Umma and Lagash. The northern lords presided over larger kingdoms with an authoritarian hand, cultivating trade relationships with cities like Ebla and Mari in what is now Syria. They ruled with a militaristic ideology that made conquest and dominance central tenets of kingship. With autocratic expertise, they controlled land ownership and maintained more strongly centralized economies than those of the city-states of the south.

By 2500 B.C., the Akkadian cities to the immediate north of Sumer were becoming more aggressive toward their southern neighbors.[22] Akkadian rulers specialized in long distance raiding rather than territorial conquest, but this changed after an able ruler, Sargon, founded a royal dynasty at Agade, south of Babylon, in 2334 B.C. In that year, his army defeated a coalition of Sumerian city-states led by King Lugal-zagesi of Ur. He smote Eridu and brought Lugal-zagesi in a neck stock to the gates of Nippur. Having subdued the south, this consummate general subjugated Mari far to the north and the land of the "Cedar Forest" and the "Silver Mountain" in the Tauros. Sargon became the complete master of Mesopotamia.

This much larger empire was even more vulnerable to sudden climatic changes. Its vulnerability is fully evident upstream in the archaeological sites of the Habur plain, west of the Euphrates River, in modern-day Syria.

❦

In earlier times Habur had been a fertile landscape, nourished by plentiful rainfall and close to Euphrates floods. The effects of the long drought were delayed here. As late as 2900 B.C., the river and its tributaries supported dozens of small farming villages, dispersed settlements of egalitarian communities, of which the largest covered no more than ten hectares. Three centuries later, rainfall faltered and became more seasonal. Stream deposits on mountainsides show signs of much more irregular water flow both on the Habur plain and on the Anatolian plateau to the north.

Just as in the south, people responded by moving into larger centers where they could find food and work. Three large cities with secondary towns and villages developed across the Habur, one of them now represented by the archaeological site of Tell Leilan, excavated by Harvey Weiss.[23] Tell Leilan began as a small farming settlement, one of many during the years of plentiful rainfall. After 2600 B.C., the village suddenly grew sixfold and became a flourishing city carefully laid out on unoccupied land. Tell Leilan featured not only an acropolis but also a lower town bisected by a straight, potsherd-paved street 4.75 meters wide. Mud-brick walls lined the street, with houses opening onto alleyways behind them.

Tell Leilan's anonymous rulers transformed their hinterland into a tightly knit, carefully organized agricultural landscape. Weiss and his colleagues unearthed a block of storehouses covering more than two hundred square meters. One hundred eighty-eight broken door and jar sealings still lay in the abandoned storerooms among the seeds of carefully threshed and winnowed barley, emmer, and durum wheat, processed in the fields, then delivered to the acropolis.

By 2300 B.C., Tell Leilan was one of the largest cities on the Habur plain, covering as much as 100 hectares. The Akkadians advanced against the city from their nearby fortress at Tell Brak (a city dating to as early as the fourth millennium), then fortified the entire settlement with massive mud-brick walls and earthen ramparts. With draconian thoroughness, they razed nearby villages and towns and brought the administration of farming and grain firmly into official hands.

Weiss found a telltale clue to the city's governance in Tell Leilan's houses and courtyards, where almost no grain chaff came to light. He believes that the grain consumed by the inhabitants was precleaned, then distributed as rations by the Akkadian authorities. Each worker received an allocation of grain and oil, passed out in standard-sized clay vessels manufactured in the city's kilns. Commoners paid their taxes to the state both in produce and in labor on public works. Hundreds of them worked on irrigation canals and waterways. Weiss cross-sectioned one of the channels on the west side of the city, where he traced the history of the canal—its laborious excavation in hard, calcic soil, the construction of massive basalt block embankments, and the huge piles of water-borne silt and pebbles that were removed from the channel. Large-scale waterworks and huge grain surpluses bought some security from year-to-year fluctuations in river floods—as long as there was enough rainfall to sustain average inundations in the Euphrates.

Akkadian rule endured for about a century, at a time when the climate was markedly seasonal and perhaps somewhat warmer than today. Erosion was well under control; windblown sands borne by dry winds were not a problem. The Akkadians presided over a prosperous state that thrived off long distance trade and used powerful armies to subdue rebellious cities. They behaved like ardent imperialists, their rule supported not only by military force and trade but also by bombastic ideologies and intensive agricultural production.

In 2200 B.C., disaster struck. A trench in Tell Leilan's lower town tells the story of a major volcanic eruption somewhere to the north that released huge quantities of ash into the atmosphere. Like the vast eruption of Mount Tambora in southeastern Asia in 1816, the eruption probably caused a bitterly cold winter and several years without a summer. The volcanic event coincided with the beginning of a 278-year drought that affected a widespread region of southwestern Asia. The same arid centuries appear in Greenland ice cores and in cores from as far away as the Andes glaciers of southern Peru. With startling abruptness, the North Atlantic circulation decelerated. The reliable moist Mediterranean westerlies of previous centuries were now unpredictable, severe drought commonplace.

Within a few years, Tell Leilan's fields were a dust bowl criss-crossed by silted-up irrigation canals. Small cyclones of dust zigzagged between shriveled barley and wheat shoots. Skeleton-thin cattle and sheep grubbed for dry stubble where their ancestors had found rich spring grazing. The Akkadian empire collapsed like a stack of cards as its carefully organized agricultural landscape fell apart. Tell Leilan became a ghost town with crumbling walls. Harvey Weiss and his field workers estimate that between 14,000 and 28,000 people fled the city for the south or for better-watered land, a huge number by the standards of the day. Nearby Tell Brak shrank to a quarter of its former size. Extensive archaeological surveys across the Habur revealed a landscape that had been deserted, and which remained so for three centuries.

The collapse in the north caused havoc over a wide area. For thousands of years, herders had grazed their animals along the Euphrates and the Tigris in the winter, then moved them out onto the plains in spring. Now the drought made their summer pastures a near desert. Ever adaptable, the nomadic herders did what they always did in times of drought— stayed close to reliable water supplies and moved downstream along the rivers. The move brought them into direct conflict with the settled farming communities of the south, which themselves were suffering from food shortages. One can imagine the shouting and turmoil caused by voracious herds of goats spilling onto growing crops and encroaching on the carefully guarded pastures of the farmers. So serious was the threat that the ruler of Ur built a 180-kilometer-long wall, named the "Repeller of the Amorites," to keep herder immigration in check. His efforts were to no avail. Ur's hinterland saw a threefold increase in population at a time when fruit trees were dying and the authorities were frantically straightening irrigation canals to maximize much-reduced water flow. Cuneiform tablets tell us that Ur officials were reduced to distributing grain in minute rations. Ur's agricultural economy soon collapsed.

The three-hundred-year drought brought disruption elsewhere in the eastern Mediterranean. For centuries, the Nile River inundation had produced bountiful harvests and plenty of water for the Old Kingdom pharaohs in Egypt, who considered themselves masters of the great river. In 2184 B.C., the Nile floods faltered.[24] For 150 years, catastrophically low floods brought famine to Egypt. Central government broke down, a revolving door of pharaohs followed each other at Memphis, and the state fell apart into its constituent provinces. Over a century passed before Mentuhotep I reunified Egypt, in 2046 B.C. He and his successors, having learned their lesson, invested heavily in agriculture and centralized storage, and redefined themselves less as gods than as shepherds of the people. They had learned that doctrines of royal infallibility could be a political liability and a literal death sentence.

Egypt survived because the people believed their kings had defeated falsehood and used their divine and human qualities to influence nature on their behalf. The best and most powerful Egyptian kings prospered because they were pragmatists who deployed their people to create an organized oasis out of natural bounty. Firm administration, centralized government, and technological ingenuity, combined with compelling ideology, ensured the survival of the state through floods high and low, and through steadily rising population growth in the city and countryside.

Mesopotamian civilization also survived. After 1900 B.C., rainfall returned to its previous seasonality. People returned to Habur and Assyria; Tell Leilan prospered once more, to become the center of an Amorite state. For all the disruptions of catastrophic drought and much drier conditions, the institutions and ideology of ancient Mesopotamia survived to become the blueprint for the great empires of later times. With the help of the gods, the rulers of Mesopotamia tamed a harsh environment, except when the vagaries of atmospheric and oceanic circulation challenged their ingenuity and their domains. But in the final analysis, the ingenious strategy of centralization, of an organized landscape, was the best defense against an unforgiving world.

8

GIFTS OF THE DESERT
6000 TO 3100 B.C.

Creator of all and giver of their sustenance . . .
Valiant herdsman who drives his cattle,
Their refuge and giver of their sustenance. . . .

> Hymn to the Sun by Suti and Hor, architects to pharaoh
> Amenhotep III, c. 1400 B.C.

Egypt may be the gift of the Nile; but ancient Egyptian
civilization was the gift of the deserts.

> Toby Wilkinson, *Genesis of the Pharaohs*, 2003

The wind sears your face as you lean into the stinging sand, peering through a slit in the cloth masking your nose and mouth. Millions of tiny grains flick against the Land Rover doors and mock the faint vehicle tracks that stretch behind you. Without a compass and an electronic navigator you would be helplessly lost within minutes. It's hard to believe that people once hunted animals and lived by shallow lakes in this very place, or that they wandered here over vast tracts of grassland. How did anyone live in the Sahara?

This world of sand and rock, of weathered outcrops and dunes, pressed on a completely different universe. The Nile Valley, a land so fertile that it nurtured the longest lived of all human civilizations, cuts across the desert from tropical Africa to the Mediterranean. For thousands of years, these two absolutely different worlds flourished alongside one another. Their different fates demonstrate the vulnerability inherent in any human response to climatic stress.

❧

Sahra': the Arabic word means "desert." This is an understatement. The Sahara stretches for one-sixth of the world's circumference from the Atlantic Ocean to the Red Sea, a huge wilderness of sand dunes, barren rocky plateaus, gravel plains, dry valleys, and salt flats covering 9,100,000 square kilometers. Here *ergs*, sand seas confined within large basins, move constantly, sometimes forming huge dunes up to 180 meters high. Daytime temperatures can rise to 58°C (over 136°F), then fall below freezing at night. Rainfall is sporadic at best, can fall in any season, and totals less than five millimeters annually in the eastern desert. Yet there is life in the midst of the wilderness. Vast underground aquifers lie below the desert surface and sometimes reach it, creating oases. About ninety of them provide sufficient water for farming villages today. A few families live at the numerous, much smaller oases from the Atlantic to the Red Sea. Today, about two million people live in the desert, most of them at its margins, mainly herders and traders. They do not spend much time in the hyperarid central Sahara.

Six thousand years ago, the desert population was much smaller, no more than a few thousand people, but cattle herders flourished in landscapes that are now devoid of life. The climate changes of the Holocene left an indelible mark on this region and its societies.

The Sahara is a world of sand and rock, with only small areas of permanent vegetation. Hot, dust-filled winds blow constantly over an often featureless landscape, whose scenery, especially in the rocky Eastern Desert between the Nile and the Red Sea, can be spectacular. Much-eroded mountains and uplands rise in the central Sahara. The Ahaggar Mountains in Algeria climb 2,916 meters above sea level. To the northeast lie the Tassili-n'Ajjer highlands. A lifeless place, you might think, but

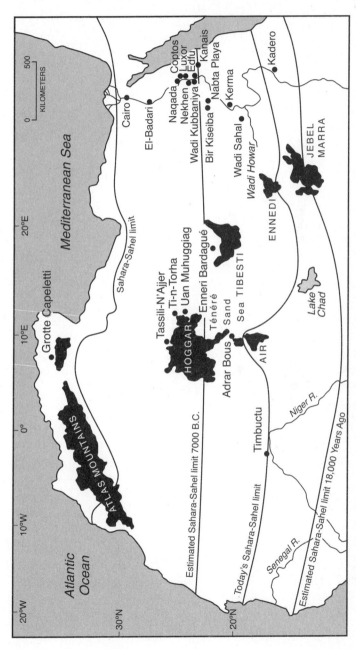

Map of the Sahara Desert and Egypt showing sites and locations mentioned in Chapter 8

even today's utterly dry Sahara supports 70 mammal species, 90 forms of resident bird, and about 100 species of reptiles. Both animals and plants have adapted to a nearly rainless world. The moment any rain falls, seeds lying in the ground come to life, grow rapidly, then die after a life cycle of about eight weeks. The desert is a world of ephemeral habitats that only develop after rainstorms. The long periods of dormancy are an illusion, for there is always the potential for plant growth. Even small increases in annual rainfall bring large areas at the edges to life.[1]

The desert breathes like a set of giant lungs, expanding and contracting with tiny changes in rainfall patterns.[2] At the margins, absolute desert gives way to dunes covered with permanent scrubby vegetation, then to semiarid grasslands and eventually savanna, as rainfall increases by about a millimeter per kilometer from north to south. The lungs draw in animals and people during periods of higher rainfall, then expel them to the margins when greater aridity returns. None of the rainfall shifts during the Holocene was very large—a matter of millimeters per year—but the effects are dramatic.

The pump operates tirelessly, decade by decade, making the Sahara's frontiers advance and retreat as unpredictably as waves on a seashore. Orbiting meteorological satellites have tracked the north-south movements of the Sahel grassland zone at the southern edge of the desert since the 1980s. In 1984, the driest year of the twentieth century, the expansion southward was equivalent to 15 percent of the entire desert. The following year, the Sahel expanded northward 110 kilometers, reducing the size of the desert by 724,000 square kilometers. There were also major contraction and expansion episodes during the 1990s coinciding with rainfall shifts. Satellite imagery dramatizes how the slightest increase or decrease in rainfall affects the desert margins. A few more millimeters of spring rain across the Sahel brings thousands of hectares of arid landscape to life with stunted grass and even desert flowers. Shallow pools form for a few days or weeks after the rain. Immediately, cattle herders fan out over the new pasture. Their beasts crop the fresh grass and shrubs as fast as they grow. The next year, which may bring almost no rain at all, will find hungry cattle clustered around permanent waterholes. Their owners move them southward, away from the encroaching desert, to graze the stubble on farmer's lands.[3]

❦

The satellite imagery chronicles a living desert, never still, always changing in response to small movements of the Intertropical Convergence Zone (ITCZ) with its monsoon rains. A northward movement of the ITCZ brings the Indian Ocean monsoon circulation closer to the Arabian and Sahara deserts. When the ITCZ and its monsoon rains move southward, the Sahara is drier.

These changes were more dramatic in the past. Between 20,000 and 15,000 years ago, the late Ice Age Sahara was extremely dry, its margins far south of those of modern times. Until as late as 9000 B.C., high-pressure tropical belts reinforced by polar air extended their drying influence over the ITCZ and its monsoon rains. Heat exchanges between the Equator and the North Pole slowed dramatically, accelerating the high-altitude jet stream and intensifying tropical anticyclones. Consequently, the period of the great warming was a time of extreme aridity in the Sahara. For three thousand years, almost no humans lived in the desert.

After 9000 B.C. and the end of the Younger Dryas, the rains improved. The ITCZ moved north, bringing rainfall to the central and southern Sahara. Only the north remained dry, probably because the jet stream moved northward and accentuated dryness there. Between about 8000 and 5500 B.C., lakes throughout East Africa and the Sahel expanded massively. Rainfall in East Africa and the Sahara increased between 150 and 400 millimeters annually. A stronger Asian monsoon cycle created a completely different Saharan world from that of today.

Until about 2550 B.C., when the Egyptian pharaoh Khufu and his successors were building the pyramids of Giza by the Nile, the desert supported many freshwater lakes, some of them quite large. Crocodiles and hippopotami flourished in northern Mali, where the rainfall is now a mere five millimeters annually. The bones of such animals imply well-watered terrain with ample plant life. Lake Chad and other lake basins supported rich plant communities and teemed with fish. The desert's powerful lungs sucked in from the margins of the desert not only animals and plants but also Stone Age hunting bands, who settled at lakesides and in desert oases and ranged widely over more open country when there was standing water. They pursued and gathered a remarkable variety of foods, "regional specialties [that] would have impressed even the best French chef," as the geologist Neil Roberts perhaps overenthusiastically put it.[4]

For all this seeming plenty—it is easy to exaggerate it—only a few thousand people lived in the vast desert between the Atlantic and the Red Sea, almost all of them sticking close to lakes and other permanent water sources. Like all societies living in semiarid lands, the hunters were constantly on the move, leaving little behind them for the archaeologist to study except for over 30,000 rock paintings and engravings in mountainous areas deep in the desert and east of the Nile. Much of the art comes from the Tassili n'Ajjer in Algeria, where over 8,000 years ago the artists depicted animals like buffalo, elephant, and rhinoceros—all locally extinct now—with startling realism. Men armed with clubs, throwing sticks, axes, and bows cavort around their prey. Vivid rock engravings in the Eastern Desert from around 4000 B.C. or earlier also depict an era when the Sahara was wetter, for the animals on the rock include elephants and giraffes.[5]

Then, after 3500 B.C., the art abruptly changes in the Tassili-n'Ajjer. The buffalo and other now-extinct animals vanish, replaced by familiar game species alongside domesticated cattle. Saharan hunting bands had taken up cattle herding.

❦

The ancient Sahara comprised many environments—sand seas, rugged mountains, semiarid grasslands, and oases. Then there was the Nile, the only North African river that traverses the Sahara from south to north. Other Saharan rivers were important during the earlier Holocene, including one that may have flowed from the Tibesti massif in the heart of the desert into the Mediterranean. But only the Nile survived the intense drying that settled over the Sahara after 4000 B.C., flowing through the least hospitable reaches of the desert as it had done for hundreds of thousands of years. The Nile was a link across the desert, an oasis and a refuge, a world very different from that of the arid landscapes that surrounded its meandering floodplain.

The Nile Valley bisects the eastern Sahara like a green arrow shooting toward the Mediterranean. At the end of the Ice Age, the great river flowed through a deep gorge toward an ocean much lower than today's. As sea levels rose after the Ice Age and East African lakes overflowed into the White Nile, the river became more sluggish. The summer floods deposited deep layers of fertile silt in the once-narrow valley. Each summer, the annual inundation covered much of the floodplain, creating a patchwork of marshes, pools, and swamps where fish teemed and plant foods abounded.

Even during the arid millennia of the late Ice Age, a tiny population of hunters dwelled by the river. Theirs was an insecure life at best, for the Nile floods varied dramatically from year to year. In times of severe drought, the marshlands would dry up, depriving the foragers of vital plant foods. For this reason, the people exploited a broad range of food resources. For instance, 13,000 years before the pharaohs, the inhabitants of Wadi Kabbaniya, a tiny camp of reed shelters downstream of Aswan, lived off catfish trapped in shallow pools left by the receding Nile flood, and off wild nut grass, a sedge that still grows by the river today.[6]

The same broad-based hunting societies persisted well into the still-dry Holocene, but populations rose slowly along a now much more tractable river, all the way from the Nile delta by the Mediterranean deep into the Sudan. With the natural expansion of wetlands and shallows, fish and wild plant food supplies were sufficient for some groups, like those in central Egypt and along the White Nile in Sudan, to live at the same location for many months of the year. So permanent were some settlements that the dead were given cemeteries, where they lay in shallow pits covered with stone slabs. Still, floods varied from year to year and growing populations were circumscribed within small territories. Many quarrels clearly ended in violence. Some of the dead in the cemeteries perished from wounds inflicted by stone arrow barbs found in their bones.[7]

In 9000 B.C., perhaps a thousand people lived in the Nile Valley between the Mediterranean and what is now Khartoum, subsisting for the most part off fish and wild plants. The lush floodplain gave way abruptly to vast tracts of desert interspersed with dry grasses and scrub. For the Egyptians of later times, this frontier between river and arid lands demarcated their world from that of foreigners. But the outsiders exercised a pervasive influence on the formation of their civilization.

❦

The land of the foreigners, the eastern Sahara west of the Nile (not to be confused with the Eastern Desert on the other bank), is one of the driest landscapes in the world. Much of it lacks any plant cover whatsoever for hundreds of kilometers. German scientists led by Rudolph Kuper have spent years studying the complex environmental changes that have transformed this brutal land since the Ice Age.[8] Their evidence comes from the complex sediments of long-vanished lakes and streams, from charcoal samples and animal bones found in ancient archaeological sites.

Before 4000 B.C., ancient lake beds tell us, the Egyptian portions of the eastern Sahara enjoyed slightly greater rainfall than today. Acacia trees, tamarisk bushes, and other shrubs grew in the better-watered locations, the northernmost outpost of the tropical savanna that had spread 500 to 600 kilometers northward from its present boundary. Patches of drought-tolerant vegetation grew across the landscape, somewhat like that found in the Sahel region immediately south of the desert today. The densest growth lay at low points in a varied terrain, where heavy runoff accumulated during rare rainstorms. Similar vegetation now flourishes in southern Libya, where annual rainfall of between 25 and 50 millimeters produces some pasture and firewood for cattle-owning nomads.[9]

Before 4000 B.C., the eastern Sahara was a thoroughly viable landscape for cattle herders, especially if they spent at least part of the year on the fringes of the Nile Valley, where pasturage abounded, and if they were prepared to remain constantly on the move in search of widely separated pastures and water. Some places supported denser stands of tamarisks during wetter times, especially in the bottoms of wadis and around seasonal pools. Even a slight increase in rainfall brought extensive stands of ephemeral grasses and herbs as well as standing water during the wet months.

The patchy vegetation of the Egyptian Sahara gave way to much more widespread grass cover further south, beginning at about the modern Egyptian-Sudanese frontier. Here acacia trees thrived, always a sign of a higher water table. The ground cover was virtually identical to the desert scrub/savanna of the Sahel that flourishes south of the Sahara today. During this climatic optimum, some areas of the Sudanese desert were surprisingly well watered. Wadi Howar, to the east of the Nile and southwest of the river's Dongola Reach, was a perennial river braided with numerous lakes along the main channels, connected to one another during flood events. Catfish, bream, and Nile perch abounded, migrants from the Nile at a time when the wadi flowed into the great river.

An eclectic mix of game animals came from the archaeological sites investigated by the Germans, including elephant and rhinoceros, oryx, and crocodiles from shallow lakes. The inhabitants of these sites kept goats and sheep but relied more than anything else on cattle.

Many researchers have written of a Sahara where large herds of cattle grazed happily, almost certainly because their images of cattle herding come from European meadows. The reality was a harsh herding life eked out on marginal strips of desert. These were not the sleek, well-fed oxen of my European youth, contentedly chewing their cud in lush pastures, but lean, ill-favored desert kine. Unlike sheep and goats, cattle have the mobility to shift from one grazing area to another without substantial losses. The aridity of the environment demanded a fast-moving nomadism, in a constant search for water supplies, for cattle have to be watered regularly, preferably every 24 hours, at the most every three days. They drink constantly in hot, dry environments, not to avoid dehydration but to cool their bodies with huge volumes of water. Provided a beast acquires about two kilograms of good-quality food a day, it will not lose weight. Ensuring that cattle obtain adequate grass or forage requires careful management. Herd boys have to drive the animals out to graze in the cool of early morning. During the hot hours of midday, the beasts seek shade, if there is any, and chew the cud, so they need adequate food in their alimentary system by then. The herders pen the calves back at camp until the cows have departed. Come evening, even free-ranging cattle will return to base, as the mothers seek their calves to feed them. Watering the herds also consumed a great deal of time, either at natural waterholes or from wells dug into dry watercourses.[10]

Saharan cattle had a tough existence. Every herd spent much of its life under serious environmental stress, eating poor-quality vegetation. Cattle bones from the German sites are those of slender, poorly developed animals with a shoulder height of about 115 centimeters. The same stunted breed survived for many centuries. The complete skull of a third-millennium domestic cow from Wadi Sahal in the Sudanese desert is from a small, long-horned beast, the same as those buried in graves at the royal capital at Kerma, by the Nile, in 1500 B.C.[11]

For all its challenges, cattle herding had a long history in the desert. But how and why did it begin?

❧

The father of the Saharan cattle herds was the primordial wild ox, the aurochs. Julius Caesar remarked of the European aurochs that "even if they are caught very young, the animals cannot be tamed or accustomed to human beings."[12] The last herd of wild aurochs perished in the dark forests of Poland in A.D. 1627, but Polish scientists managed to back-breed a herd just before World War II. They produced a frisky, russet-colored animal of uncertain temper, not unlike its ferocious predecessor.

Caesar's men hunted and captured the aurochs in the temperate forests, woodlands, and thickets of ancient Gaul. Roman hunters had to stalk their prey at close quarters and pursue them in stealth. The aurochs was suspicious, easily spooked, and quick to charge. But what happened in more open terrain, where there is nowhere to hide? Many years ago, I was looking for early farming villages along the banks of the Zambezi River in central Africa when I wandered inadvertently into the midst of a peaceful herd of feeding elephants. I was new to the bush and unfamiliar with the telltale signs of their presence—snapped off branches, fresh dung, and the gentle rumblings from their gas-filled stomachs. Upon seeing them I froze. They looked at me nonchalantly and then resumed feeding. I quietly traced my steps and left them in peace. Only later did I realize that the elephants were not alarmed by my presence, since I was in full view and walking slowly among them, posing no hidden threat. Herein may lie a clue as to how Saharan hunters managed to tame the aurochs.

The biologist Michael Mloszewski has spent long periods observing herds of wild buffalo (*Synceros caffer*) in central Africa.[13] Wild buffalo roam in woodland and grassland as well as in much drier environments.

The largest herds flourished in areas with plenty of water, while buffalo in drier surroundings travel in smaller and more docile groups, reflecting a need to stay with the herd in its constant search for water and good pasture. Mloszeweski not only watched the herds, he walked amongst them, just as I had done with the Zambezi elephants. He found the buffalo wary of carnivores and other possible threats obscured by trees or tall grass. The herds were much more relaxed when a potential predator was out in the open, walking slowly among them. Presumably, ancient game herds, even aurochs, by all accounts as unpredictable an animal as the notoriously ill-tempered buffalo, may have acted in the same way, allowing hunters to move freely among them as long as they remained in full view. Such free movement was vital to people who had but the simplest of bow-and-arrow technologies to pursue large animals. The only way they could fatally wound such a quarry was to approach within a few meters. Stalking required tree and tall grass cover, a rarity in the forbidding Sahara. Fortunately, the cattle had evolved to recognize only certain kinds of behavior as dangerous: predators kept hidden, other herbivores did not. If they stayed in the open, people could walk among the animals, provided they took care never to corner them or to separate a mother from her young. They could then pick off their quarry with relative ease, perhaps wearing clever disguises to get close enough for a fatal shot.

Andrew Smith, an archaeologist at the University of Cape Town, has studied cattle herding groups in and around the Sahara.[14] He has excavated small campsites used by hunting bands that preyed on the antelope and wild oxen of a moister Sahara around 6500 B.C. By 6000 B.C., during the Mini Ice Age, conditions over North Africa and throughout southwestern Asia became drier again. The desert expanded, springs and streams dried up, and the semiarid grasslands withered. These were the conditions, Smith believes, when some desert bands tamed wild cattle.

The Sahara was never well watered. Both animals and people were constantly on the move in search of food and water. When conditions worsened, Smith believes, the small aurochs herds of the desert became even smaller, closer-knit breeding units. The beasts were reluctant to abandon water sources, making it easier for hunters to move among them and cull them at will. Inevitably, cattle and humans came into close contact. The hunters gained such a complete familiarity with aurochs behavior that they began to control the movements of individual herds, preventing them from moving from one place to another and thus assuring continuance of their meat supply. By culling the more intemperate beasts, they soon gained genetic control over the herd, which led to rapid physiological and behavioral changes in the animals. The newly domesticated cattle were easier to control and may have enjoyed a higher calving rate, which would have yielded greater milk supplies. Judging by rock paintings deep in the desert, the herders were soon selecting for hide color and horn shape.

Most experts agree that Saharan hunters domesticated the aurochs quite independently of southwestern Asia. They did so thanks to a combination of drought, profound familiarity with prey, and, as always, brilliant human opportunism in the face of one of the Ice Age's most intractable beasts.

We do not know exactly when people first domesticated cattle in the desert, but it could have been as early as 7500 B.C., if a scatter of bones from the Bir Kiseiba and Nabta Playa sites in the Egyptian desert are to be believed.[15] Cattle were certainly domesticated by 5500 B.C.[16] They are present in the Enneri Bardargué in the Tibesti massif by about 5400 B.C. Domesticated cattle bones come from the Capeletti site in the Aurès Mountains of Algeria, where they date to between 4600 and 2400 B.C.; the number of bones increases dramatically as time goes on, suggesting that cattle were rapidly replacing game as the primary meat source. After 5000 B.C., large numbers of sheep or goats and smaller cattle bones appear at Nabta Playa, the former almost certainly being an import from the Nile Valley, as neither sheep nor goats are indigenous to the Sahara.

The archaeologists Fiona Marshall and Elisabeth Hildebrand believe cattle were domesticated somewhere in the eastern Sahara by about 7000 B.C., perhaps by hunter-gatherer bands based in desert playa basins, where plant foods attracted plenty of game.[17] Taming the aurochs ensured a much more predictable food supply, stored on the readily accessible hoof. We also know that wild cattle had major ritual significance long before they were tamed: burials accompanied by cattle horns became important in the region before 10,000 B.C.

The Sahara once again grew slightly wetter after 5000 B.C., at a time of more plentiful rainfall throughout much of southwestern Asia. Sahel-like shrubs and grasses moved northward, creating wide areas of semiarid rangeland that could be used to graze cattle and small stock. At the same time, wild game populations increased. Within a few centuries, cattle herders spread rapidly across the desert—from the Nile Valley toward the confluence of the Blue and White Nile rivers, then far westward into the Aïr Mountains and even as far west as the Timbuctu region of modern-day Mali. Despite these enormous distances, toolkits used by the herders remained remarkably similar, including finely made arrowheads and woodworking tools like axes and gouges, as well as bag-shaped pots for holding the milk from their herds. We should not be surprised at this, for, like Ice Age hunters in Siberia and Alaska, these people depended not on technology but on intelligence, on knowledge of where grazing and water were to be found, and on social networks that linked autonomous herding camps hundreds of kilometers apart. The same kinds of social ties operate in the Sahara to this day.

The Saharan landscape comprised two main areas—open plains and mountains, both used by herding groups. During the moister centuries, shallow lakes abounded, so people tended to live near them. Rain fell between July and September on the southern margins of the desert, where today tsetse flies carry sleeping sickness fatal to cattle. The herders may have moved southward during the dry season when the tsetse retreated. Meanwhile, those living close to the mountains practiced a different form of seasonal migration, moving into better-watered valleys during the dry season and onto more open terrain during the rains. The very nature of the environment, with its localized rainfall and unpredictable water and graze, meant that everyone had to cover considerable distances through the year.[18]

Maintaining cattle in the Sahara was a carefully calculated numbers game, where herders built up the size of the herd during good years and assumed they would lose most of their beasts in the coming years to drought or disease. A wise herder dispersed his beasts over several camps, to guard against epidemics and also to insure against the vagaries of local rainfall, which could vary dramatically within just 25 to 35 kilometers. It is an ineluctable fact of biology that cows give birth to equal numbers of male and female calves, which means that a herder ends up with a surplus of males well above breeding requirements. The bull calves are slaughtered, or else castrated, fattened, and kept as a source of meat for times when milk is in short supply. The surplus is a priceless social instrument, used to pay for wives, cement social ties, and fulfill ceremonial obligations. It thus symbolized wealth and pride, social prestige, and family and personal relationships with people living in other camps over enormous distances. Bulls became symbols of virile leadership, of important chieftains. It was no coincidence that the powerful rulers of the Sudanese kingdom of Kerma were buried with lavish cattle offerings 2,500 years later. Cattle were wealth, kingship itself.

❧

The Egyptians called their homeland *Kmt*, "the black land," on account of its dark alluvium, contrasting it with the "red land" of the surrounding deserts. By 4000 B.C., Nile Valley populations had risen to far higher densities than those of the Sahara. A thousand years later, when Egyptian civilization began, perhaps half a million people lived between the Mediterranean Sea and the First Cataract 700 kilometers upstream. The rhythm of valley life depended not on desert rainfall, but on the whims of the inundation. Each summer, when the Nile floodwaters arrived, fueled by tropical rains far upstream, the river rose above its banks and turned the valley into a vast shallow lake, each village staying dry on higher ground or becoming an island on a low mound above the floodwaters. As the current slowed, the river dropped silt on the flooded lands, then receded.

Compared with turbulent rivers like the Tigris in Mesopotamia or the Indus in Pakistan, the Nile was relatively predictable. A normal flood allowed a good crop season over about two-thirds of the floodplain. A rise that peaked two meters below average could leave up to three-quarters of some Upper Egyptian provinces totally unirrigated. For all these uncertainties, the Nile was a huge oasis in 4500 B.C., with plenty of fertile soil, ample pasturage, and many hectares of ponds, swamps, and marshes where fish teemed and edible foods abounded. Compared with their contemporaries in southern Mesopotamia, who spent months every year laboring on the simple irrigation canals on which their survival depended, the Egyptians had it easy.

During the early fifth millennium B.C., Badarian communities (named after a settlement near the village of el-Badari) flourished over a long stretch of the Nile between the modern cities of Cairo and Luxor.[19] The Badarians lived a relatively easy life in the fertile Nile Valley. Their toolkits were light and portable, known to us from settlements and cemeteries near the river and from their highly polished, thin-walled clay vessels. Like many subsistence farmers, the Badarians placed a high premium on body decoration as a way of showing personal status and social affiliation. They ground their pigments on stone palettes, artifacts that remained a mark of Egyptian life for the next two thousand years. The silt-stone for these palettes came from the Black Mountains of the Wadi Hammamut in the Eastern Desert, a natural route to the Red Sea.[20]

The Badarians were also cattle people who often buried domesticated beasts, dogs, and savanna antelopes alongside their human dead. They had regular contact with cattle people from the Eastern Desert, who moved between the settled lands of the valley and the wider universe of the desert grasslands, where they wandered freely with their herds. These contacts endured for centuries, marked by distinctive Badarian artifacts on the Red Sea coast from what were then much-better-watered tracts of the Eastern Desert. During the Badarian heyday, desert nomads, and perhaps some valley cattle people, who were part-time farmers, could move effortlessly over the desert grasslands, especially during the rainy reason when standing water was available. Such an existence was probably commonplace along the Nile far south into Nubia. In many places, valley people like the Badarians integrated the desert into their annual round as part of their material and spiritual world. Fortunately for science, the cattle people recorded some of their beliefs as rock engravings in shelters and wadis in the Eastern Desert. The Cambridge University Egyptologist Toby Wilkinson controversially dates most of this art to before 4000 B.C., long before pharaohs ruled a unified Egypt, on the basis of loose stylistic similarities with contemporary artifacts along the Nile.[21]

The engravings include river boats being towed by gangs of men, just as funerary barges navigated the walls of New Kingdom tombs in the Valley of the Kings twenty-five centuries later. In a considerable intellectual stretch, Wilkinson believes these images show that the Egyptian belief in the afterlife dates well before the first pharaoh in 3100 B.C., and that it originated among Nile people who moved freely between the desert and the settled lands. The Eastern Desert engravings include figures of gods, too, among them the fertility deity Min, one of the earliest recognizable Egyptian divines. On the walls of a rock-cut temple at Kanais, west of Edfu in the heart of the desert, Min, easily identifiable by his trademark erect phallus, rides in the bow of a banana-shaped boat while brandishing a flail. Wilkinson boldly dates this engraving to at least 3500 B.C., when Egypt was still a string of small kingdoms. In later centuries, pharaohs carried crooks and flails as symbols of their role as "shepherds of the people." If Wilkinson is correct, then this symbolism, born of cattle people, shows the Egyptians' debt to the desert nomads.

The Egyptian kings were fierce bulls who trampled their enemies underfoot, a familiar scene in royal iconography. When the pharaoh wore a bull's tail in his belt, as an early king, Scorpion, did in a frieze at Nekhen, he took on the attributes of this formidable beast as well as proclaiming the central importance of cattle in Nile life. The famous Narmer palette of about 3100 B.C., also found at Nekhen, commemorates the unification of Egypt into a single state after years of conflict. We see Narmer, the first pharaoh, wearing a bull's tail, and a bull, symbolizing the conquering king, trampling on his enemies. These scenes unfold under the watchful gaze of two cattle deities.[22]

All of these symbols hark back to earlier times, when the Egyptians were cattle-herding people moving constantly between the Saharan grasslands and the valley. If the Eastern Desert engravings are indeed as old as Wilkinson claims, then we have the first evidence that the origins of many ancient Egyptian beliefs and ideologies lay as much in the deserts as they did in the Nile Valley.

These beliefs may have come into greater play after 4000 B.C., when intensifying droughts settled over the Nile and the desert pump pushed the cattle herders to the Sahara's margins and disrupted the ancient migration patterns of valley folk. When the Sahara was better watered and semiarid grasslands bordered much of the Nile, especially south of the First Cataract, Kmt was part of a wider desert world. Many valley communities also grazed cattle in the desert. By the same token, herders further afield were, of course, aware of the villages and small kingdoms along the river, perhaps trading with them and visiting their settlements for permission to graze their herds on the stubble of recently harvested fields.

The Egyptian god Mut sails in the bow of a boat. Kanais, Eastern Desert. After A. E. P. Weigall, *Travels in the Upper Egyptian Deserts* (1909)

The Narmer Palette, a cosmetic palette from Nekhen dating to c. 3100 B.C. The palette depicts the pharaoh presiding over the conquest of Lower Egypt, the two beasts with entwined necks symbolizing the unity of the new state. The king presides in his role as a great bull and is watched over by two bull deities. After J. E. Quibell, *Hierakonpolis* (1900), vol. I, pl. 29

There was plenty of land to go around, so the occasional movement of valley communities and nomads in and out of the valley may not have led to competition for pasture. The herders used the Nile Valley mainly as an anchor and place of refuge in unusually dry years.

After 4000 B.C., the nomads moved southward with the retreating Sahel into the tsetse-free East African highlands, where cattle people like the Maasai thrive to this day. They also moved into the Nile Valley in much larger numbers, at a time of rapid political and social change along the river.

For generations, the nomads had interacted with the farmers of the valley, perhaps bringing with them new ideas such as cattle cults and the notion of elders as strong bulls and herdsmen. Judging from modern herding societies, their leaders were elders of long experience and exceptional ritual ability, who called on the supernatural world to predict rain. If the Eastern Desert petroglyphs are to be believed, such notions of leadership were well established along the Nile. As the drought intensified, the cattle herders stayed closer to the river. Desert herders and settled farmers merged and intermarried; some cattle people set down roots in the great oasis of the valley while others remained in the nearby desert. But the basic notions of leadership forged among cattle people seem to have moved to center stage.

The drought and lowered flood levels triggered major changes in Egyptian life. During the fourth millennium, barley and wheat assumed even greater importance. By 3800 B.C., as the desert was beginning to dry up, farming communities flourished along the river all the way from the Sudan to the Delta. At Naqada in Upper Egypt, 25 kilometers south of the modern city of Luxor, small hamlets spaced about a kilometer apart along the Nile in 4000 B.C. grew enough grain at the edge of the floodplain to support 75 to 120 people per square kilometer.[23] By clearing trees, removing dense grass, building dikes, and digging drainage ditches to clear still-flooded land, the farmers soon opened up much larger tracts. By the time they had put four or even eight times more ground under cultivation, they could support as many as 760 to 1,520 people per square kilometer, many of them nonfarmers such as priests and traders. By 3600 B.C., the villages had coalesced into a walled town, with the rectangular mud-brick houses characteristic of later Egyptian cities. Many early Nile towns were little more than agglomerations of villages. But larger, more palatial residences housed a prosperous elite who enjoyed contacts with other communities up- and downstream. Naqada had become the capital of a small but important kingdom.

"The Nile looms very large before every Egyptian, and with reason," wrote the British irrigation expert William Willcocks, who worked in Egypt during the 1890s.[24] He described the frantic labor of shoring up canals and levees when the flood came, days and nights when a breached dam could flood a village in minutes. The Nile must have loomed large before the people of Naqada and another state upstream, Nekhen, whose rise to power coincided with the drying of the Sahara and the droughts that afflicted Mesopotamia with the southward shift of the summer monsoon after 4000 B.C. Much less water flowed downstream during the inundation after 3800 B.C., just when local farming populations were rising rapidly. There may not have been hunger along the Nile, but a succession of lower inundations could have provided an impetus toward larger settlements and more closely organized agriculture. This may well have been the time when some forms of simple irrigation came into play. There was nothing new about water management along the Nile, for farmers had diverted floodwater onto their fields for thousands of years. Irrigation was a local invention just as it was in Mesopotamia. Certainly the results of moving into towns were dramatic—much higher local populations, intensified trade with neighbors along the river, and the appearance of small kingdoms, which traded and competed with one another for many centuries.

The river has buried or swept away their settlements, but we can imagine villages of reed shelters and mud huts close to natural basins in the floodplain, each linked to the others and to the small towns and kingdoms up- and downriver. Nekhen, the "city of the falcon," was already the home of the falcon god Horus, venerated by the Egyptians for more than three thousand years. Horus's city flourished off a lively trade in plum-red pots. A brewery near the town produced 1,150 liters of beer a day, sufficient for 200 people. The curving rows of sand-filled burial places of Nekhen's ruling families lie close to the town, with its crowded mud houses and Horus shrine. Unfortunately, ancient looters ravaged the tombs, leaving only a jumble of black-topped jars, flint arrowheads, and wooden furniture fragments. So we know little about Nekhen's rulers except for occasional symbols of kingship. One macehead, a venerated symbol of royal authority, depicts a ruler in full ceremonial dress. He wears the White Crown of Upper Egypt and wields a mattock, as if he is about to breach the wall of an irrigation canal to release floodwater. A scorpion dangles before his face, perhaps a depiction of his name. The king wears a ritual bull's tail, a symbol of royal authority, which hangs from the back of his belt. He is the "Strong Bull," "Great of Strength," the "Bull of Horus."[25]

In later centuries, Egyptian priests compiled king lists, which stretched back in an orderly (and fictional) line back to the time of Menes, the first pharaoh, and then beyond to a legendary era of the "Divine Souls of Nekhen." Perhaps Scorpion was one of the Divine Souls. Part of his royal authority derived from ancient herder beliefs that embodied power in the body of a bull.

Then there was Bat, an important goddess of the seventh nome (or province) of Upper Egypt. She later became Hathor, the female consort of the Bull of Amenti, the first deity of the necropolis, the city of the dead. Hathor was the goddess of fertility, the protectress of women, and the nurse of the pharaoh, who gave him the supernatural powers to rule his kingdom. Perhaps the rituals that honored Hathor in the form of a celestial cow originated in the beliefs of herding societies that had been pushed into the Nile Valley by the drying Sahara centuries before the pharaoh Menes unified a mosaic of kingdoms into a single Egyptian state in 3100 B.C.

Egyptian civilization came together from many ancient strands, from ancient perceptions of a world order that revolved around the passage of the sun across the heavens and the changeless rhythm of the Nile. But many of the institutions of divine kingship, of Egyptian ideology, also stemmed from primordial notions of leadership and of the afterlife nurtured in the minds of cattle people living with the harsh realities of desert grasslands. When the savanna dried up and the grasslands disappeared, their ideas helped crystallize a civilization that endured for more than three thousand years.

PART THREE

THE DISTANCE BETWEEN GOOD AND BAD FORTUNE

Add to your stores, and Famine, burning-eyed,
Will stay away . . .
To sow your seed
Go naked; strip to plough and strip to reap,
If you would harvest all Demeter's yield
In season. Thus each crop will come in turn,
And later, you will not be found in need
And forced to beg from other men, and get
No help.

Hesiod, *Works and Days,* 8th century B.C.

	Climate Events Vegetation Zones	Human Events	Climate Triggers
A.D. 2003 —	Little Ice Age	Industrial Revolution	Warming after A.D. 1860 Cooler, more volatile climate— many cold periods
A.D. 1000 —	Medieval Warm Period Drought of A.D. 910 in Central America Event of 536	Ancestral Pueblo dispersal Collapse of Tiwanaku Collapse of Maya civilization in the southern lowlands, Yucatán Avar empire in eastern Europe Decline of Rome	Major droughts in western North America, Central and South America ? major volcanic event causing cooling
A.D. 1 —	**Sub-Atlantic** *(cooler, wetter in Europe)*	Caesar conquers Gaul Celtic migrations Biskupin	Drought on eastern steppes Abrupt cooling (A.D. 850)
1000 B.C. —	Drought event in eastern Mediterranean	Shaugh Moor, England, in use Collapse of Hittite, Mycenaean civilization Uluburun shipwreck	Major drought episode— ? El Niño events
2000 B.C. —	Drought event in eastern Mediterranean **Sub-Boreal**	Egypt reunified (2046 B.C.) Old Kingdom Egypt ends in crisis Akkadian empire Old Kingdom Egypt Sumerian civilization	Major El Niño event? 300-year drought in eastern Mediterranean after 2200 B.C.
3000 B.C. —			

Table 3 showing major climatological and historical events

9

THE DANCE
OF AIR AND OCEAN
2200 TO 1200 B.C.

And the yield of these trees will never flag or die,
Neither in winter nor in summer, a harvest all year round
For the West Wind always breathing through will bring
some fruits to the bud and others warm to ripeness.

Homer on King Alcinoos's garden, *Odyssey*,
Book 7, trans. Robert Fagles

In 1892, a Peruvian sea captain, Camilo Carrillo, published a short paper in the *Bulletin* of the Lima Geographical Society, in which he drew attention to a warm, anomalous coastal climate that flowed along the Pacific coast, disrupting the rich anchovy fisheries close inshore. He wrote: "The Paita sailors, who frequently navigate along the coast in small craft . . . name this counter-current the current of El Niño (the Child Jesus) because it has been observed to appear immediately after Christmas."[1]

At the time, El Niño seemed like a merely local curiosity that disrupted fisheries and lowered the natural production of sea bird guano, a major Peruvian export of the day. A century of research by scientists all over the world has elevated the Christmas Child to the status of a global phenomenon, a seesaw of atmospheric pressure called the Southern Oscillation that affects the lives of millions—and has for thousands of years. The seesaw emanates from an east-west circulation in the eastern Pacific and a huge pool of warm water in the west. Dry air sinks gently over the cold eastern ocean, and flows westward on the southeasterly trade winds. When warming occurs in the eastern Pacific, the sea surface temperature gradient between east and west decreases, the trade wind flow weakens, and pressure changes between the eastern and equatorial Pacific follow, acting just like a seesaw—the Southern Oscillation.

The climatologist George Philander calls El Niño a dance between the atmosphere and the ocean.[2] The dancers, gyrating unpredictably to a music that only they hear, make an ill-matched pair. The atmosphere is agile and quick to respond to prompts from its cumbersome partner. But their fandango triggers the eastward surge of warm water from the southwestern Pacific that starts an El Niño event. In the planet's catalogue of short-term climate changes, El Niño–Southern Oscillation (ENSO) events exercise an influence second only to the passing seasons.

The Pacific is a perpetual motion machine. West-blowing trade winds push warm surface water ever westward, forming a pool of warmer water thousands of kilometers across.[3] As the warm water moves west, colder water from the depths of the ocean flows to the surface near South America to take its place. The eastern Pacific is downright cold, even close inshore. Little moisture evaporates from it, so rain clouds rarely form. The Peruvian coast receives almost no rainfall; Mexico's Baja Peninsula and California have long dry seasons and even years of almost total drought. Far away, in the western Pacific, moist air heated by the warm ocean rises, condenses, and forms massive rain clouds. Heat and humidity climb to almost unbearable levels. Finally, the clouds loose scattered showers, then a deluge of rain, and the monsoon bursts over Southeast Asia and Indonesia. Life-bringing moisture waters the fields and fills irrigation canals for another year. A vast, self-perpetuating cycle keeps the eastern Pacific dry and the west wet.

For some unknown reason, every few years (usually in the Southern Hemisphere's spring) the machine hesitates. The dancers alter tempo. The ever-present northeast trade winds slacken and sometimes even die completely. An ENSO event is under way.

As the trades abate, gravity kicks in. Westerly winds increase east of New Guinea, generating Kelvin waves, internal waves below the ocean surface that push surface water across the tropical Pacific. A surge of warm water piled up by the trade winds in the western Pacific flows backward to the east. As the water travels eastward, it flows over the top of the cooler water and warms the sea surface dramatically. Surface temperatures cool in the western Pacific, inhibiting cloud formation and causing drought in southeast Asia and Australia. Meanwhile, rain clouds form over the Peruvian coast and the Galápagos Islands far to the east. A hundred year's rain can fall in a few days. The vast reservoir of warm, moist air over South America bulges dramatically and disrupts the air flows that circle the earth. The jet streams lurch north, bringing heavy rains and severe storms to much of the North American west coast. One stream crosses the Rocky Mountains, keeping arctic air out of the Midwest, which enjoys an unusually mild winter. Drought settles over northeastern Brazil and the southern margins of the Sahara. El Niño has now assumed global proportions.

ENSO events also exercise a strong influence on monsoons, and on the movements of our old friend the Intertropical Convergence Zone. The word *monsoon* comes from the Arabic word *mausem* (season).[4] The monsoon is a season of rains borne on dark nimbus clouds of summer that blow in from the southwest. A huge air circulation determines the intensity of the monsoon, which moves north in the Northern summer, southward in winter. In a good monsoon year, rain showers fall throughout western India and Pakistan from June to September, sometimes into November with the retreating monsoon. Millions of tropical farmers depend on this circulation. Today, highways, railroads, and at least a rudimentary infrastructure protects many such communities from the worst of monsoon failures. But what happened in the past when the unpredictable dark clouds never massed and the monsoon failed? With almost mind-numbing regularity, subsistence farmers died by the millions. The historian Mike Davis has estimated that between 30 and 50 million tropical villagers between the Sudan and northern China perished of drought, famine, and disease during the nineteenth century, more than in all that century's wars put together.[5] Twenty-one out of twenty-six droughts since 1877 have been attributed to El Niños, the most severe also coinciding with heavy snow cover in Eurasia, but the effects of ENSO events on monsoons vary considerably.

No one knows when the dance between atmosphere and ocean began in the vast wastes of the Pacific. Some experts believe ENSOs occurred during the Ice Age, others that they are a phenomenon of the last ten thousand years. I would not be surprised if they turn out to be of high antiquity, but at present we do not have the fine-grained climatological

172

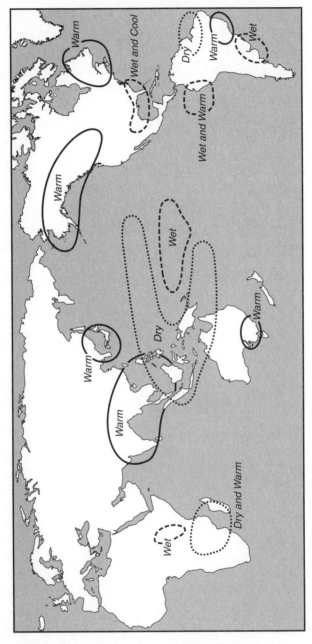

The major global effects of ENSO events. It is reasonable to assume that the same pattern pertained in ancient times.

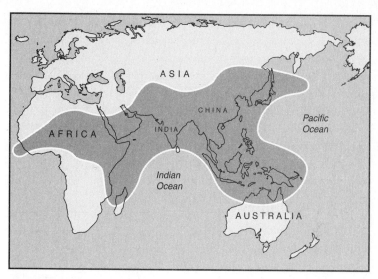

Monsoon climates of the world

data to document El Niños of the remoter past. Still, everyone agrees that major ENSO events have exercised a powerful effect on human societies since at least five thousand years ago, when the first urban civilizations appeared in Egypt and Mesopotamia. By that time, the seesaws of natural global warming had helped turn foragers into sedentary farmers and villagers into·city dwellers. Anchored to their fields and their irrigation systems, they were now dependent on much shorter climatic cycles and were unable to move away. By 2200 B.C., the scale of vulnerability was larger than ever before, especially in Egypt, where civilization rested on the Nile inundation and on the divine powers of the pharaohs. We know that by then, ENSO events were major players on the global climatic scene.

As we saw in Chapter 7, widespread disruption across Mesopotamia resulted from the 300-year drought cycle of 2200 B.C., a global event now recorded in Greenland ice cores. Aridity and, apparently, a series of frequent ENSO events toppled cities and upset the delicate balance of political power over a large area. The same drought cycle also brought suffering and catastrophe to the Nile. It's worth describing this particular cataclysm in more detail, as it offers a telling example of ENSO's power over events far away.

In Egypt, the power and spiritual authority of the pharaoh were unquestioned. According to Egyptian belief, the stars were divine beings, and the ruler was destined to take his place among them. "The king goes to his double. . . . A ladder is set up for him that he may ascend on it," proclaims a spell in a Royal Pyramid text.[6] The pharaohs were living gods, the embodiment of the divine order of a prosperous world nourished by a bountiful river. An Egyptian ruler at the height of his power was a blend of force and intelligence, nurture and fear, sustenance and punishment. He was thought to exercise a magical control over the life-giving Nile floods. Egyptian kings were held to be incapable of failure.

Every summer, rainfall from tropical Africa floods down the Nile. Most of the annual floodwaters originate as heavy monsoon rains over the Ethiopian highlands, the water pump that kept Ancient Egypt running. A complicated interplay of high and low pressure affects weather conditions in the Ethiopian mountains. Most summers, a persistent low-pressure system over India and the Arabian Sea brings strong southwesterlies to the Indian Ocean region. The Intertropical Convergence Zone lies just north of Eritrea, so abundant rain falls in the Ethiopian highlands and pours down the Blue Nile and Atbara rivers. These conditions prevail as long as atmospheric pressure is high in the western Pacific. When pressure falls over the Pacific, as it does during ENSO events, it rises over the Indian Ocean. The convergence zone stays farther south and the large Indian Ocean low-pressure system falters, develops only weakly, or moves eastward. The monsoon winds blow at a fraction of their usual strength or fail altogether. India and the Ethiopian highland suffer from drought. Thousands of kilometers to the north, Egypt experiences a poor flood year. Sometimes it suffers several.

Major El Niño events and the shifts of the convergence zone affected ancient Egyptian civilization from its earliest days. Unfortunately, we lack tree-ring records for Old Kingdom Egypt, and have only fragmentary contemporary observations of dubious reliability. They tell us that Nile inundations were in decline as part of the great drying trends that descended on the Sahara after 4000 B.C. Between 3000 and 2900 B.C., the flood fell by a meter, fully a third of the discharge of earlier times.[7]

The Old Kingdom pharaohs were sufficiently alarmed by this that they ordered court officials to record flood levels. Their bureaucrats made markings on cliffs and carved columns at strategic points along the river to develop the art of flood prediction to a high pitch. Sophisticated measurement systems were all very well, but they provided no protection against the unpredictable pressure seesaws of the Indian Ocean.

At a time when life expectancy was short and generational memory correspondingly shallow, a decade or century of better-than-average inundations could easily lull officials into a false sense of security despite rising populations, growing towns, and grossly inadequate grain storage facilities. Most Egyptians still lived from harvest to harvest and from flood to flood.

For nearly a thousand years, from 3100 to 2160 B.C., the Egyptians prospered under a series of strong and increasingly despotic kings. This was the era of pyramid building, of divine pharaohs, which culminated in the long reign of Pepi II, who ascended to the throne in 2278 B.C. at the age of six and reigned for ninety-four years. (The length of Pepi's reign is controversial, and may be as short as sixty-four years.)[8] His Egypt was powerful, wealthy, and somewhat complacent, master of vast trade monopolies in timber from Byblos on the eastern Mediterranean coast and ivory and tropical products from Nubia. But Pepi ruled in turbulent times. Thirty years into his reign, a Mesopotamian king, perhaps Sargon of Akkad, sacked Byblos and so destroyed a major source of Egyptian wealth. Pepi was also unsure of the loyalty of his provincial governors (nomarchs), who were responsible for tribute and tax collection. As long as the pharaoh was strong and decisive, the nomarchs trimmed their sails to the political winds and kept the tribute flowing. This changed as Pepi grew older and increasingly detached from the business of state. The succession may have been in dispute, as the pharaoh had outlived most of his sons. Ambitious nomarchs grew bolder, even behaved like independent kings, and were less respectful of their divine ruler.

When Pepi II died in 2184 B.C., during what may have been hard economic times, he left behind a state riven by internal dissension, its overseas trade in confusion, and without strong leadership. At this critical moment, the Nile inundations faltered. Within a few generations, Egypt collapsed into its component provinces. A sequence of weak and short-lived rulers passed through the royal capital at Memphis. The pharaoh's secular and spiritual powers wilted in the face of political unrest, social change, and rapidly intensifying famine.

For centuries, the pharaohs had been the flood makers, but now the "right order" of which they boasted was in question. The king was helpless, not only theologically bankrupt but incapable of feeding his people. Each town and village was on its own, in the midst of a river floodplain that seemed to be slowly turning into desert. As the Nile fell to record low levels, the people in desperation planted crops on sandbanks. In places, one could walk across the river almost dry-shod. As hunger intensified, villagers took to the countryside in a frenzied search for food. Only the most powerful and competent nomarchs acted decisively, for they had had the foresight to stockpile grain supplies against bad years. Khety of Assiut boasted in his tomb inscriptions, "I acted . . . as giver of water in the middle of the day. . . . I made a dam for this town, when Upper Egypt was a desert [?]. . . . I was rich in grain when the land was as a sandbank, and nourished my town by measuring grain."9

Nomarchs like Khety were well aware of the vulnerability of their people and had learned the hard way that only decisive, even draconian leadership could stave off famine. They built temporary dams at the edges of alluvial flats to retain as much floodwater on the fields as possible. Grain was rationed carefully and distributed to the worst-hit areas. Provincial boundaries were closed to prevent aimless wandering—a common reaction to mass hunger. Despite all these administrative initiatives aimed at preventing panic, social disorder broke out. Angry mobs killed soldiers guarding granaries. Egypt teetered on the brink of chaos for a century. At the end of a long civil war, King Mentuhotep I, a ruler from Thebes in Upper Egypt, conquered his rivals downstream and reunited the Two Lands (Upper and Lower Egypt) in 2046 B.C.

Thus began the Middle Kingdom, two-and-a-half centuries of prosperity and abundance. There were periods of low floods, but none approached those of the great hunger. The memory of those years apparently lived on: the famine was recalled by the seer Ipiutet some generations later: "The Storehouse is bare, / Its keeper stretched on the ground. . . . The grain of Egypt is 'I-go-get-it.'. . . The plunderer is everywhere and the servant takes what he finds."10

The Middle Kingdom pharaohs discouraged notions of infallibility yet maintained their facade of divinity. They knew that their state had come against a vicious threshold of vulnerability. So they deployed their people to create an irrigated oasis, an agricultural state as immune as they could make it to the whims of the inundation. The government invested heavily in grain storage facilities, created a highly centralized bureaucracy for feeding people. The pharaohs now depicted themselves not as carefree, youthful god-kings but as broodingly serious monarchs with a profound awareness of their responsibilities. Despite ups and downs, Egyptian civilization prospered almost uninterrupted until the first millennium B.C. The pharaohs had learned from the searing experience of the great droughts, developed large scale irrigation schemes and elaborate storage facilities, and renounced claims of infallibility as politically unwise. When a new drought cycle descended over the eastern Mediterranean in 1200 B.C., the Nile floods were lower, but the Egyptians weathered the poor inundation years, only to have to fight off outsiders fleeing crop failures and famine elsewhere.

The evidence for the widespread drought in about 1200 B.C. is once again a matter of climatological shreds and patches. Some experts, like the geologist Karl Butzer, believe there was no major climatic shift at all. But the evidence for social disruption resulting from drought and famine is striking. Numerous small cities and towns flourished throughout the southern Levant by the end of the third millennium B.C.[11] These were highly centralized, inflexible communities whose leaders controlled the populace through their rationing of carefully hoarded food supplies. In a single drought year, their subjects could be kept under control by careful distribution of granary inventories. Such droughts actually strengthened the power of those who controlled the granaries, for they would now have more people dependent on them and could acquire land and labor at low cost. But when drought succeeded drought until the granaries emptied, the same strategies failed.

How could city rulers respond to such situations? One immediately looks for technological innovations—new implements of tillage, more elaborate irrigation systems designed to tap hitherto underexploited springs or other water sources. They rarely appear, for the response was grounded in the ways in which the society was governed and how it perceived its cosmos and environment. All eastern Mediterranean societies of the day believed that powerful and capricious divine forces controlled winter cold and summer heat, flood and drought. So the immediate reaction, like that of medieval Europeans, was to propitiate the gods. In good times, medieval farmers helped build cathedrals to the glory of God and brought offerings. In bad, they went on pilgrimages and joined processions of penitents. When droughts threatened society, Bronze Age rulers built temples and cult sanctuaries. This is what one finds in the uppermost levels of the abandoned cities.

Appeasement failed. As people fled the shadows of their discredited lords, the great temples fell into disrepair and cities became ghost towns. The social collapse was complete throughout the southern Levant. A much-reduced population retreated into small villages and herding camps close to permanent springs. Only a few cities and towns survived, all of them on the banks of perennial rivers that could still support adequate grain.

By 2200 B.C., hundreds of thousands of people, perhaps millions, along the Nile and in eastern Mediterranean lands had crossed a threshold of environmental vulnerability that was unimaginable two millennia earlier. In a world of short life expectancy and very brief generational memory, no one remembered the great droughts of yesteryear or developed plans to deal with them.

In about 1318 B.C., a heavily laden cargo ship coasted westward along the rugged south Turkish coast near the rocky headland known today as Uluburun. We have no records of what happened, but one can imagine the skipper keeping a wary distance from the rocks as he eyes the dark clouds massing offshore. Perhaps he tries to make for a nearby harbor, but it becomes increasingly clear they won't reach it before the storm breaks. Suddenly, a vicious squall throws the ship on its beam ends, bringing green water pouring over the bulwarks. A shrieking gust splits the flapping sail and takes the mast with it. The crew frantically man the oars, but to no avail. The ship, wallowing in the heavy seas, is blown toward the pitiless headland of Uluburun. As the ship crashes against submerged rocks and breaks up almost immediately, the men, many of whom cannot swim, jump for their lives. Minutes later, the sea is calm, the sky blue. Only a few timbers float on the surface.[12]

Over three thousand years later, a sponge diver noticed a pile of "metal biscuits with ears" on the seabed at a depth of 45 meters off Uluburun. His skipper knew at once that they were copper ingots, such as were carried throughout the eastern Mediterranean by ancient ships, and reported the find to Turkey's Underwater Museum at Bodrum. In 1981, Çemal Pulak and Don Frey began excavations on the wreck, which was an archaeologist's dream. Hundreds of highly informative artifacts lay in undisturbed rows for nine meters down a steep slope in the seabed.

The Uluburun ship carried a cargo of dazzling wealth and variety. Three hundred fifty copper ingots were aboard, each weighing about 27 kilograms, as well as enough tin to fabricate bronze weapons and armor for a small army. Large amphorae contained stacked Canaanite and Mycenaean pottery. A ton of resin traveled in two-handled Syrian jars, used by Egyptian priests in temple rituals. The cargo included hardwood from the Levant, Baltic amber, tortoise shells, elephant tusks and hippopotamus teeth, jars of olives, and dozens of blue glass beads. The Uluburun ship carried items from Africa, Egypt, the eastern Mediterranean coast, Turkey, Cyprus, and the Aegean islands.

Judging from the woods in the cargo, the doomed ship had been sailing along a well-trodden circular route from east to west—from the Syrian coast across to Cyprus, along the southern Turkish shore, and then into the Aegean Sea, even as far as the Greek mainland. Perhaps it carried a royal consignment from one monarch to another. Such valuable loads were not unusual. Some centuries earlier, the king of Alashiya (Cyprus) had written to the pharaoh of Egypt: "I herewith send you 500 [units] of copper. As my brother's greeting gift I send it to you." The letter survived in the palace archives of King Akhenaten, the famous heretic pharaoh, at El Amarna on the Nile.[13]

The Uluburun ship set off on its voyage from the center of a closely interconnected eastern Mediterranean world. The Levant, the land of the Canaanites, was the cockpit of this bustling mercantile and political

Map of the eastern Mediterranean world in 1300 B.C.

universe, a place of exquisitely nuanced checks and balances. Everyone knew that he who controlled the Levant trade controlled the eastern Mediterranean. Ports like Ugarit on the northern Syrian coast were polyglot cities where people from all corners of the civilized world rubbed shoulders. Donkey caravans converged from deserts and cities far to the east. Watchful merchants loaded precious cargoes onto vessels that sailed to the outer limits of the known world: to Sardinia, Sicily and Italy. Mycenaeans from Crete and Greece mingled freely with Egyptians and desert nomads, Assyrian merchants and Hittite diplomats. Battered merchant ships from all over the Mediterranean world lay in the crowded Levant ports.

The great powers of the Bronze Age had been at peace for a half century when the Uluburun ship sailed from the Levant. Ugarit was a nominal vassal of the militaristic Hittite kings, who controlled a kingdom known as

Hatti in what is now Turkey and obtained much of their grain from northern Syria. The Hittites, newcomers on the international scene, had risen to power in Anatolia only in the fourteenth century B.C., when they burst from behind the Tauros mountains and defeated the state of Mitanni, at the time a major political power in the Levant.[14] The Hittites extended their influence over much of what is now Syria, where the northern plateau became a granary for Hittite monarchs. Inevitably, the newcomers came into conflict with the pharaohs, who had controlled the southern Levant since the reign of Tutmosis III in 1483 B.C.

King Suppiliuliuma of the Hittites presided over a prosperous and powerful civilization whose rivalry with Egypt had culminated in a treaty dividing the Levant in 1258 B.C., after the inconclusive battle of Kanesh, which the pharaoh Rameses II claimed grandiloquently as one of his most glorious victories. Suppiliuliuma's reign was the culmination of generations of expanding trade and prosperity, which turned the Levant into an international terminus for trade from as far afield as Mesopotamia, the Iranian Plateau, the Nile, and mainland Greece.

The Hittites' lives were structured around a warrior culture. Tens of thousands of farmers, who were effectively serfs, provided Hatti's food. The Hittite capital, Hattusas in central Anatolia, lay on the great bend of the Halys River in a dramatic landscape of forests and deep gorges. There was little good agricultural land, which may be why Hatti expanded so aggressively into the fertile lands of central Syria. Quite apart from its lucrative trade routes, Syria was a breadbasket for the Hittite state. But Hattusas was vulnerable. Unlike Egypt, or the increasingly powerful Assyrians to the east, the Hittite kings did not live close to much of their food supply. Hattusas itself was a sacred city, a ceremonial center adorned by generations of kings with temples and shrines. Its grain came from the Anatolian plateau and from Syria, much of it transported by sea through ports like Ugarit to Ura on the Cilician shore.

Both Egypt and Hatti were in regular touch with the Aegean world—with the palaces of Crete, rich in wine, timber, and olive oil. Even farther west, the warrior kings of Mycenae presided over the Plain of Argos in Greece's Peloponnese. Their ships traveled as far as the Nile.

Then, suddenly, in about 1200 B.C., this carefully balanced world fell apart. The Hittite state collapsed; Mycenaean civilization imploded; the Assyrians and Babylonians lived through hard times; the Levant cities went into economic depression and were ravaged by mysterious seafarers known to archaeologists as the Sea People. Only Egypt survived, but her pharaohs spent much time repelling unwelcome invaders, some from Libya. Merneptah, the thirteenth son of Rameses II, boasted in an inscription on the Temple of Amun at Karnak: "Libyans slain, whose uncircumcised phalli were carried off 6,239." Late Bronze Age civilization faltered and, in many places, came to an end.

This widespread implosion of civilization coincided with another widespread drought.

꩜

The great droughts of 1200 B.C. are as controversial as those of earlier times. In 1966, the classicist Rhys Carpenter wrote a short book entitled *Discontinuity in Greek Civilization*, in which he suggested that the decline of the Mycenaean civilization of mainland Greece was directly connected to a northward shift of dry desert winds from the Sahara.[15] The arid conditions thoroughly desiccated the Mycenaean homeland in the Peloponnese, as well as Crete and Anatolia. Drought undermined Mycenaean and Hittite agriculture and contributed to the collapse of both civilizations. Carpenter's book thrust climate change onto center stage.

Almost every climatologist dismissed Carpenter's intriguing theory as fundamentally unsound—except for Reid Bryson of the University of Wisconsin, who assigned a graduate student, Don Donley, to study the subject. Bryson, Donley, and the British climatologist Hubert Lamb analyzed the basic atmospheric circulation patterns over Europe and the Mediterranean to see if there was a mode that matched Carpenter's climatic scenario for the Mycenaean decline.[16] They found that Greece is normally on the boundary between regions of deficit and excess moisture. This means that dramatic rainfall differences occur from one area to the next. When the three researchers looked at rainfall patterns from November 1954 to March 1955, the unusually dry conditions in southern Greece's Peloponnese—60 percent of normal rainfall, which occurred only a few times in the twentieth century—coincided closely with what Carpenter had proposed for the Mycenaean homeland in 1200 B.C.

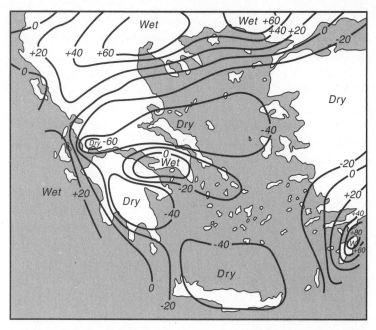

Rainfall patterns over Greece and the Aegean region in 1954/55, showing percentages above and below normal. Similar conditions probably occurred c. 1200 B.C.

In 1954/55, there was a winter trough of low pressure west of its normal position over the western Mediterranean and higher-than-usual pressure over Turkey. The storm tracks that normally brought rain to southern Greece curved sharply northward instead. Athens and the Attica region were wetter than usual; Anatolia and southern Greece were much drier.

It's interesting to correlate what we know of historical events in 1200 B.C. with the rainfall patterns of 1954/55. Hatti suffered severe famine. Near the end of the thirteenth century B.C., the Hittites moved the center of their troubled empire from the Anatolian plateau to northern Syria, where food was more plentiful. In 1954/55, rainfall in the area fell short by about 40 percent, while temperatures were 2.5 to 4°C above normal. Across the Mediterranean, Libyan nomads moved into Egypt's settled lands in search of water and grazing and were repulsed after bloody conflict. In 1954/55, Libyan precipitation was half what usually fell. The drought was far from universal. Pollen diagrams of 1200 B.C. show evidence of normal precipitation in the northwestern Greek mountains—it was normal, too, in 1954/55—and evidence of floods in Hungary, where rainfall was 5 to 15 percent above normal in 1954/55.

The three researchers concluded that Carpenter was probably right. Had the 1954/55 climatic pattern occurred in 1200 B.C., Mycenaean agriculture would have been in a precarious position after just one year. A short, intense cycle of three or four such years would have been disastrous.

Another climate expert, Barry Weiss, later followed up on the Bryson and Donley research.[17] He produced rainfall and temperature diagrams for Anatolia and lands further afield in 1954/55, which were even more revealing. Southwestern Anatolia experienced very heavy rainfall, whereas the plateau east of the modern capital of Ankara was very dry. Some places received only 7 percent of their usual rainfall. The northern Syrian coast received 40 percent less than normal. Weiss's research provides more good reasons to assume that a widespread drought affected the eastern Mediterranean three millennia ago.

Even if we lack specific details of the ancient drought, we can be certain that the effects were devastating. Subsistence farming was never easy in ancient Greece. Mycenaean farmers depended on unpredictable winter rainfall to grow cereals in the valleys, and olives and grapes on valley slopes.[18] Their most elaborate implement of tillage was the ox-drawn plow. Homer depicted a golden age of planting and harvest in the *Iliad*, "broad fields" where "crews of plowmen wheeled their teams, driving them up and back" and the earth churned black behind them.

The image of fertility and bounty extended to the harvest. The smith god Hephaestus depicted a king's estate on Achilles' shield where

> *harvesters labored,*
> *Reaping the ripe grain, swinging their whetted scythes,*
> *Some stalks fall in line with the reapers, row on row,*
> *And others the sheaf-binders girded round with ropes,*
> *Three binders standing over the sheaves, behind them,*
> *Boys gathering up the cut swaths, filling their arms,*
> *Supplying grain to the binders, endless bundles.[19]*

"Endless bundles . . . "—the image conjures up a world of inexhaustible harvests presided over by a benign Zeus. The reality was much harsher: a countryside laced with palaces and manor houses, rocky soils of mostly moderate fertility, and relatively small grain surpluses stored in palace storerooms. Most people lived at the subsistence level, eking out a living in rugged terrain where even the most fertile plains, like the Plain of Argos near Mycenae, were subject to irregular rainfall. The lifeblood of Mycenaean civilization was its exports of wine and olive oil, timber and fine pottery, shipped as far as the Levant and deep into the Aegean. Without question, the Mycenaeans imported large quantities of grain, but still the populace lived essentially from one harvest to the next.

When drought came, the Mycenaeans could easily survive one dry year. A series of such years was another matter. At first, the lords of the palaces could ration grain to the hinterland, but a second year of crop failure would have put severe stress on the rationing system. If Carpenter and the climatologists are correct, then the harsh droughts of 1200 B.C. spelled disaster for the Mycenaean lords, whose prosperity depended entirely on surplus grain levied from their subjects and on seaborne trade. The palaces were burned and abandoned, the populace scattered into small, self-sufficient villages.

Civilization vanished for four centuries or more. The dark centuries lingered in collective memory for many generations. As late as the fifth century B.C., the Athenian general Thucydides wrote of a Greece of old "without commerce, without communication by land or sea, cultivating no more acreage than the necessities of life demanded, destitute of capital, building no large towns or attaining any form of greatness."[20]

The drought that descended on Mycenae and Crete also devastated Anatolia and the Hittite empire. By 1200 B.C., serious internal stresses racked Hatti. Succession disputes had created royal feuds that undermined the great king's authority. Hattusas was destroyed by fire in 1180 B.C., during the reign of King Tudhaliya IV, perhaps as part of civil war. Tudhaliya fought Kurunta, the ruler of southern Anatolia, who may have split off his domains from Hatti. When he did, Hattusas no longer had access to its major grain port at Ura. By that time, the Hittites were importing food from other states, especially Egypt. The rebuilding of Hattusas and its elaborate shrines had absorbed huge numbers of people, as did obligatory annual service in Hatti's armies—all this apart from the labor of growing food. With sudden climate changes, the grandiose ambitions of state caught up with the ailing empire.

Like all despotic monarchs, the Hittite kings knew that hunger and so-cial disorder went hand in hand. So they appealed to other states for assis-tance. The Egyptian pharaoh Merneptah recorded in an inscription that he sent a grain shipment "to keep alive the land of Hatti." As the drought in-tensified, fighting erupted, much of it to fend off marauding fleets and armies of hungry, displaced people, including the mysterious Sea People, many of them from the Aegean, who ravaged the civilized eastern Mediter-ranean world. As the armies battled, the scribes of Ugarit, itself threatened with attack, calmly went about their daily business of baking fresh cunei-form tablets in the ovens of the royal archives. A batch of tablets was still in the ovens when the city was attacked. One of them preserved a letter from the Hittite king requesting that a large ship be loaded with 200 measures of grain (about 450 metric tons). It was, wrote the monarch, "a matter of life and death: let the king of Ugarit not linger."[21] Soon after 1200 B.C., the Hittite empire dissolved into its constituent parts. The remnants of Hittite armies resisted the Sea People furiously, but to no avail.

The Sea People traveled by land and sea, besieging ports and inland cities, pillaging royal treasuries, looking for places to settle. No one knows precisely who they were, but many were undoubtedly refugees from parched lands desperate for a permanent home. Inevitably they traveled to the Nile, looking to settle in the fertile delta. In about 1200 B.C., an al-liance of Libyans and Sea People attacked Egypt from Syria by land and sea—a horde on the move, complete with ox carts, women, and children, who planned not just to raid the Nile Valley but to settle there. Hundreds of ships sailed alongside travelers on land. The Egyptian navy confronted the enemy fleet at an eastern mouth of the Nile. Archers poured volleys of arrows into the attacker's ships. Inscriptions on the king's temple at Medinet Habu near Luxor show grappling irons bringing the enemy ves-sels close alongside as arrows annihilated the crews. Rameses eventually prevailed, capturing vast numbers of cattle and killing more than two thousand attackers. Piles of severed enemy hands were placed before the pharaoh, the numbers dutifully tallied by ubiquitous scribes, then checked against a tally of severed penises.[22]

Egypt survived the attack, and another one in 1193 B.C., perhaps be-cause the invaders had been weakened by their earlier campaigns. But the pharaohs were in trouble. Like their neighbors, the Egyptians were ravaged by low inundations and crop shortfalls, which led to massive inflation and social unrest. Workers in the royal necropolis near the Valley of Kings went on strike when their rations went unissued. Corruption was rampant; tomb robbing reached epidemic proportions. Most important of all, the seemingly inexhaustible supplies of Nubian gold from the south dried up. There may have been more gold underground in the realms of the dead than there was in that of the living. Pharaohs had always conducted their foreign diplomacy with all the arrogance of unlimited wealth. They courted rulers with offers of gold and marriages. Now their diplomatic clout had gone. Egypt withdrew from the world stage, leaving behind it a diverse and highly competitive political landscape where the pharaohs no longer played.

Centuries would pass before prosperity returned, before the Assyrians were strong enough to advance to the Mediterranean shore and new Greek civilization arose from the ashes of the old.

Behind these momentous events lay the invisible forces of the atmosphere and the ocean, the irregular seesaw of the Southern Oscillation, the capricious north-south movements of the Intertropical Convergence Zone, and the ocean circulation of the North Atlantic. The monsoon rains advanced and retreated, bringing drought and crop failures when they weakened or did not appear at all. A newly vulnerable humanity danced to the tunes of the global climate. Despite this, noble lords and great kings rejoiced in their power and military conquests. Millions labored to keep them and their armies and cities fed. Grain, raw materials, luxury goods—all flowed into the hands of a tiny minority that controlled thousands of anonymous, hardworking hands.

Originally, the city had come into being in part as a mechanism for feeding people, for controlling their labor and ensuring ample food supplies. Nothing succeeds like success, but success came at a price—greatly enhanced vulnerability to major, short-term climatic events. As long as the rains fell, the civilizations of Egypt and the eastern Mediterranean enjoyed good, even giddy times; but when the rains failed, the plenty ended abruptly and without warning. The citadels and temples still stood, surrounded by closely packed mud-brick houses and crowded bazaars. But caravans and ships no longer carried grain, and store shelves became bare. There was nowhere to go, no safety net of less desirable foods to tide people over until better times returned. Hunting bands could move away, closer to permanent water, to places where food could be found. Farming communities had some cushion of game and edible plant remains to fall back on. They could even disperse into smaller settlements in a world where populations were still small and territorial boundaries less fixed. But in Egypt or Hatti, the cities and towns contained thousands of inhabitants who had never plowed a field, repaired an irrigation canal, or gathered a harvest. The city was permanent, immovable, completely at the mercy of flood and drought—of what the inhabitants thought of as the wrath of the gods, which we now know to be part of the endless symphony of global climate.

The moment when people moved into cities and towns, into larger settlements from which they could not move and which depended on humanly managed farming landscapes, they stepped over a threshold of far greater vulnerability to sudden climatic change than ever before. Now there was no middle ground between prosperity and collapse. Of course, climate change didn't "cause" the end of the Hittite empire or the dilution of pharaonic power along the Nile. But whatever weaknesses, injustices, and inefficiencies existed in these societies, the droughts uncovered them and turned them into fatal flaws that set loose the forces of social chaos and tumbled their kings into oblivion.

10

CELTS AND ROMANS
1200 B.C. TO A.D. 900

> There were innumerable trumpeters and horn-blowers
> and . . . the whole army were shouting their war cries at
> the same time. Very frightening too were the appearance
> and gestures of the naked warriors in front, all in the
> prime of life and finely built men, and all the leading
> companies richly adorned with gold torcs and armlets.
>
> Polybius on the Celts at war

The fierce Celtic warriors known as Gauls, who lived in the wild lands
north of the Alps, were the bogeymen of Roman lore. Their arrogant
taunts inviting single combat terrified Rome's legions. They were the
scourges of settled lands who swept down without warning on quiet
farming villages or drove off herds in dawn raids. Generations of Roman
mothers frightened their children with cautionary tales of these "barbarian" hordes. In 390 B.C., Celtic armies had besieged Rome itself. They
were archetypical enemies, described by the writer Ammianus Marcellinus as "of tall stature, fair and ruddy, terrible for fierceness of their eyes,
fond of quarrelling and of overbearing insolence."[1]

The Celts came from a world alien to the urbanized Romans, a northern environment colder, wetter, and much more demanding to farm. They
lived in a northern continental zone, an entirely different climatic regimen
from the Mediterranean. In the north, the heaviest rain fell during warm

Map showing Celtic peoples, archaeological sites, and Roman possessions

summers; winters were dry and generally mild, but sometimes bitterly cold. Celtic farmers, like their predecessors, lived at the mercy of the moist westerlies that brought rainfall to northern Europe. Without warning, the westerly air flow could falter as high pressure built over Greenland and in the far north. Drought would settle over newly planted fields; week after week of frost and snow would mantle highlands and lowlands with bitter cold. The people would go hungry, and when the cold came, the dying would begin. Even inside the best-built dwelling and with fires burning day and night, young and old would shiver and sometimes freeze to death. The harsh realities of subsistence agriculture and food shortages bred tough, warlike societies.

Then as now, Europe had a climate of shifting boundaries. In the south lies the Mediterranean zone—mild, with wet winters and dry, hot summers. The west enjoys an oceanic climate, with cool, often wet summers and relatively warm winters; most rain falls in autumn. The continental regimen once inhabited by the Celts extends across the north and east. Immutable zones, one might think, but the boundaries between them, often called ecotones, have altered dramatically over the past three thousand years owing to shifts in the jet stream. (The term *ecotone* refers to a boundary between two or more ecological zones. Such places often appealed to ancient peoples because they could access different game and plant foods in each.)

The frontier between the continental and Mediterranean zones currently lies on the southern edge of France's Massif Central, where the vegetation changes within a few meters from temperate to Mediterranean. The archaeologist Carole Crumley has tracked the movements of this ecotone over the past three thousand years. Her findings show that the boundary lay as far south as latitude 36°N, along the North African coast, in colder centuries. Warmer times would shift the frontier as far northward as the North Sea and Baltic Sea coasts, a distance of some 880 kilometers—no less than 12° of latitude.[2] Crumley believes that these north-south shifts in climatic zones had a dramatic, and hitherto unsuspected, effect on European history.

⚭

At the time of the Hittite and Mycenaean collapse in 1200 B.C., Europe north of the Mediterranean zone was a mosaic of small-scale communities of subsistence farmers.[3] It was a world apart from the turbulent domains of the eastern Mediterranean civilizations. In the well-wooded north, the egalitarian farming societies of earlier times had given way to small competing dynasties of local chiefs. In this patchwork of constantly shifting alliances, chief vied with chief in the acquisition of the currency of success. This currency took the form of prestigious ornaments—Baltic amber and, above all, shiny bronze, used to manufacture weapons, jewelry, and some categories of tools like axes. Bronze was buried with the dead and offered to the gods. It was the

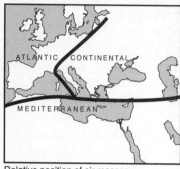

Relative position of air masses,
1200–300 B.C.

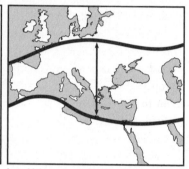

Relative position of air masses,
ca. 300 B.C.–A.D. 300

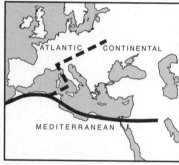

Relative position of air masses,
A.D. 500–900

Late Holocene range of the Temperate-
Mediterranean ecotone

Changing ecological zones in Europe. Reprinted by permission from Carole L.
Crumley, ed., *Historical Ecology* © 1994 by the School of American Research,
Santa Fe, New Mexico

metal of display, known to us from great hoards of metal objects buried by
their owners near major copper deposits close to central Germany's Harz
Mountains. Shiny bronze gleamed in the sunlight, on the battlefield, and by
firelight, proclaiming authority, social status, and prowess in battle. These
people had no powerful kings or centralized bureaucracies. Life revolved
around the field, the household, and the village workshop. Most people
dwelled in small, round houses, in hamlets or villages, living much the same
way as the first farmers had over three thousand years earlier.

Life in every village, however small, ebbed and flowed with the harvests, with long- and short-term climatic shifts. For thousands of years,
the Gallic homeland had been drier and warmer than today, but a gradual

cooling had been underway since about 3500 B.C. At first, the colder conditions had little effect on daily life. Most communities depended heavily on wheat and barley. Wheat is notably intolerant of heavy rainfall, and cold summers brought serious declines in crop yields. With each bad harvest, the grain shortages were felt almost at once.

The heavy dependence on barley and wheat made subsistence farmers in an increasingly continental climate more and more vulnerable to hard years. So they adapted to colder conditions by sowing new crops, especially millet, a grain with a short growing season, excellent storage properties, and the ability to withstand drought. Many years ago, I spent time with millet farmers in central Africa. They valued the hardy cereal because it tolerated very dry growing seasons. In good years, millet was highly productive, which delighted the farmers. They consumed the surplus by fermenting it to make many liters of beer, which became an important social currency to pay for communal tasks like house building. European farmers prized millet for the same reasons. It provided not only grain for unleavened breads and porridges but also the basis for fermented beverages, consumed at the feasts that became a prominent feature of Gallic life. Celtic beans (our broad, or lima, beans) also came into use. Such beans are fast growers that are tolerant of a wide variety of conditions, especially cool, moist environments.

The farmers of the north adapted effortlessly to a climatic regimen that was rarely constant and often extreme, with short-term cycles of wetter and drier, warmer and cooler conditions that arrived without warning. We know of the short-term changes from Danish bogs, where the paleobotanist Bent Aaby examined distinctive land surfaces of the second millennium B.C. and discovered that cooler and wetter cycles alternated with warmer and drier ones about every 260 years.[4] No one knows what drove these cycles, but some experts believe that they were associated with major volcanic events, like the eruption of the Hekla volcano on Iceland in 1159 B.C.

☙❦❧

The sixteenth-century German physician Casper Peucer called Hekla the Gate of Hell, "for people know from long experience that whenever great battles are fought or there is bloody carnage somewhere on the globe, then there can be heard in the mountain fearful howlings, weeping, and gnashing of teeth."[5] The bleak mountain, with its black lava flows and smoking summit, supports flocks of ravens, thought by the superstitious to be the souls of the dead hovering at the gateway to the underworld. Hekla towers 1,497 meters above sea level from sparsely vegetated highlands about 110 kilometers east of Reykjavik and has erupted twenty-three times since Iceland founded its ancient parliament, the Atheling, in A.D. 930.[6]

Hekla is not alone. Major eruptions have ravaged Iceland four or five times a century since the tenth century A.D. The larger ones have hurled so much volcanic ash and aerosols into the atmosphere that they filtered out enough sunlight to significantly reduce the amount of heat reaching the earth. Debris from major Icelandic volcanic outbursts spread like smoke across Europe. From 1783 to 1786, savage eruptions killed a quarter of Iceland's population and burned so much grass that three-quarters of the island's cattle starved to death. By chance, Benjamin Franklin was in Paris at the time. He complained of a sulphurous haze that stung his eyes and hung over France during the summer months. He rightly attributed this to an Icelandic eruption—we know now it was the Laki volcano—whose gases spread slowly eastward and southeastward over Europe. Wrote Franklin perceptively, "Hence perhaps the winter of 1783–4 was more severe than any that had happened for many years."[7]

The climatic effects of even the largest Icelandic eruptions pale alongside that of the three-month Mount Tambora eruption of April 1815, one of the most powerful since the late Ice Age, which blew 1,300 meters off the top of a volcano in eastern Java.[8] At least 12,000 people perished in the eruption; another 44,000 died of famine caused by ash falling on neighboring islands. The dense volcanic clouds that ascended high into the atmosphere reduced the absorption of solar radiation by well over 20 percent. The year 1816 acquired immediate notoriety as "the year without a summer." The monthly temperatures for that summer were between 2.3 and 4.6°C colder than the mean. Hailstorms and thunderstorms battered growing crops. Much of the harvest in southeastern England was "in so damp a condition, as to be unfit for immediate use." The cold weather kept the poet Percy Bysshe Shelley, his wife Mary, and fellow poet Lord Byron indoors during their summer vacation in Geneva. The party entertained one another with stories. Mary's invention became the classic horror novel *Frankenstein*.[9]

Thought less powerful than Mount Tambora, Icelandic eruptions had serious short-term effects on European climate, especially on subsistence farmers who lived from harvest to harvest. Thanks to Greenland ice cores, radiocarbon dating, and narrow layers of volcanic tephra (ash) in peat bogs and other deposits that can be traced to specific volcanoes from their distinctive trace elements, we can sometimes identify large eruptions that affected considerable areas. A conspicuous ash layer that originated from a major Hekla eruption occurs in the GISP–2 ice core on the Greenland ice cap at 1159 B.C., marked in Swedish bogs by peat layers signaling colder and wetter conditions. Irish tree-ring sequences display a marked zone of thinner rings around that year.

One could dismiss a sequence of, say, five years of colder summers resulting from volcanic activity as a mere blip in the endless cycle of planting and harvest that was the lot of the subsistence farmers. But five years was a long time to those who had to suffer through it. However bountiful the harvest, life was always lived on the margin. The historian Johan Huizinga once remarked of the Middle Ages that "[t]he distance between sadness and joy, between good and bad fortune, seemed to be much greater than for us. . . . The cutting cold and dreaded darkness of winter were more concrete evils."[10] His remarks apply with even greater force to the farmers of 2,500 years earlier, when most communities survived at near-subsistence levels, with only enough grain to get through one bad harvest and plant for the next.

Even in good years, the farmer endured the constant specter of winter famine. All it took to make people go hungry was too much or too little rainfall, an early or late frost, or an epidemic of cattle disease that decimated breeding stock and draught animals. Only the ancient ties of kin, social reciprocity, and a diminishing stock of wild plant foods and game kept every household from hunger. The threat of starvation always hung over the north, where centuries of good harvests had increased agricultural productivity, village populations rose in response, and expanding communities took up additional woodland and grazing range. People consistently underestimate how marginal subsistence agriculture is. Inevitably, farmers in growing villages take up more land, and as the best soils come under cultivation, they turn to more marginal fields, many of them on easily erodable hillsides. There is a subtle and invisible equation between population growth, good harvests, and the carrying capacity of the land. Almost invariably, people farmed close to the limit, and sometimes beyond. Many winters, villagers were hungry and people died.

Hunger and episodes of malnutrition were a fact of Bronze Age life. When scientists examined the frozen corpse of Ötzi, the famous "Ice Man" of 3100 B.C., who was killed high in the Alps, they discovered telltale "Harris lines" on his bones that resulted from episodes of malnutrition at ages 9, 15, and 16.[11] He had also experienced episodes of reduced growth, another sign of dietary stress. His experience was probably typical. The margin between hunger and plenty was small, the line easily traversed.

The Hekla eruption of 1159 B.C. may have triggered crop failures and hunger over a wide area of northern Europe.

And still the cooling continued, oblivious to volcanic events. The northern farmers responded by growing more cold-resistant crops and diversifying heavily into cattle herding. Cattle were far more than meat, hides, horn, and bones. They were wealth on the hoof, with a constant surplus of young male beasts for breeding. In societies with ever more diversified economies and a lust for wealth and prestige, cattle became a currency of political and social life. Just as cattle people do today in Africa, the ancient European farmer would build up his herds in good years, figuring that this gave him insurance against winter mortality and drought years. He would spread his animals around among relatives to minimize the dangers of epidemic diseases. Each year unfolded in a pattern of movement and careful grazing that required large ranges and much more planned use of the landscape than in earlier times.

Cooler summers and expanded farming, combined with larger-scale herding and higher populations, required more economical use of space and a careful separation of different farming activities. After 1300 B.C., the farmers in many areas drove long boundary ditches and banks across the countryside with ards (scratch plows) to divide the landscape into closely knit field systems. At the same time, farming and herding expanded into hitherto uncleared areas and onto higher ground.

Most of these Bronze Age landscapes have vanished in the face of later agriculture and twentieth-century industry. Only a few patches of the vast mosaic of field systems survive for archaeologists to investigate. One lies on the windy Shaugh Moor highlands of Dartmoor in southwestern Britain, a series of low stone walls, some linked to wider prehistoric land boundaries that covered the whole of Dartmoor, others forming smaller areas of enclosed pasture.[12] Hoof prints of sheep and cattle came from one ditch.

For more than twelve hundred years, stock herders used Dartmoor's field systems, living for weeks or months on end in small stone dwellings by the fields. Their activities ravaged the countryside. Originally, the area was a mosaic of alder woods, hazel scrub, and acid grasslands at the higher elevations. After ten centuries of stock herding, the landscape was mainly moorland degraded by heavy grazing. Around 800 B.C., the European climate abruptly became cooler and considerably wetter; the herders moved on and never returned. By this time, the ecotone dividing the continental zone of the north and the Mediterranean region had shifted far southward and lay over North Africa. For the next five centuries, all of what is now France and southern Germany lived under a highly variable regimen that brought severe winters and a mix of moist oceanic conditions and much drier, more continental climate.

⚶

The Nordic sagas refer to a "Fimbul-winter," a legendary time when the sun, moon, and stars were swallowed by a wolf. Perhaps these tales are a folk memory of the harsh climatic shifts of these centuries.

A sharp cold snap occurred simultaneously over a wide area in 850 B.C., coinciding with a sudden reduction in sunspot activity, an increase in cosmic ray flux, and much higher production of carbon–14 in the atmosphere. All of these changes are indicative of a reduction in so-lar activity: the sun literally shined less brightly for some centuries. Re-duced solar activity seems to have been the forcing mechanism behind the change to cooler and wetter conditions in higher and middle lati-tudes. Interestingly, a similar reduction in solar activity and a rise in carbon–14 activity coincided with the height of the Little Ice Age many centuries later, the so-called Maunder Minimum of A.D. 1645–1710.[13]

We cannot be sure whether there is a relationship between solar activity and abrupt changes like that of 850 B.C., but there is certainly a nearly per-fect coincidence between major fluctuations in global temperature over the past thousand years and major changes in carbon–14 levels identified in tree rings. This implies that long-term changes in solar radiation may have had a profound effect on terrestrial climate over many thousands of years.

Fortunately for the Celts, their highly flexible farming strategies and cattle-herding practices were well suited to an uncertain climate. We are only just beginning to discern some of the major changes in human set-tlement that resulted from the abrupt cooling. People retreated from higher ground throughout highland Britain, and we know from pollen diagrams that there were major vegetational changes as woodland gave way to grassland. These shifts were due as much to rapid forest clearance and more intensive herding as to cooler conditions.

In the Low Countries, the higher rainfall led to higher water tables and greater natural seepage, which in turn enhanced the transport of iron by groundwater. As a result, bog and lake iron ore formed more rapidly and widely, making the raw material for iron tools more readily available within a few generations, when previously it had largely come from mines. Ironworking became a village craft, and iron-bladed implements of tillage came into widespread use—a major economic development.

In most places, cooler temperatures and ample rainfall had the effect of fostering agricultural productivity resulting from new farming methods, especially the use of the plow and iron tools. The carrying capacity of good soils rose sharply as the land was enclosed and kept permanently cleared of regenerated woodland. Much of what the Romans called Gaul, as well as southern Britain, now came under cultivation. Visitors commented on the densely farmed landscape. Julius Caesar, visiting southern Britain in 55 B.C., noted that the population was "exceedingly large, the ground thickly studded with homesteads."[14] Dense settlements clustered on well-drained river gravels and floodplains like those of the Thames and Severn rivers.

The Romans did not tamper much with the basic pattern of indigenous land occupation. Only in the far north, where the construction of Hadrian's Wall consumed enormous quantities of oak trees, did they do extensive forest clearance. [15] The distribution of wooded and nonwooded land and the territorial divisions of most estates and parishes recorded in William the Conqueror's Domesday Book in A.D. 1086 had by then been established at least a thousand years and perhaps much longer. Britain lay north of the shifting frontiers of the European ecotones and enjoyed a long-term continuity of farming life.

✿

With iron came a new social order, no longer egalitarian but more hierarchical, even tribal in its loyalties. As the landscape became more crowded and boundaries more clearly drawn, we find more and more weapons appearing—slashing swords and shields, bronze helmets, even pieces of armor. Raiding and warfare were now an integral part of daily life. In some places, war became endemic, so much so that chiefs built strongly fortified settlements on hilltops, on lake promontories, and even on islands in lakes. By 600 B.C., temperate Europe was a landscape of hill forts, many occupied by substantial communities.[16]

The environmental cost of these hill forts came home to me vividly when I visited the reconstruction of a fortified village at Biskupin in Poland, a two-hectare settlement on a peninsula extending into a lake, surrounded by a wooden rampart filled with earth and sand. Preservation conditions in the waterlogged soil were so good that many wooden and bone artifacts, and even textile fragments, survived, as well as palisade and house timbers. Given the size of the village, the scale of the fortifications suggested an obsession with outside threats—literally a fortress mentality. A single entrance with watch tower and double gates lay on the southwestern side, while a road ran around the inside of the rampart, enclosing a system of no less than eleven streets made of logs laid side by side. Over a hundred houses made of horizontal logs reinforced with pegs lay along the streets, each large enough to accommodate both humans and beasts.[17]

Biskupin consumed an entire landscape of oak trees. The earliest settlement was built almost entirely of oak. By 450 B.C., having stripped the oak forests, the inhabitants turned to pine for their dwellings. Biskupin's carpenters used over 8,000 cubic meters of timber in each building phase, with devastating effects on the surrounding environment. And then they required firewood. I began to realize just how fast the Europe of 2,500 years ago lost its woodland to rapidly expanding agriculture and the rapacious demands of tribal warfare.

These centuries may have been a time of rising tension, of increasingly frequent warfare, which triggered several centuries of frenzied fortification. Each fort was the center of a self-sufficient economic system, dependent on subsistence agriculture and the acquisition and storage of large food surpluses as a hedge against periodic food shortages. Life revolved not around long-distance trading, although there were certainly some prestigious gift exchanges, but around farming, war, and cattle herding.

Why these abrupt shifts in the tenor of farming existence? Why did people suddenly bring warfare to center stage? I suspect that a combination of new ideas and the harsh realities of subsistence agriculture was to blame.

What do people do when confronted with food shortages within confined territorial boundaries? If they are subsistence farmers, they fall back on game and edible plants within their territories. If those are in short supply, as they are bound to be when more and more land is farmed or grazed, they try to move. By 400 B.C., moving was not an option in many parts of the world, so the alternative to hunger was to help yourself to your neighbor's grain and herds. From casual raids to endemic war is but a short step when populations keep rising and food shortages become more commonplace. Inevitably, social values changed profoundly. Now doctrines of war and individual bravery came to the forefront. They arose not only because of changing social and political conditions at home but because of drought far to the east on the great steppes, where once again the ancient pump effect of deserts came into play.

The grassland steppe extended from the eastern margins of Europe to the far horizon, across Central Asia, bounded by desert to the south and cold boreal forest to the north. Its boundaries had shifted constantly since the Ice Age, expanding and contracting north and south as rainfall pat-terns shifted through the millennia. Like the Sahara and the Eurasian steppe/tundra of 20,000 years ago, the grassland steppe acted like a pump, sucking in nomadic peoples during periods of higher rainfall, pushing them out to the margins and onto neighboring lands when drought came. During the ninth century B.C., the climate of the steppe suddenly became colder and drier. Within generations, standing water supplies had dried up. The drought played havoc with long-established seasonal movements of flocks and herds.[18]

The Mongolian steppe appears to have been the first region affected. In wet centuries it was a wonderful oasis for herding peoples. Herds grew, populations increased. Then a drought cycle would force the nomads to move elsewhere and to impinge on settled lands. In the eighth century B.C., the drought on the steppe sent nomads pouring into China. They were repulsed, setting in motion a domino effect of population move-ments that brought some horse-using nomads to the Danube Basin and the eastern frontier of the Celtic world.

Horses caught on in Europe. So did a complicated set of ideas and art styles that soon linked central Europe from Burgundy to Bohemia. Within a few generations, a horse-riding aristocracy of powerful chief-tains presided over the farmlands of the north. For the first time, we glimpse signs of the Celtic societies described by the Romans—warlike chieftains who commanded loyal bands of followers by kinship, prestige, and warrior prowess. They displayed their power by cycles of feasts and gift giving, by public display. This culture was a vicious circle of con-sumption and yet more consumption, which enveloped all of western Eu-rope, southern Britain, and Ireland, marked by flamboyant metalwork, lively art, and rapid rises in local populations.

Celtic feasts helped maintain social equilibrium in this restless world of reckless bravery. The Greek writer Posidonius traveled to Gaul in the first century B.C. and feasted with the Celts, whose hospitality was legendary. He described how "when the hindquarters were served up, the bravest hero took the thigh piece and if another man claimed it they stood up and fought in single combat to death." Celtic chieftains honored bards, who disseminated legends and tales of gallant deeds, poets "who delivered eulo-gies in song." Well rewarded, they would sing the praises of their patrons.

A well-tipped bard sang of the chief Louernius that even "the tracks made by his chariot on the earth gave gold and largess to mankind."[19]

This was a world of legendary heroes and warriors, its values changed in part by climatic changes centuries earlier far to the east. Small wonder Europe became a restless continent, a place of constant tribal movements in response to overcrowded valleys and local shortages of agricultural land. The movements culminated in the great Celtic migrations of the fourth century B.C., which changed the course of European history.

•

The flamboyant Celts of the north hovered on the frontiers of a rapidly changing Mediterranean world, but their leaders were hungry for its luxuries. Two centuries before the great migrations began, Greek traders from Massilia (modern-day Marseilles) traveled into the heart of Europe through the Rhône and Saône river valleys laden with amphorae of red wine and fine drinking vessels. Their chiefly hosts embraced their vintages with enthusiasm. Feasts became elaborate ceremonies of wine mixing in magnificent bowls and quaffing out of fine vessels from the south, where intoxication was a sign of prestige and social prominence. The artifacts of wine consumption became ceremonial gifts of great significance and a way that a chief could mark his power over lesser neighbors. When a chief died, he was buried in all his finery, with his drinking vessels and mixing bowls, on top of a gold-decked funerary cart, sometimes covered in iron sheeting. Everything enhanced personal prestige, with family linked to family by gift exchanges, their followings changing from generation to generation. As long as the supply of exotic wines continued, the delicate power equation remained intact. As enterprising Etruscan merchants bypassed the Greek routes and made direct contract with Celtic leaders to the north, in the Marne/Moselle region, the center of political gravity passed northward into an area where rapid population growth and uncertain harvests threatened many groups.[20]

By the middle of the fifth century B.C., political conditions among the tribes of northern Europe were extremely volatile. Agricultural productivity had soared. Territorial boundaries tightened; neighbors lived in ever-closer juxtaposition in a world of closely packed field systems, fortified villages, and endemic conflict. Chief vied with chief in a Monopoly-like game of one-upmanship and warfare. Restless young men were the cannon fodder of intertribal wars that ebbed and flowed from the Atlantic to the Rhine. Quite apart from the by-now deeply engrained values of conquest, valor, and war, serious environmental stress haunted communities hemmed in by their neighbors. In earlier times, the farmers would have moved to uncleared land. Now all their leaders could do was to export young men to search for new homelands. The Roman writer Pompeius Trogus, himself of Celtic birth, writing of the migrations four centuries later, remarked that the Gauls had outgrown their land. As many as 300,000 warriors are said to have set out to seek new lands.

According to the historian Titus Livius, the Bituriges of the Marne/Moselle area were the most powerful Gallic tribe of the day. They were such successful farmers that their population exploded and restless, idle young men threatened law and order. Their chief, Ambigatus, "wishing to relieve his kingdom of the burdensome throng," chose two of his kinsmen and charged each of them to lead a migration, the one eastward, the other southward toward Italy. Thousands of young men made their way across Europe seeking farmland and plunder. While the elderly, slaves, women, and children stayed home to till the land and tend herds, the warriors wandered freely, kept in order by feasts, commemorating rank and deeds in battle. Their ferocity was legendary. The Greek geographer Strabo remarked that "the whole race is madly fond of war, high-spirited, and quick to battle."[21]

Waves of northern tribes moved southward, especially during the late fourth century. Now entire households migrated south of the Po to found small, scattered communities. In about 390 B.C., as Rome was conquering its Etruscan neighbors, Celtic war bands broke through the Apennine Mountains and moved south, marching to the very gates of Rome. The warriors burned and pillaged much of the city, but the Capital held out for seven months before the Celts moved on. The incursion stayed rooted in the Roman memory for centuries.

The Celts appeared to be in Italy to stay, but the inexorable forces of climate change were against them. By 300 B.C., the ecotone between the continental and Mediterranean zones had moved north, at least as far as modern-day Burgundy.[22] The shift brought a much more Mediterranean climate, with warm, dry summers and wet winters, to the more southerly Celtic domains. Roman agriculture, which was based on extensive production of a few crops such as wheat and millet for large urban populations, was much better suited to the semiarid southern European environment. As the ecotone moved sharply north, Rome gained power rapidly. By the second century, Romans dominated the western Mediterranean shipping routes hitherto controlled by Greek colonies. Rome conquered Carthage in North Africa, its other great maritime rival, becoming a growing imperial power in the process. Favorable climatic conditions in the Roman homeland and southern Europe now played into their hands. The Pax Romana ate steadily into the Celtic lands on the coattails of the north-shifting ecotone. By the mid-second century B.C., the Celtic lands in what is now southern France were a Roman province.

Nevertheless, the Celts inspired in the Roman psyche a deep fear of northern barbarians. This apprehension increased manyfold in the late second century, as the movements in the north continued. A confederacy of northern tribes moved south and east from the North Sea coast in 113 B.C., first to the Danube and then to within a few days' march of Italy. Fortunately, the horde moved west into Gaul and did not venture south, but further ravages were held in check only by a Roman victory over the Teutones near modern-day Aix-en-Provence in 102 B.C.

Gallic tribes living near the frontiers of the growing empire came under strong Roman influence. Political conditions changed as well. By the second half of the second century B.C., large defended Celtic settlements appeared over much of Europe from western France to Serbia, with formidable earthworks and palisades surrounding densely packed houses and workshops. Production of glass beads, wheel-turned pottery, and ironwork was on a near-industrial scale. These *oppida* (Latin for "towns") brought together smaller, hitherto migrating groups into more stable configurations and established more centralized control over grain surpluses.

In 59 B.C., continued unrest in Gaul gave Julius Caesar the opportunity to play on the Romans' deep fear of the Celts. He was given the command of a force to counter the southward advance of Germanic peoples—or so he claimed. By 51, he had conquered Gaul, crossed briefly to Britain and over the Rhine into Germany. The conquest of Gaul and its aftermath caused such profound disruptions in Celtic life that generations passed before the Romans felt a need to reorganize their new province. When they did, the much warmer, Mediterranean-like conditions made their agriculture highly suitable for provinces remodeled in their imperial image.

For five centuries, the Roman grip on western Europe extended deep into Britain, to the frontiers of Scandinavia, and to the Rhine.

❦

The warm conditions persisted through the heyday of the Roman empire. The northern frontier of the Mediterranean zone now lay far to the north. This lengthened the growing season for the cereal crops that supported Rome's garrisons and cities, and the newcomers took full advantage of it. The Romanization of northern Gaul involved, among other things, the reorientation of farming away from mere subsistence to larger-scale production for both military garrisons and urban centers. The farmers also had to grow food beyond their own needs to meet their tax obligations. Agricultural produce became a cash commodity; private ownership replaced the communal tenure of earlier Celtic times where land was redistributed every year.[23]

The Celts were unable to absorb enough technical knowledge to withstand the efficiency of the Roman war machine. Nor did they ever develop the political organization that would have allowed them to conquer and colonize large territories. Fiercely individualistic and warlike, Celtic tribes were riven by factionalism and infighting. Theirs was an oral culture with an aversion to setting things down in writing, so we will never ascertain the full extent of Celtic resistance to Roman institutions. But northern Gaul and Britain were never completely secure. Frontier tribes in the continental zone always hovered on the margins, ready to pounce on the unwary and take advantage of perceived weakness. The Romans had three advantages—a well-organized army, an impressive infrastructure of roads and sea routes, and carefully orchestrated agricultural production throughout their domains that fed armies and city dwellers. Entire provinces like Egypt and North Africa fed the mobs of Rome. In the final analysis, everything depended on Rome's ability to produce large surpluses of the cereal grains that were the staples of society.

The Roman empire was an order of magnitude more complex an enterprise than its predecessors. As an economic entity, it was a far more powerful and integrated way of creating wealth. For all the corruption and political intrigue throughout their domains, Roman emperors presided over a generally well administered empire by force, efficient administration, and a harsh rule of law. The empire was vulnerable to Celtic raids and to constant rebellions, to the point that the margins were sometimes sacrificed to preserve the core. But underneath the panoply of state and its far-flung possessions lay a startling vulnerability to climate. Political stability and control of outlying areas ultimately depended on the length of cereal-growing seasons in the Mediterranean zone. As long as this climatic regimen extended far to the north, food supplies were reasonably secure and Roman rule based on a sound economic foundation. The empire could survive climatic stresses that would have taxed less closely organized civilizations. Ordinary cold and drought cycles had little effect. Nor did major ENSO events. But major shifts in European climatic zones, with their attendant temperature and rainfall changes, affected Roman rule profoundly. If the growing season shortened in the north and there were long cycles of poor harvests, the security of Gaul and the west was in question.

The third century A.D. was a period of crisis throughout the Roman world. Intense political struggles in Europe, a decline in the centralized power of Rome, and an increasing role for the army in political and foreign affairs all contributed to the empire's difficulties. Germanic peoples threatened the frontiers in the east and overran them at times. Generations of incursions, many of them peaceful, brought complex minglings of provincial Roman and Germanic culture.[24] But by the fifth century, Rome's western empire was in serious trouble. Germanic tribes had learned from their neighbors and were now better organized. Franks and Goths overran much of Gaul just as climatic conditions changed and the Mediterranean zone retreated far southward. By 500, conditions were cooler and wetter throughout the west, making any form of large-scale cereal production very much harder over much of Gaul. The frontier between the continental and Mediterranean zones once again lay across North Africa. Ice even formed on the Nile River during the winter of A.D. 829.[25]

Scholars debate what happened as Rome's influence declined. One school of thought believes that agriculture was thrown into chaos. The military and urban markets were gone. Fields stood empty. Desperate farmers reverted to subsistence agriculture. Others argue for continuity— that there was no upheaval, merely a return to greater self-sufficiency. In England, for example, farming became less intensive after Roman times with no military or urban populations to provision. Farmers tended to cultivate lighter soils over heavier ones as they reverted to pre-Roman patterns of land use. At the same time, cattle throughout western Europe became smaller at the shoulders, perhaps because Roman cross-breeding practices were abandoned. More intensive farming involving heavier clay soils did not resume until the eighth century, when towns assumed greater importance and monasteries oversaw a large-scale reorganization of agricultural production which, in effect, paid for these communities.[26]

A weakened Roman Gaul without a solid agricultural base could not hope to resist invasion, particularly if grain could no longer buy loyalty. With the collapse of Rome, western Europe soon became a land of warlords and fiercely competitive tribes. The Celtic elite and the Christian church maintained those elements of Roman culture that were important to them, including Latin. Christianity, which spread through Romanized Gaul in the fourth and fifth centuries, was but one of many religions competing in Europe, among them Celtic druidism and, eventually, Islam. Early in the fifth century, a Romanized Briton named Patricius was taken prisoner by pirates and became a slave in Ireland. He returned to become a missionary and bishop, helping to convert the country to Christianity in 432. As the rest of Europe fell into confusion and war, Ireland experienced what has sometimes been called a golden age, a time when Christianity "burned and gleamed through the darkness," as Winston Churchill put it. Eventually, Christianity became firmly established throughout Britain and France and the ancient warrior cults disappeared.

✿

The ecotone shift of the sixth century coincided with a major natural catastrophe. What may have been a huge volcanic eruption in A.D. 535 brought the densest, most persistent dry fog in recorded history to Europe, southwestern Asia, and China. Widespread famine, hunger, and bubonic plague followed once the abundant surpluses of the harvest of the year before were consumed.[27] The historian Procopius wrote from Carthage that "the sun gave forth its light without brightness, like the moon during this whole year, and it seemed exceedingly like the sun in eclipse, for the beams it shed were not clear nor such as it is accustomed to shed." Snow fell in Mesopotamia; crops failed throughout Italy and southern Iraq; Britain experienced its worst weather in a century. China suffered through a major drought, "yellow dust rained down like snow," and snow fell the following August, ruining the crops.[28] Tree rings from Scandinavia and western Europe chronicle an abrupt slowing in tree growth between 536 and 545, and drought is well documented in western North America for the years 536 and 542/3. Ice cores from the Andes tell us that severe aridity also descended on the Moche civilization of north coastal Peru.

The event of 535/6 was the single most abrupt climatic occurrence of the past two thousand years, perhaps due to a volcanic outburst exceeding even the Mount Tambora eruption of 1816 in its intensity.

Both Greenland and Antarctic ice cores record layers of sulfuric acid of volcanic origin during the sixth century A.D., events which apparently lasted some years. But the sulfur-rich layers are not so precisely dated as those from tree rings. The acid can only have come either from a huge volcanic eruption that shot millions of tons of fine volcanic ash into the atmosphere—just like Hekla and Mount Tambora—or, as some scientists believe, from a comet hitting one of the world's oceans, or even from the earth passing through a cloud of interstellar dust.[29] Current scientific opinion favors a massive eruption, but so far no one has succeeded in identifying its source. One candidate is the El Chichón volcano in Chiapas, Mexico. Another possible culprit lies somewhere in the long chain of volcanoes between Samoa and Sumatra in the Pacific and Southeast Asia.

Whatever the cause of the abrupt cold, there is widespread evidence for dramatic slowing in tree growth over much of Europe and Eurasia. The colder temperatures coincide with a period when atmospheric pressure was high over Greenland and the north and low over the Azores in the middle of the Atlantic Ocean. The prevailing westerlies slowed and bitter, dry weather settled over Europe. Widespread drought followed, penetrating deep into Eurasia.

Severe droughts hit northern China in A.D. 536–538 and extended into Mongolia and Siberia, where tree rings reveal some of the coldest conditions in the past fifteen hundred years. Drought settled over the grassland steppe, where the vegetation with its short roots is extremely sensitive to arid conditions. As had happened on numerous occasions before, the nomads of the steppe and their horses suffered badly. The Avar nomads moved westward toward Europe, skirting the northern shores of the Caspian Sea and moving onto the fertile grasslands north of the Caucasus Mountains. Eventually they fought their way into what is now Hungary, creating a new empire that extended from Germany in the west to the Volga River in the east and from the Baltic to the Balkan frontiers of the eastern Roman empire.[30]

The same drought that set the Avars on the move caused major suffering in the Roman provinces in Bulgaria and Scythia. Famines also affected the Slavic farmers of Poland and western Ukraine, who promptly raided their Roman neighbors. Frequent Slavic incursions followed. The Avars started impinging on Roman territory, building alliances with the Slavs and others, then often turning on their allies. By the 570s, the Avar empire covered over two-and-a-half million kilometers from the Baltic to Ukraine, a domain whose rulers lived off "peace payments" in exchange for not raiding the empire. The situation deteriorated even further. Milked of vast sums of gold as protection money, suffering repeated plague epidemics, and harassed by constant warfare, the empire was reduced to sorry straits. The tax base of citizens shrank by 60 percent from plague and Slav or Avar land seizures. In *The Chronicle of Theophanes,* written in about A.D. 813, we learn that "the Barbarians had made Europe a desert, while the Persians had given over all Asia to ravaging and had led whole cities into captivity and had constantly swallowed up whole Roman armies."[31]

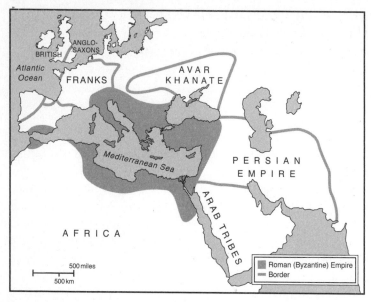

Map of the Avar empire and other polities in the first millennium A.D. From
Catastrophe by David Keys, published by Century Books. Reprinted by permission of The Random House Group Ltd.

The other side of Europe also witnessed exceptionally cold years, especially between 535 and 555 that coincided with a major outbreak of plague. There was a "failure of bread" in Ireland in 538. In 554, "the winter was so severe with frost and snow that the birds and wild animals became so tame as to allow themselves to be taken by hand."[32] During these years the former Roman city of Wroxeter near the Welsh border shrank from an area of 79 hectares protected by three kilometers of earthworks and palisades to a mere 10 hectares. The houses in the new town were erected with no regard for earlier property lines.[33]

The chaos of the sixth century laid many of the foundations of medieval Europe, which culminated three centuries later in a patchwork of feudal states and war lords united only by the Christian faith. But for all the deeds of conquest and adventuring, Europe was a continent of farmers. The vagaries of floods, droughts, and severe winters affected everyone's economic fortunes, from monarch and baron to artisan and peasant. Several wet springs and cool summers in a row, a sequence of severe Atlantic winter storms and floods, a two-year drought—such brief climatic variations were sufficient to put peoples' lives at risk.

❧

By A.D. 900, the Mediterranean ecotone once again shifted further north at a time when the wars and political chaos of earlier centuries were stabilizing somewhat and monasteries were introducing more sophisticated forms of agriculture to feed towns and their own communities. For the next four centuries, summers passed with good harvests and enough to eat. Summer after summer, warm, settled weather began in June and extended into July and August and beyond. European farmers followed an annual routine rooted deep in the past, cultivating small fields often divided into strips. For the four centuries of this aptly named Medieval Warm Period, average summer temperatures in the west were between 0.7 and 1.0 degrees Centigrade above twentieth-century averages, even warmer in central Europe. Growing seasons lengthened; vineyards flourished across southern and central England. French lords quaffed so much prime English wine that the French tried to negotiate trade agreements to exclude such vintages from the Continent.

In that devout age, everyone's fate was in the hand of the Lord, the latest in a panoply of deities that went back to Ancient Egypt and Mesopotamia, and even earlier. People lived at God's mercy, with only their piety to intercede for them, expressed in prayer and mortar. Gratitude came from chant and prayer, from lavish offerings, and, above all, from a surge of cathedral building. Despite wars, schism, and other strife, these were the centuries of Gothic architecture, of great shrines that were the magnets of medieval life. Here great bells tolled in times of joy and mourning, celebration and crisis. Each Easter, a New Light was kindled to signal the beginning of the farming year. And each fall, laden carts brought harvest offerings to God. Compared with previous centuries and what lay ahead, these centuries were a climatic golden age. True, local food shortages were not unknown, life expectancy was short, and the routine of backbreaking labor never ended. But crop failures were sufficiently rare that peasant and lord alike believed that God was smiling upon them. And so God was, while in the Western Hemisphere savage droughts toppled states and undermined human societies in every kind of environment imaginable.

11

THE GREAT DROUGHTS
A.D. 1 TO 1200

When the people thirst, let them remember me, for I
have the power to cover up the face of the sun with a
rain-cloud and to send a rain-wind every day. When a
man plants on dry ground, let him remember me. If he
calls my name and sees me, it will rain four or five days,
and he can plant his seed.

Kumastamxo, son of the Yuma Indian
creator, in a creation myth

One can imagine the arid California landscape, eleven hundred
years ago, shimmering under intense May heat. The grassy hillsides are
brown. Deer lie motionless under live oaks growing by a dry stream.
High above arcs a blue, cloudless sky, visibility so crystal that the islands
far offshore seem to float on a white haze. The Pacific is an intense blue
unruffled by the slightest wind, its oily swells rolling lazily onto the
sandy beach. A line of canoes sits above the high-water mark. From the
village back of the bay comes a scent of decaying fish, sewage, and stag-
nant water made worse by the stench emanating from racks of drying
anchovies. Even the small spring nearby yields only a trickle of water for
the families in the settlement. The heat wave has lasted for days; acorn
granaries are virtually empty. Year after year, the expected rains have
never materialized.

The people in the village are gaunt, with clear signs of malnutrition, but at least they have fish close inshore. Their relatives inland have resorted to an eclectic range of barely edible plants that they would normally never touch. The drought has endured as long as anyone can remember. Yet on the other side of the world, farmers prosper and erect great monuments to their god.

⊗

For the five centuries of the Medieval Warm Period, from A.D. 900 to 1300, Europe basked in warm, settled weather, with only occasional bitter winters, cool summers, and memorable storms. Summer after summer passed with dreamy days, golden sunlight, and abundant harvests. Vast Gothic cathedrals soared heavenward in expensive outpourings of love for God. Architects, masons, and carpenters created works of genius, edifices "of exquisite delicacy and light . . . tall slender windows filled with brilliant expanses of stained glass."[1] Every one of these ethereal places of worship was a metaphorical sacrifice: an offering of stone and material goods in anticipation of divine favors. The expected return was bountiful harvests, the gift of gifts for a Europe of subsistence farmers that still lived from harvest to harvest. Vineyards flourished in England; the Norse sailed to Greenland and Labrador. Food shortages were not unknown, and the backbreaking labor of land clearance, planting, and harvest never ended. Nevertheless, real famines were rare. Lord and peasant alike piously believed that God was smiling on them.

In the Americas, the same five centuries witnessed severe drought, hunger, warfare in the north, and the collapse of two major civilizations to the south.

Short-term climatic events like droughts do not often leave a clear footprint. But the droughts of the Medieval Warm Period (or Medieval Climatic Anomaly, as it is often called) left giant tracks across the American west, wrought in deep-sea cores, pollen samples, tree rings, and ice cores from high in the Andes. From the California coast to the Maya lowlands to Lake Titicaca, five centuries of sudden aridity wrought havoc on human societies already living close to the environmental edge. The great droughts of the Medieval Warm Period are so well documented in the New World that we can gain valuable insights into how ancient native American societies, whether hunter-gatherers, subsistence farmers, or elaborate civilizations, handled environmental stress.

The story begins in southern California, where good fortune has yielded one of the most precise records of short-term climatic change over the past three thousand years from anywhere in North America. The data come from a 198-meter deep-sea core in a sea floor basin in the Santa Barbara Channel, 17 meters of which represent the Holocene. About 1.5 meters of foraminifera-rich sediment accumulated every thousand years. Douglas and James Kennett—son and father, archaeologist and ocean-ographer respectively—used both marine foraminifera and AMS radio-carbon dates to obtain a high-resolution portrait of maritime climate change in the region at twenty-five-year intervals over the past three thousand years. Few ancient records achieve this remarkable precision.[2]

In the Santa Barbara Channel, the prevailing wind blows parallel to the coastline, from west to east. The rotation of the earth causes these breezes to move water offshore at right angles to the direction of the wind, a phe-nomenon known as the Coriolis effect. As the surface water moves out to sea, colder water from deeper levels is drawn upward to replace it. The up-welling water is rich in nutrients, encouraging seaweed and phytoplankton growth. Fish, marine mammals, and sea birds thrive on the phytoplankton in some of the most productive ecosystems in the world. Coastal up-welling regions are a mere 1 percent of the ocean surface, but collectively they account for about 50 percent of today's global fish landings.

During the spring and summer, the nutrient-rich cool waters upwell strongly off the coast south of Point Conception and are carried offshore to the westernmost of the Channel Islands. As a result, a remarkable diversity of marine life flourishes on what was once the Chumash Indians' doorstep. Unfortunately, the productivity of the fisheries varied for a number of rea-sons, among them wind speed and the effects of ENSO events, which brought different oceanographic conditions to the Santa Barbara Channel.

Such was the background to the Kennetts' sea core investigation. They found that climatic conditions were relatively stable from the end of the Ice Age up to about 2000 B.C., at which point the climate became much more

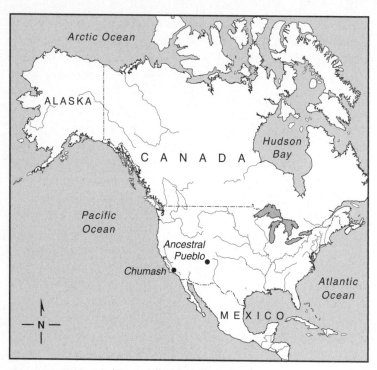

Map showing locations and peoples mentioned in Chapter 11

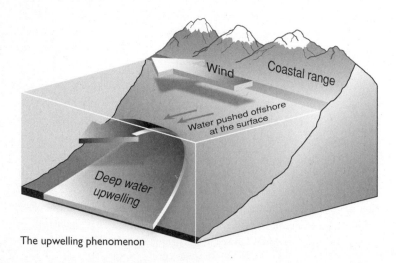

The upwelling phenomenon

unstable. By detecting oxygen isotope differences between minute surface-dwelling and deeper-water foraminifera preserved in the cores, they could measure the intensity of natural upwelling of nutrient-rich colder water to the surface. By radiocarbon-dating the foraminifera, they could date up-welling fluctuations, as well as compare the cold, dry periods they repre-sented with tree-ring records from various locations in southern California. The Kennetts emerged with a remarkably accurate portrait of climate changes in the Santa Barbara Channel region after 1000 B.C. and of the droughts that descended over the region during the Medieval Warm Period.[3]

From A.D. 450 to 1300, they found, sea temperatures dropped sharply, to about 1.5°C cooler than the median sea surface temperature in the Santa Barbara Channel for the Holocene as a whole. For three-and-a-half centuries, from 950 to 1300, marine upwelling was especially in-tense, making local fisheries extremely productive. After 1300, water tem-peratures stabilized and became warmer. Two centuries later, upwelling subsided somewhat and marine productivity dropped.

The colder sea surface temperatures and increased upwelling generally coincided with droughts of varying severity documented in tree rings from the southern California mountains. The cold interval between A.D. 450 and 1300 saw frequent climatic shifts, especially between 950 and 1500, a period of persistent drought. The most intense drought cycles oc-curred from 500 to 800, 980 to 1250, and 1650 to 1750. Interestingly, the same tree-ring records show that the high rainfall totals of the mid-twentieth century occurred only three times in this thousand-year tree-ring record. For a state facing controversies over water allocations, this should be sobering news.

When the Portuguese explorer João Rodrigues Cabrilho (more commonly Cabrillo) sailed into the Santa Barbara Channel in 1542, he encountered seemingly prosperous fisherfolk living along a densely populated coastline. "Fine canoes each holding twelve or thirteen Indians came to the ships," he wrote. "They have round houses, well covered down to the ground. They wear skins, eat acorns, and a white seed the size of maize."[4] Some 15,000 Chumash hunter-gatherers lived along the coast and on the offshore Channel Islands, many in permanent villages of several hundred souls. Their society was among the most elaborate of all hunter-gatherer societies in North America. The Chumash impressed the Spaniards, who described them as "of good disposition, affable, liberal." Each larger village had at least one hereditary chief, who wore "a little cape like a doublet reaching to the waist and made of bear skin." With their sophisticated planked canoes, unique to the Pacific coast, and seemingly endless food supplies, the Chumash appeared to live in a coastal Garden of Eden. Remarked the Spanish traveler Pedro Fages, "It may be said that to them the day is one continuous meal."[5] It would have been more accurate to say that they lived in constant expectation of hunger, for the prosperity was illusory. The Chumash had suffered greatly during the droughts of the Medieval Warm Period and had changed their society completely as a result.

No one knows when the Chumash first settled in their homeland, but their ancestry goes deep into the remote past. Judging from the low densities of archaeological sites, relatively few people lived along the coast before 2000 B.C., when rainfall was considerably lower than today. These millennia saw the "climatic optimum" (often called the Altithermal) that brought favorable climatic conditions to Europe.[6] But these same periods were not optimal elsewhere—in fact they mirror the Medieval Warm Period, with ample rainfall in Europe and savage droughts in the American west. During these millennia, high Pacific temperatures suppressed natural downwelling and kept marine productivity low.

Around 3000 B.C., just as the first urban civilizations appeared in Egypt and Mesopotamia and a handful of foraging bands in Central America were cultivating maize, something changed. For thousands of years, forager populations in the west had always been small, even in the best-watered areas. After 3000 B.C., the climate of the west closely resembled that of today— the same unpredictable rainfall, and somewhat cooler temperatures than the preceding four thousand years. The people who had lived through the climatic optimum had adapted so successfully to much drier conditions that they lived close to the land's maximum carrying capacity. Now the good times returned, there was more to eat in an already edible landscape, and the population rose rapidly both in the interior and along the coast.

As populations rose, so did the potential for food shortages. In California, there came a moment when the staple foods of many millennia were inadequate to feed growing numbers of people.[7] They turned to more labor-intensive foods like acorns, just as their very distant relatives had in southwestern Asia thousands of years earlier, and also engaged in much heavier exploitation of sea fisheries and sea mammals.

Before 2000 B.C., most California societies had moved constantly, exploiting whatever foods were the least trouble to collect and process. But acorns had the same effect on the Californians that they had on the Natufians of the Levant. The daily routine of pounding and leaching tied the women to their mortars and storage bins. Many western groups settled down in a few base camps, which they occupied for months on end. Their worlds shrank from hundreds of square kilometers to the boundaries of a single watershed, a small stretch of coastline, or a desert landscape with a few perennial springs. At the same time, many more people survived to adulthood, and the rate of population increase accelerated.

These restricted homelands were too small for any band to be self-sufficient. In drought years or at times of failed acorn crops, neighboring kin began to exchange foodstuffs and other commodities on a much larger scale. In time, the egalitarian bands of old became more structured, as leaders were needed to manage relationships between individuals and their groups and with neighboring bands. Inevitably, some people—kin leaders, individuals perceived to have exceptional supernatural powers—acquired better access to acorn stocks and other commodities and became the leaders of far more complex societies, especially in areas where the diversity and abundance of food resources supported large populations. By 1500 B.C., the ancestors of the Chumash in the Santa Barbara region exploited acorns and all kinds of marine foods and were living in far larger settlements than in earlier times.

෴

By the time of Christ, the Chumash were in trouble.[8] For many centuries, warmer temperatures had reduced natural upwelling offshore, so the anchovies that sustained growing village communities were in shorter supply. Fisheries generally were less productive than in earlier times. But populations on the Channel Islands and the mainland were still rising steadily. Inevitably, territorial boundaries between neighboring communities were cast in more rigid terms. Even in cycles of good years with abundant rainfall, good catches, and plentiful edible grasses and acorns, many communities were left with little surplus.

Then things got worse. The Kennetts' deep-sea core shows that ocean temperatures cooled and upwelling intensified after A.D. 450. The inshore fisheries improved dramatically. But with cooling came drought, and there were now many more mouths to feed, with the result that some areas were undoubtedly overfished—as they are today. For eight centuries, the droughts intensified as the climate became more unpredictable. Periodic El Niños brought violent storms and floods, suppressed upwelling, and uprooted inshore kelp beds where fish abounded. But the archaeological evidence suggests that the effects on coastal communities were probably relatively minor.

The real trouble came in the interior, where the droughts impinged heavily on groups that relied on nut harvests, grasses, and game. Inland groups everywhere had always faced the constant threat of drought-induced food shortages. Now there were many more people, more fixed territorial boundaries, and intensified competition for oak groves. Chiefs vied for control of territory and resources. They fought one another for food as hunger and malnutrition stalked their villages. At the same time, permanent water supplies shrank dramatically.

For thousands of years, the communities of the coast and interior had formed a cultural continuum, the people inland linked inextricably to the fortunes of those along the shore. Kin ties and social obligations united even widely separated communities in ancient webs of interdependence. So food shortages and intergroup competition affected everyone, whether inshore, on the coast, or on the Channel Islands. The droughts created a new social reality: a tense world where friendship and animosity were drawn in tight, hard lines.

From the beginning of time, when confronted with drought or flood, food shortages or failed oak harvests, California groups had always moved. The Chumash no longer had that option, for there were too many people across the landscape. Archaeologist Jeanne Arnold reports that many communities on Santa Cruz Island, the largest landmass offshore, were aban-

doned during the dry centuries of the first millennium A.D., probably because of insufficient surface water. The biological anthropologists Patricia
Lambert and Phillip Walker have found clear indications of pathological
conditions due to malnutrition, such as cribra orbitalia, a characteristic
pitting of the eye socket due to iron deficiency anemia.[9] But the most
telling evidence of social change comes from war casualties.[10]

When Lambert and Walker examined skeletons from village cemeteries
dating to between A.D. 300 and 1150, they found a high incidence of head
injuries, apparently inflicted by clubs or axes, peaking in the centuries before A.D. 1150. The incidence of wounds then declined sharply. Lambert
also looked at projectile wounds inflicted with arrows and spears. She found
numerous examples of healed wounds, as one would expect when people
are fighting with relatively inaccurate weapons.[11] Studies of arrow casualties
from nineteenth-century Indian wars told her that the most lethal wounds
were to the soft tissue of the chest and abdominal cavity. There were occasional projectile wounds going back to as early as 3500 B.C., but between
A.D. 300 and 1150 they grew much more frequent. Warfare was not an in-
nate propensity of the Chumash or somehow an outgrowth of their culture;
it was a response to environmental conditions. The rise in arrow wounds
came at a time when populations were growing, people were congregating
in much larger settlements, and ever more restricted territories were yielding
unreliable food and water supplies. Sporadic warfare among hereditary
chiefs remained part of Chumash life for many centuries.

The violence seems to have peaked before A.D. 1150. Then it subsided
dramatically. For reasons as yet only partially understood, the Chumash
moved away from violence and created an entirely new society. They seem
to have grown suddenly wiser—a bold statement to be sure, but it appears
to be no exaggeration. Faced with escalating violence, persistent hunger,
and perhaps even local population crashes, their leaders seem to have realized that they were all in the same situation, that survival depended not on
competition but on enhanced interdependence. A web of interconnected-
ness had sustained coastal and mainland communities for centuries. But
the ancient networks appear to have partially broken down in an environment of distrust and intensifying competition for food supplies. At the
same time, the structure of society had changed—more people lived in
close juxtaposition in relatively large settlements. Group territories were

smaller and more crowded, each with its own leaders who acquired their position through their skills of persuasion and war. When the unpredictably drought-prone world of 300 B.C. to A.D. 850 was replaced by permanent drought, all the Chumash leaders could do to adjust was collaborate closely with one another. It no longer made sense to fight over resources nobody possessed.

The one resource that remained was the sea. The changes coincided with the Medieval Warm Period, which along the Pacific coast was a period of cooler sea surface temperatures. Marine productivity soared between 950 and 1300 as natural upwelling intensified off the coast. The signs of social change in response are unmistakable: an explosion in the number of archaeological sites, much larger permanent settlements on the coast, and a spectacular rise in the number of shell beads and other exotic artifacts on the mainland and the Channel Islands. A few wealthy individuals, most of them owners of planked canoes, rose to prominence. Such vessels, unique to the Chumash, were fashioned from driftwood planks sewn together to form sophisticated canoes capable of navigating the open waters of the Santa Barbara Channel. With these craft, Chumash leaders controlled trade in acorn meal and ornamental seashells between the islands and the mainland.[12] Each chief maintained his independence, but there was a level of economic interdependence unknown in earlier times. Food supplies stabilized and were more evenly distributed. There was a marked improvement in the health of both islanders and mainlanders, despite well-documented periods of intense drought and occasional malnutrition. At the same time, all chiefs and their family members belonged to the *antap*, a formal association that supervised dances and other rituals that validated the new social order and where shamans ensured the continuity of the world.[13]

By innovation and with long-term pragmatism, the Chumash came to terms with the great droughts. Their savior was the vast productivity of coastal fisheries, which compensated to some degree for arid conditions ashore. Ultimately, however, it was hereditary chieftainship, the ties between chiefly families, expertly conducted ritual, and tight control of trading relationships that enabled the Chumash to weather the crisis and maintain one of the most elaborate hunter-gatherer societies on earth. A culture without rigid social ranks, warriors, or slaves, it was a brilliant solution to an unpredictable, sometimes violent world of climatic extremes.

❦

Chaco Canyon in the gloaming: I walked in the twilight, the cliffs on either side dark against the infinite bowl of the heavens. A deep silence enveloped me among the shadows where the great houses of the Ancestral Pueblo merged into the intimacy of night. In the quiet I imagined the smell of wood smoke, the barking of dogs, and the murmur of evening conversation—the undergrowth of human life. A soft night wind chilled my hair and the past vanished. It was hard to remember that over five thousand people had once lived here, until driven away by capricious drought.

The Chumash of California adapted to the crisis of the Medieval Warm Period with an intensification of ritual activity and new styles of leadership. Far inland, when the same droughts settled over the land of the Ancestral Pueblo, the response was quite different.[14]

The Ancestral Pueblo, once called the Anasazi, the "ancient ones" of the Southwest, built some of the largest towns in ancient North America about one thousand years ago. They were always subsistence farmers, living and farming as households even when they dwelt in large multiroom pueblos. Ancestral Pueblo farmers adapted to the dry San Juan Plateau by becoming expert at selecting soils with the correct moisture-retaining properties on north- and east-facing slopes that received little direct sunlight. Every farmer planted on river floodplains and at arroyo mouths, where the soil was naturally irrigated. They diverted water from streams and springs, using every drop of runoff they could. Everything was done to reduce the risk of crop failure. As a matter of routine, the cultivators dispersed their gardens widely over the landscape to minimize the risk of local drought or flood. They learned how to shorten the growing season from the usual 130 or 140 days to perhaps 120 days by planting on shaded slopes, at varying elevations, and in different soils. They were among the most expert of all native American farmers.

Over many centuries, Ancestral Pueblo communities employed the same basic adaptation to their harsh environment, which saw them through yearly rainfall shifts, decade-long droughts, and seasonal changes. El Niño rains and other common climatic events called for temporary and flexible adjustments—farming more land, relying more heavily on wild plant foods, and, above all, moving across the landscape. As long as they stayed within the carrying capacity of their environments, the people had plenty of options.

Movement was deeply ingrained in ancient Pueblo philosophy. Every community had its poems, songs, and chants. Many of them spoke of survival in terms of movement, like Simon Ortiz's modern poem from Acoma pueblo, consciously in the ancient tradition:

> *Survival, I know how this way.*
> *This way, I know.*
> *It rains.*
> *Mountains and canyons and plants grow.*
> *We traveled this way, gauged our distance by stories*
> *and loved our children . . .*
> *We told ourselves over and over again,*
> *We shall survive this way.*[15]

The strategy of movement worked well for many centuries. The people lived in self-sufficient communities, but every village and hamlet, however small, maintained connections with neighbors near and far—through kinship ties and individual friendships. Many of these links extended over long distances, into places where rainfall patterns were quite different—additional insurance for people accustomed to relying on others to see them through crop failures, and to being relied on in turn. Ancestral Pueblo households and communities made constant adjustment to good and bad rainfall years.

By A.D. 800, many Ancestral Pueblo lived in larger settlements. Small hamlets became clusters of rooms and storehouses built in contiguous blocks that formed much bigger communities than the hamlets of earlier times. Population densities rose, too, in places like Chaco Canyon, New Mexico, and further north in the Moctezuma Valley and Mesa Verde area of the Four Corners region in southern Colorado. During the early ninth century, tree-rings tell us that rainfall in the north was better than average. Between 840 and 860, some Ancestral Pueblo communities in the Dolores Valley region of the north housed dozens of families.[16] Then the rains faltered, and ancient doctrines of mobility kicked in. The inhabitants left their large pueblos and dispersed over the landscape.

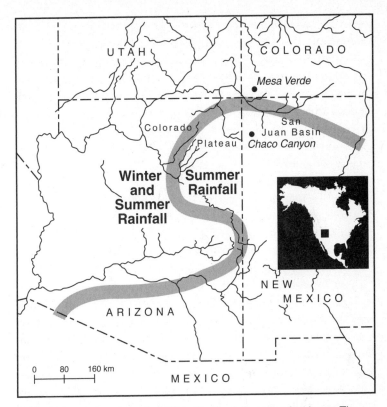

Places and sites, also areas of rainfall in the North American Southwest. The shaded line marks the frontier between the winter and summer rainfall patterns of the northwestern region and the more predictable summer rainfall of the southeastern area.

It was different in the south, where the inhabitants of Chaco Canyon took advantage of springs and natural seeps to grow maize in favored places.[17] Many of the original villages had become small pueblos by the 750s. During the ninth and tenth centuries, summer rainfall was highly variable, but instead of dispersing, and for reasons we do not understand, the Chaco people built three "great houses" at the junctions of major drainages. The largest, Pueblo Bonito, stood five stories high along its rear wall and remained in use for more than two centuries. In its eleventh-century heyday, Pueblo Bonito had at least six hundred rooms in use and could house about a thousand people.

By 1050, five great pueblos dominated Chaco Canyon, whose population had risen to about 5,500 people. The canyon is not very large, but it was the center of an important Ancestral Pueblo universe, the focus of at least seventy communities dispersed over more than 65,000 square kilometers of northwestern New Mexico and parts of southern Colorado. Chaco was now the center of a vast sacred landscape delineated by outlying communities and ceremonial trackways. The canyon was an intensely important and scared place.

From A.D. 1050 to 1100, the rains were plentiful. Chaco and its outliers flourished, probably longer than they would have in drier times. The steady rise in population was not a problem as long as winter rainfall fertilized the fields. Then, in 1130, fifty years of intense drought settled over the canyon. The Chaco people had but one recourse, deeply embedded in their psyche—movement. Within a few generations, the great houses stood empty. Well over half Chaco's population had dispersed into villages, hamlets, and pueblos far from the canyon. Soon almost everyone was gone.

A magnificent flowering of Ancestral Pueblo culture endured further north in the higher and better-watered Four Corners region. There were many valleys and canyons where dry farming worked well, and where ample game and plant foods served as a cushion during hungry months. In the twelfth century, hundreds of households moved from dispersed communities into large towns by river banks, in sheltered valleys, and built into natural rock shelters in the walls of deep canyons, like the Cliff Palace in Mesa Verde, with its 220 masonry rooms and 23 sacred subterranean chambers, or *kivas*.

Many more farmers inhabited the large drainages northwest of Mesa Verde, where populations rose rapidly from 13–30 people per square kilometer during the tenth century to as much as 130 three centuries later. Soon a growing population had reached the limits of the land's carrying capacity. For instance, the environmental scientist Carla Van West estimates that the Sand Canyon area could have supported enough maize to feed an average local population of about 31,360 at a density of 21 people per square kilometer over a 400-year period between A.D. 900 and 1300.[18] The twelfth-century drought that caused the Chaco dispersal, she argues, had little effect on the people of Sand Canyon. They still had enough room to move locally. The farmers could survive the harshest of drought cycles provided there were no restrictions on movement or on access to the best soils, and provided they could acquire food from neighbors when crops failed. But, once population densities approached the canyon's carrying capacity and all the most productive soils were taken up, surviving even a short drought was much harder. By 1250, the farmers had taken up all the usable land. A quarter century later, the great drought of 1276 to 1299 settled over the Four Corners region.

The Laboratory of Tree-Ring Research at the University of Arizona has tracked the progress of this drought from its first appearance in the extreme northwest of the region in 1276.[19] Over the next decade, very dry conditions expanded over the entire Southwest and lasted until 1299. The drought manifested itself in dramatically reduced rainfall, of course, but with marked differences from north to south. More than 60 percent of the shortfall occurred in the northwest, in southern Utah and Colorado, versus a mere 10 percent in the southeast in New Mexico. Between 1250 and 1450, the southeast enjoyed almost stable summer rainfall, while the Colorado Plateau in the northwest suffered through unpredictable rainfall and severe droughts.

While life in the southeast continued without interruption, the northwest suffered badly. Pueblo construction in the north slowed suddenly, then ceased. By 1300, the great pueblos of the Four Corners were silent. Oral traditions recall how the gods had failed, and trusted tribal leaders were discredited; the world was unsafe. The people had dispersed widely. Most joined distant communities elsewhere. Once again, the ancient tradition of movement took hold.

Theirs was not the aimless search for food seen in many famines. Instead of taking mindlessly to the countryside, the people of the northwest drew on the intricate web of social relationships and friendships that linked community to community, some so far away that they flourished in quite different rainfall environments. When the great drought settled over the northwest, the inhabitants of the great pueblos fell back on their last resort: to invoke the obligations of their social networks and disperse.[20]

At nearly a thousand years' distance, we have no means of reconstructing the complex set of movements and events. We know from excavations at Sand Canyon Pueblo that many households left large, hard-to-carry objects such as grinders behind them—suggesting both that they planned a long journey and that they expected to find help at the end of it. Where did they go? Our only clues come from studies of the distributions of painted clay vessels. The archaeologist Alison Rautman has developed a nice model of social networks at the extreme eastern edge of the Pueblo world, using old pottery styles and modern climatic data.[21] She used the distributions of different trade pots to show how communities developed regular exchange relationships with villages living in quite different climatic zones. In another study, John Roney showed how thirteenth-century pottery styles from the northern San Juan south-southeast to the Rio Grande Valley near Socorro displayed remarkable similarities.[22] If these studies are any guide, then the inhabitants of the northwestern pueblos moved southeast into the Little Colorado River drainage, the Mogollon Highlands, and the Rio Grande Valley. Rautman used tree-ring data to show that these areas suffered little climate change during the critical centuries when the northwest was under severe drought.

The communities receiving immigrants had to be flexible enough to assign them land and water as well as meaningful social roles. The newcomers came to communities that were perceived as places where things were done right, where the gods were worshiped correctly, where people were safe from wars and witches. The centuries after 1300 witnessed a remarkable efflorescence of new religious ideas such as the famed kachina cults growing out of much older beliefs. Many of these no doubt resulted from the integration of the newcomers into existing communities.

The ripple of abandonments occurred over more than a century. But the Ancestral Pueblo rode out the dry conditions like a small craft riding atop massive swells. They never sought to remake their society into a larger, more complex vessel. There were no technological innovations nor new crops. Unlike the Chumash, the Ancestral Pueblo continued to live as they always had. New religious beliefs, adapted to new social institutions, seem to have had little effect on the old exchange routes and the old mobility. In the words of a Tewa elder, "They started coming and moving and then they settled and they stood up again and then they started moving again."[23]

12

MAGNIFICENT RUINS
A.D. 1 TO 1200

> Throughout their domains Coniraya Viracocha . . . the
> Creator of all things . . . by his word of command,
> caused the terraces and fields to be formed on the steep
> sides of ravines, and sustaining walls to rise up and sup-
> port them. He also made the irrigation canals flow.
>
> Inca legend, in Garcilaso de la Vega, *The Royal*
> *Commentaries of the Inca,* trans. H. V. Livermore

Like the ancient Egyptians, the Maya cast an irresistible spell on archaeologist and layperson alike. You feel it amid the sprawling ruins of the
Great Plaza at Tikal, where the rainforest presses on the pyramids. The last
time I was there, gray mist fingered between the trees and mantled the
high temples with delicate tendrils. The carefully trimmed grass of the
plaza was wet underfoot in the still dawn, smooth and absolutely clean.
The silence of the forest drifted like a gray blanket over a once vibrant city.
Here great lords had shed their blood in lavish public ceremonies and entered the Otherworld in dramatic trance. Vast crowds had gathered here,
armies assembled for battle amidst richly scented incense that swirled upward from smoking altars. I remembered the words of the nineteenth-
century traveler John Lloyd Stephens when he gazed on the ruins of another Maya city, Copán: "In Egypt the colossal skeletons of gigantic
temples stand in unwatered sands in all the nakedness of desolation; but

here an immense forest shrouds the ruins, hiding them from sight, heightening the impression and giving an intensity and almost wildness to the interest. . . . Nor shall I at this moment offer any conjecture in regard to the people who built [them]; or to the time or the means by which [they were] depopulated to become a desolation and ruin; or as to whether it fell by the sword, famine, or pestilence."[1] Generations of archaeologists have pondered the sudden collapse of Maya civilization.

Until surprisingly recently, the ancient Maya were a mysterious, little-understood civilization, their leaders thought to be peaceful astronomer-priests preoccupied with the measurement of time and the passage of the heavenly bodies. Our state of knowledge about them was like that of nineteenth-century Egyptologists, who were unable to read the hiero-glyphic inscriptions on temple walls. The triumphant decipherment of Maya script during the 1980s changed our perceptions completely. Maya glyphs do indeed deal with astronomical events and calendrics, but they also narrate grand events, the accessions and deaths of great lords, recount elaborate royal genealogies, and chronicle the rise and fall of dynasties.[2] We now know that ancient Maya civilization was a patchwork of competing city-states obsessed with genealogy, diplomatic maneuvering, and military conquest. Tikal was one of these, rising to prominence in the first century B.C. In A.D. 219, the Lord Xac-Moch-Xoc founded a brilliant ruling dynasty at Tikal. The ninth ruler, Great Jaguar Paw, conquered his nearby rival, Uaxactún. Judicious trading and diplomatic marriages extended Tikal's domains even further. By 500, Tikal controlled a territory of about 2,500 square kilometers and the destinies of about 360,000 people. This was a large kingdom by Maya standards, though miniscule when compared with ancient Egypt or the Assyrian empire.[3]

By A.D. 600, the Maya lowlands supported a maze of kingdoms whose lords were obsessed with war and militaristic religion. For the next three centuries, the balance of military and political power shifted back and forth among different city-states, from Caracol to Tikal to Dos Pilos, and back to Tikal. Rulers of exceptional ability would forge several conquered cities into a state, which fell apart when its founder died or a lord was conquered in battle. What held Maya society together was the institution of kingship. Maya kings saw their lives recorded as history on public buildings in the hearts of their cities. The nobility, below the kings in the

Maya sites mentioned in Chapter 12

social hierarchy, defined their lives in terms of the great lords who ruled them. Thousands of commoners existed only to serve the nobility and supported the entire superstructure of the state. Maya lords were shaman-rulers who interceded with the powerful forces of the supernatural in elaborate public ceremonies where they appeared in trance before their people. Their relationships to royal ancestors ensured—in fact. *was*—the continuity of human existence. A compelling ideology and a powerful, unspoken social contract bound noble and commoner to lord and provided the rationale for building cities and ceremonial centers that were symbolic re-creations of the mythic world.[4]

For more than ten centuries, from before the time of Christ until A.D. 900, the Maya flourished in the Central American lowlands. Then, abruptly, their city-states collapsed. Copán, Palenque, Tikal, and other great cities imploded. Their populations perished or dispersed into small villages scattered across a heavily cultivated landscape. Maya civilization continued to flourish in the northern Yucatán until the Spanish *entrada* of the early sixteenth century, but the great cities of the south vanished into the forest, only to be revealed to an astonished world by John Lloyd Stephens.

Why did Maya civilization end so swiftly? Why did Tikal's population shrink within a few generations from 25,000 to perhaps a third of that number? Many factors led to the collapse, but new climatological research suggests that droughts were a major villain.

⚗

The ancient Maya farmed the Petén-Yucatán peninsula, a vast limestone shelf uplifted from the ocean that defines the Gulf of Mexico's southern lip. The porous limestone flattens out as one travels north into the Yucatán from the more rugged southern lowlands and looks just like a featureless green carpet when seen from the air. This seeming uniformity is an illusion. The dense tree cover masks an astonishing diversity of local habitats, all of which presented special challenges to Maya farmers.

The Maya homeland was an unforgiving environment, with few fertile soils except in parts of the Petén and along larger river valleys.[5] Maya farmers were well aware of the fragility of their environment. Clearing the forest exposed the ground to pelting rain and intense tropical sunlight. The surface quickly turned brick-hard, making the cleared garden impossible to cultivate. To farm such demanding fields by clearing and burning off the forest, then planting, required experience and great patience. A sharper contrast with Stone Age Europe or the Nile Valley is hard to imagine.

Maya farmers lived with constant environmental disruptions—years of drought and crop failure, or torrential rains and soil erosion, followed by months of dry weather during the critical growing season before returning storms drowned the surviving corn. Yet their society not only survived but also flourished for a millennium and a half, developing great cities and elaborate city-states ruled by powerful militant lords. Maya civilization lasted far longer than Sumerian civilization in Mesopotamia, Old Kingdom Egypt, or the Harappan state of the Indus Valley in what is now Pakistan.

Like other tropical farmers in the Americas, the Maya used slash-and-burn agriculture to grow maize and beans. Each fall, they would cut down a patch of forest on well-drained land, then burn off the wood and brush. As the burn subsided, the ash and charcoal fell on the soil. Farmers and their families worked this natural fertilizer into the earth, then planted their crops to coincide with the first rains. Such cleared gardens, called *milpa*, remained fertile for only about two years. The farmer then moved on to a new plot and began all over again, leaving the original land to lie fallow for four to seven years. For many centuries, the Maya were village farmers, their settlements lying among patchwork quilts of newly cleared gardens and regenerating land, surrounded by thick forest that separated them from their neighbors.

Slash-and-burn agriculture worked well enough when the farming population was small. But the crop yields were never sufficient to support large settlements, nor could the stocks of surplus grain feed more than a handful of nonfarmers, such as stone-ax makers. Still, until a few centuries before Christ, this simple farming system was the staple of an increasingly complex village society. Such subsistence farming was fairly resilient when confronted with climatic stress, for the forest offered numerous edible plant foods to fall back on in lean years.

After 400 B.C., the first large ceremonial centers appeared in the lowlands. Between 150 and 50 B.C., the city of El Mirador grew to cover 16 square kilometers of low, undulating terrain, part of which flooded during the wet season. El Mirador was a maze of pyramids and plazas, with more than 200 imposing structures including causeways, temples, and lords' dwellings. The city lies in a depressed zone, where water could be trapped for later use during the dry season. By this time, the Maya were also building large reservoirs for water storage. This careful management reflected a society that was well aware of the need to plan for drought years. The strategy seems to have worked, for Maya civilization developed rapidly into a complex mosaic of city-states.

The classic period of Maya civilization, from A.D. 200 to 800, saw new adaptations to the challenging lowland environment. Many communities now lay at the summits of hillocks and ridges, so that the quarries at their base used to build pyramids, temples, and other structures became large reservoirs surrounded by artificial hills and plazas that were catchment pavements to funnel water into them. With brilliant ingenuity, the Maya architects built gravity canals that released water from the elevated central reservoir system into tanks and surrounding irrigation systems.[6]

These elaborate water management systems developed over many centuries out of a need to store water in a land without seasonal river floods—or even major rivers—like those that supplied the irrigation schemes of the Egyptians or Sumerians. The Maya developed what the archaeologist Vernon Scarborough calls "microwatersheds" to make up for deficiencies in rainfall. But such systems have severe constraints. Inevitably, they can service only a limited area. Rainfall filled the reservoirs and tanks but fluctuated greatly from year to year, making the carefully controlled releases of floodwater typical of Mesopotamian irrigation impossible. Water management and irrigation in the lowlands required the right topography, highly flexible labor management, and a great deal of trial and error.

Over centuries, Maya agriculture slowly created a highly engineered infrastructure that became increasingly productive over time. Everything was slow and deliberate, set in a social and political context that accommodated the realities of a fragile tropical environment. The Maya were successful because they spent many centuries learning how to farm this environment. They worked successfully within environmental limitations they learned the hard way, kept their villages dispersed and developed a level of interdependency that reflected the uneven distribution of soils and food resources across the landscape. As long as this system worked well, they were relatively immune to climatic stress. It was no coincidence that Maya civilization developed as a mosaic of much smaller city-states, each centered on microwatersheds, which gave it a flexibility and resilience to short-term climatic events that endured for many centuries.

As populations rose, especially on the outskirts of cities, the Maya expanded the scope of their agriculture. As early as the first century A.D., they began draining and canalizing swamps, turning hitherto unfarmable lands into grids of raised-field systems elevated above low-lying, seasonally inundated land that bordered rivers. These plots resembled the well-known swamp gardens used by the Aztecs of highland Mexico centuries later to feed their great capital, Tenochtitlán. As populations climbed even further, the Maya began terracing steep hillsides to trap silt that cascaded downslope during heavy rainstorms.

By A.D. 800, immediately before the collapse, perhaps eight to ten million Maya lived in the lowlands, a staggeringly high density for a tropical environment with low natural carrying capacity. Patrick Culbert of the University of Arizona has shown that the population density in the southern lowlands rose as high as two hundred per square kilometer, over an area so large that people could not possibly adapt to bad times by moving away to new, uncleared areas some distance away.[7] The farmers were feeding not only themselves but also a mushrooming urban population, including a rapidly growing class of unproductive nobles. As urban populations rose and ambitious lords placed ever-heavier demands on the farmers' backs, the Maya ate up their land and crossed a critical threshold of vulnerability to droughts that had been part of their world from the beginning. The scale of Maya civilization took it beyond the limits of the environment into an uncertain realm of potential disaster.

Until recently, drought theories were discounted, largely because the climatological evidence was virtually nonexistent. Now lowland lakes and a deep-sea core in the Caribbean have provided dramatic testimony of the power of drought to topple civilizations.

Lake cores are like those taken from the seabed, only much shorter. If the mud and silt at the bottom accumulates slowly and evenly without sudden floods or erosion, the climatic record they provide can be extremely fine-grained.

The climatologist David Hodell and his colleagues cored the sediments of salty Lake Chichancanab in the Yucatán in a search for climatic data.[8] Their original core, sunk in 1993, measured the changes in the oxygen-isotope ratio in shell carbonate preserved in the bottom sediment over many centuries. This and the oxygen-gypsum ratio in the fine silt allowed the scientists to reconstruct past changes in the ratio between evaporation and rainfall. They assumed that periods of drier climate were reflected in a higher proportion of gypsum to calcite, and the opposite in wetter cycles. The original core yielded a sequence of climate change over the past nine thousand years with an accuracy of about twenty years. Hodell then returned to the lake, sank two more cores side by side in its deepest parts, and obtained a high-resolution sequence for the past two thousand years. This time, he was able to use AMS radiocarbon dating on seeds, wood fragments, and other minute terrestrial debris preserved in the core. The high gypsum levels denoting droughts could now be dated precisely.

Hodell found that three major droughts spread over the Yucatán over the 2,000-year period. The first was from 475 to 250 B.C., when Maya civilization was still forming. The next lasted from 125 B.C. to A.D. 210, coinciding with the heyday of El Mirador, the greatest of the early Maya cities. Hodell believes the abandonment of El Mirador in about A.D. 150 may have resulted, at least in part, from the continuing drought. Interestingly, a core from Lake Satpeten, Guatemala, in the southern lowlands, documents a drought from 130 B.C. to A.D. 180, which is contemporary with a widespread abandonment of larger Maya settlements. But the most severe drought of all, from A.D. 750 to 1025, coincides with the great Maya collapse of the southern lowlands.

If one sets the history of Maya civilization against this background of recurring drought, there are some remarkable coincidences. The first of Hodell's three dry cycles occurred while Maya agriculture was still providing sufficient flexibility to accommodate drier years. The second cycle descended on the Maya just as the first efflorescence of cities and civilization appeared in the lowlands. Cities like El Mirador were situated in lowlying areas, where water could be trapped and stored. At first the system worked, but soon the city grew too large, the vulnerability threshold was crossed, El Mirador's lords lost their spiritual credibility in the face of environmental disaster, and the people dispersed—there was still enough space for them to do so.

When the drought ended, growth resumed and Maya civilization entered an astounding trajectory of rapid expansion. By the time the greatest drought of all settled over the lowlands, essentially all the arable land was under cultivation, and Maya agriculture was very close to the critical threshold where even a slight drop in agricultural productivity would mean serious trouble. For nearly three centuries, intense drought lowered the water table, produced inadequate rains, and ravaged an agricultural economy that already had trouble satisfying the accelerating demands of the nobility.

Hodell's lake cores provided the first reliable evidence for droughts in Maya times. Recently, a magnificent deep-sea core, from the Carioco Basin off Venezuela in the southeastern Caribbean, provided the closest thing to a climatic smoking gun that one could find.[9] The uppermost 5.5 meters of the 170-meter Carioco core cover the past 14,000 years, with a sedimentation rate of about 30 centimeters per thousand years. So precise was the definition of the Carioco sedimentation that an X-ray fluorescence scanner could read measurements of bulk titanium concentrations at a two-millimeter spacing, representing intervals of only four years. Titanium concentrations reflect the amount of terrestrial sediment flowing into the Carioco Basin, and thus provide a sequence of changing river flow and variations in rainfall through time. A high concentration signals rainfall, a lesser one drier conditions. Because dry conditions in northern South America are mainly caused by ENSO events, titanium fluctuations are an accurate reflection not only of drought but also of El Niños.

During the summer, when most rain falls, the Intertropical Convergence Zone lies in a more northerly position, over the Yucatán. During the dry winter months, the ITCZ moves south of the Maya lowlands. This means that the Maya homeland is in the same climatic regimen as the Carioco Basin, both areas lying near the northernmost position of the ITCZ's seasonal movement. As a result, the Carioco core, with its exceptional definition, provides a much more fine-grained portrait of Maya drought than lake drillings.

The Carioco sequence reveals a series of multiyear droughts superimposed on a generally dry period. This may explain why the Maya collapse was gradual, with an impact that varied from area to area. Gerald Haug and his colleagues identified four major droughts, in about A.D. 760, 810, 860, and 910 (the latter lasting about six years), spaced at about 40- to 47-year intervals, which coincides with an estimated 50-year interval from lake cores.

The collapse affected the central and southern lowlands first, areas where access to groundwater was limited and farmers relied heavily on rainfall. The northern Yucatán fared better, because here the collapsed sink holes, known as *cenotes*, provided groundwater.

The archaeologist Richardson Benedict Gill used intervals of severe cold in Swedish tree rings and the last dates inscribed on stelae at abandoned cities to propose a tripartite collapse that began in A.D. 810 and affected cities like Palenque and Yaxchilán.[10] In 860, another drought toppled the great cities of Caracol and Copán. Finally, in 890–910, Tikal, Uaxactún, and other major centers fell. This was clearly a traumatic time at Tikal, where the archaeologist Peter Harrison uncovered human remains from a house midden of the time that showed signs of burning and chewing that could only have come from survival cannibalism, when desperate people had nothing else to eat except one another. Gill's theory was controversial, until the Carioco core produced a startlingly precise match with his inscriptions and tree-ring data.

The fundamental cause of the Maya collapse, then, was at least three major droughts that brought hunger and catastrophic social change. In city after city, the great lords were powerless to bring rain; perhaps unrest erupted. Archaeology shows us that these cities' populations either perished or dispersed into small hamlets. The unfortunate Maya had overreached themselves, and their civilization come down around their ears.

Far to the south, another dazzling state suffered the same fate.

∞

"Near the buildings there is a hill made by the hands of men, on great foundations of stone," wrote the Spanish conquistador Cieza de León after a brief visit to a glorious ruin near the southern shores of Lake Titicaca in Bolivia. "What astonishes me are some great doorways of stone, some made out of a single stone."[11] According to local legend, the city was named Taypi Kala, "The Stone in the Center." Archaeologists know it as Tiwanaku, once a state of over 50,000 people that flourished during the first millennium A.D.

Tiwanaku lies about 15 kilometers east of Lake Titicaca, on a strategic riverside site first occupied by village farmers in about 400 B.C.[12] The original village quickly became a growing town, then a city. By A.D. 650, a visitor would have marveled at a city of palaces, plazas, and brightly col-

Tiwanaku and vicinity

ored temples shimmering with gold-covered bas-reliefs. Tiwanaku was an
architectural masterpiece, marked by many gateways and massive stone
buildings. A huge artificial platform known as the Akapana, 200 meters
along the sides and 15 meters high, dominated the city. In Tiwanaku's
heyday, the Akapana was a terraced platform with massive stepped retain-
ing walls of sandstone and andesite. A sunken court surrounded by stone
buildings stood atop the platform. During the rainy season, water would
gush from the court onto the terraces, ultimately cascading with a roar
into a great moat. University of Chicago archaeologist Alan Kolata has
spent many years working on Tiwanaku and its hinterland. He believes
the ceremonial precinct was a symbolic island, like the sacred Island of

the Sun in Lake Titicaca, long a revered shrine to people living around the lake. Like Maya pyramids and plazas, the Akapana was a backdrop for elaborate public ceremonies, where Tiwanaku's leaders appeared in golden finery, dressed, so sculptures tell us, like gods with elaborate head-dresses, or as condors or pumas.

Human sacrifice played a major role in the city's ceremonial life, pre-sumably to appease the all-powerful solar deity and ensure the continuity of human life. A depiction of this deity is the famous "Gateway God" on the Gateway of the Sun, which still stands. The god wears a headdress like a sunburst, with nineteen projecting rays that end in circles and puma heads. He is attended by three rows of winged functionaries with human or bird heads, each bearing its own staff of office. Tiwanaku's iconography and religious beliefs are a closed book to us, but there can be little doubt that sunshine and water played a major role in ceremonial life. The city depended on an abundance of both.

Tiwanaku flourished for about 600 years on the altiplano, the high plains of southern Peru and northwestern Bolivia. The altiplano lies between 3,800 and 4,200 meters above sea level and is a place of dramatic seasonal contrasts. Agricultural experts have long considered the plains marginal for any sort of farming, yet Tiwanaku's farmers produced large food surpluses for many centuries. The complex social landscape of Tiwanaku became the center of a powerful state, carved out partly by conquest and partly by colo-nization, and always maintaining tight control of trading activities with other societies in the highlands and on the Pacific coast. By Andean stan-dards, Tiwanaku was a long-lived kingdom. But in about A.D. 1100, its agriculture became a spectacular victim of the Medieval Warm Period.

The state was centered on the Tiwanaku and Catari drainage basins near Lake Titicaca. These basins lie in the intermediate zone between the altiplano and higher ground, the floor of each being perennially marshy and subject to flooding during the wet season, between December and March. Lake Titicaca rises and falls annually, the amount of change vary-ing with variations in rainfall, which is presumably highest during major ENSO events. It was in these basins that the Tiwanaku people developed a complex agricultural infrastructure based on raised fields. So successful were these fields that they supported dense populations for more than five hundred years.

Tiwanaku's abundant food supplies supported artisans and priests, traders and armies, and the gangs of villagers who labored on temples and other public works. Such an elaborate city seems like a miracle in a cold, windswept environment with highly unpredictable rainfall, at an elevation where only hardy crops can grow. Commoners lived on potatoes and two native tubers, oca and ulluco. Maize was a luxury of the elite. The burgeoning population required huge tonnages of food every year.

The ingenious system of raised fields took advantage of lowlying terrain and high water tables to produce several crops a year.[13] In the thin mountain air, nighttime temperatures could drop below freezing even in summer, but the groundwater acted as a heat sink, warming and preserving the crops' root systems. Furthermore, the dredging of native water plants from the canals provided a green compost that formed nutrients and also generated heat. On a frosty night, a thin layer of dense mist formed above the fields throughout the lowlands. As the warming sun dispersed the white blanket, the lush, green potato plants stood unharmed, whereas only a few kilometers away, frost-damaged crops withered in hillside fields.

The fields themselves were sophisticated examples of agricultural engineering. First, the farmers laid down a compacted layer of round pebbles as a ballast foundation. This was then sealed with a layer of dense clay to prevent the slightly saline water of Lake Titicaca from reaching the roots of the plants. The clay also maintained a constant level of freshwater from nearby springs and seasonal streams. Next, the workers set down layers of carefully sorted gravel and sand, then topsoil, rich in mud from the surrounding canals. The farmers constantly renewed the fields with organic soil and clay and fertilized them with human waste.

Tiwanaku's growing population literally paved its landscape with such fields. For instance, archaeological surveys in the Rio Catari yielded 214 sites, 48 of them belonging to the time of Tiwanaku's heyday. A important secondary capital called Lukurmata grew to an enormous size, covering 145 hectares, with dwellings and other structures extending along river terraces above the Pampa Koani. Between the central precincts of the town and the steep hillsides behind it the inhabitants created a crescent-shaped strip of raised fields. Springs in the hillsides fed freshwater through a gully into the lower terrain where the raised fields lay. Agricultural engineers lined the gully with boulders, creating a sort of aqueduct to carry water to the fields. Only 6.5 hectares of Lukurmata's area was devoted to agriculture, not nearly enough land to feed everyone living there.[14]

Much of the town's food came from numerous smaller sites clustered nearby in a virtually continuous, humanly constructed landscape of agricultural production with many independent sources of groundwater and irrigation canals. Building this huge agricultural complex entailed creating and maintaining discontinuous irrigation schemes with raised fields, each of which required its own water source and canal system.

Elsewhere in the Tiwanaku Valley, raised fields consisted of dispersed and often self-contained pockets directly associated with what Kolata calls "significant human settlements." In the Rio Catari Basin, on the other hand, the entire raised-field system was created as a single unit, planned and executed with great care, using labor probably drawn from secondary urban centers, small towns, and numerous hamlets. The Rio Catari Basin was a dedicated landscape of agricultural production, probably under the direct control of the Tiwanaku state, and separated from the main population and administrative centers. This settlement pattern suggests a highly structured, even bureaucratic state under strong central control.

Raised fields were a brilliant and productive solution to Tiwanaku's subsistence problems, with the advantage that their maintenance could be left in the hands of local communities. Their success depended on a high water table and good spring and stream flow. As long as population densities remained relatively low and the rains at an average level, there was more than enough food to feed everyone. But as the city's leaders grew more ambitious and the state ever larger, the needs for high crop yields accelerated. The scale of the agricultural operation inexorably expanded. At some point, Tiwanaku crossed a critical threshold of vulnerability to long-term drought—a climatic event beyond the comprehension of farmers with an extremely short generational memory.

Cores bored into the floor of Lake Titicaca reveal a climatic sequence with the destructive potential of a Greek tragedy. From 5700 to 1500 B.C., the altiplano was extremely dry, with Titicaca as much as 50 meters below modern levels. During these long centuries of severe drought, local farming communities never reached any significant size. Most were villages huddled around the shores of the lake, and even there water shortages made agriculture difficult and residence inevitably temporary. Many people lived in small, dispersed settlements, subsisting off alpaca herding. Other groups commuted long distances each year, so artifacts tell us, down from the altiplano to the humid Amazon rainforest or even to the deserts of the Chilean and Peruvian coast. No village in the region before 1500 B.C. lasted more than a decade.

About 1500 B.C., rainfall increased considerably. The lake rose more than 20 meters within two to four centuries. Almost immediately, sedentary agricultural villages appeared along its shores. With more rain, the risks of farming the altiplano receded somewhat. The farmers cultivated dry fields, depending entirely on seasonal rainfall with correspondingly low crop yields, and also experimented with raised-field cultivation.

The lake level now fluctuated significantly from decade to decade, but never returned to the very arid conditions of earlier times. The cores reveal short intervals with lower lake levels, as well as extended periods when fine sediments from flowing streams reached the lake floor. For a thousand years, the altiplano supported farmers and herders, but as their numbers and sophistication increased, raised-field cultivation dominated the agricultural economy. After A.D. 600, large-scale raised-field systems expanded across the wetlands, covering an area of about 190 square kilometers by A.D. 800 to 900. Intensive surveys of one 150-square-kilometer segment of Rio Catari Basin reveal that as much as 80 percent of the land was under cultivation during those two centuries. This expansion coincided with several centuries of much higher lake levels resulting from elevated rainfall. Between A.D. 350 and 500, Lake Titicaca was higher than today; it was at about the same level as modern times between 800 and 900.

Ice core studies confirm the message of sediments from Titicaca's depths. The Quelccaya ice cap lies high in the Andes, about 200 kilometers north of the lake.[15] A fine-grained ice core from there records two wetter periods, A.D. 610–650 and 760–1040. There were three dry periods, A.D. 540–610, 650–760, and 1040–1450. The last dry interval, which roughly coincides with the Medieval Warm Period, lasted four centuries and was marked by extraordinarily low ice accumulation in the Andes.

This dry period is well recorded in lake cores as well. In about A.D. 1100, the fine organic layers produced by good rainfall cease abruptly. On land, the raised-field systems of the Catari Basin vanished almost entirely within a half century. Now such fields only flourished where there was locally high groundwater.

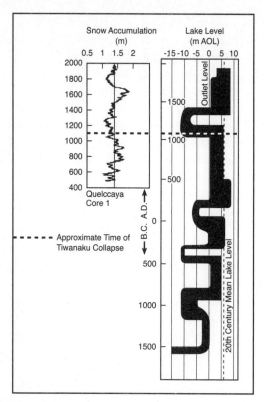

Lake levels from Lake Titicaca correlated with Andean ice cores and radiocarbon dates. *Courtesy: Museum of New Mexico, Albuquerque*

If you plot the chronology, established by radiocarbon dating, of remains from raised fields, fluctuations in Lake Titicaca's water level, and snow accumulation at Quelccaya on the same graph, a striking convergence emerges. Snow accumulation high in the Andes declined sharply after about 1040. The drought cycle peaked around 1300 and persisted with less intensity until about 1450. The Titicaca lake cores display a complete hiatus in organic sedimentation in almost all samples, reflecting a decline in lake level of between 12 and 17 meters. Lake Wiñaymarka, the smaller basin of Lake Titicaca, seems to have evaporated completely. Calibrated radiocarbon dates place the lake's shrinking to between A.D. 1030 and 1280, precisely within the period of low snow accumulation in the Andes. Both climatic indicators point to a severe and prolonged drought, probably a 10 to 15 percent decline in rainfall from the modern average. The evidence from the raised fields is equally stark: they were simply abandoned.

The scenario is compelling: a prolonged drought began with a 10 to 15 percent decline in annual rainfall, not just in one year but for much longer. Reduced rainfall soon led to lower spring discharges, and eventually to a lowered water table—and the aquifers were not recharged. As Alan Kolata remarks, "The lack of water simply made the complex physical and biological functions of the raised fields impossible."[16] The much drier conditions pushed Tiwanaku to the edge of desperation and then over it.

In the Rio Catari area, the settlement pattern changed completely after A.D. 1150. Gone is the highly organized, hierarchical landscape of earlier times. Now the people lived mainly on the hitherto virtually uninhabited pampa, most of them in small villages covering less than a hectare. The evidence for dispersal into much smaller communities is dramatic, sudden, and directly related to the three-century drought. Rainfall did not return to pre–1100 levels until the mid-fifteenth century. By that time, the people were living under the Inca empire. The farmers never again cultivated raised fields on lake-edge wetlands. Instead, they shifted to irrigated and rain-fed terrace agriculture on surrounding mountain slopes, techniques used by the Inca to great effect, but certainly incapable of supporting a dense population.

The ability of the Tiwanaku state to adjust to the great drought was limited culturally by centuries of rapid population growth underwritten by the remarkable productivity of the raised fields. Tiwanaku's economy was entirely dependent on this single agricultural technology, which in turn depended on abundant water. When the water failed, the entire system collapsed.

Tiwanaku's journey across the threshold of vulnerability was brutally direct, although the collapse itself was the result of a complex interplay of climatic change, agricultural implosion, and the inflexibility of a political and religious system built on a single highly vulnerable technology. One is irresistibly reminded of the Hittites, who depended on grain from afar. They appeased the gods with temples and lavish offerings, but their civilization fell apart with startling rapidity once their food, much of it grown in areas of uncertain rainfall, became too scarce to support a complex city. In Tiwanaku's case, the great drought undermined the credibility of the state's leaders and their gods. In the medieval drought they met a climatic disaster that was scaled to their vulnerability.

A century after its fall, only distant memories remained of the now-deserted city's greatness. Inca royal mythology later spoke of the great sun god, the supreme deity Viracocha, who came to Tiwanaku to fabricate the world from soft lake clay. The ancient city may have overreached itself and failed, but it claimed a dazzling legitimacy in the mythic history of the Andes.

EPILOGUE
A.D. 1200 TO MODERN TIMES

Human history has been played out in an ever-changing world,
the changes sometimes slow, sometimes fast, the nature of the long-
term ones always obscured by the bigger swings that distinguish
the individual years. The environment will continue to change,
partly due to human activities with their effects both intentional
and unintentional, and partly due to natural causes. There is cer-
tainly no warrant in this for expecting that either a constant or an
ever-rising standard of living will, in the long run, be possible.

Hubert Lamb, *Climate, History, and the Modern World,* 1982

Dies irae, dies illa, solvet saeclum in favilla . . . This day, this day of wrath
shall consume the world in ashes . . . The cadences of Mozart's *Requiem*
echoed heavenward in the dome of St. Paul's Cathedral and then dispersed. The performance was sublime, the acoustics perfect. As we filed
from the cathedral into the bustle of London's streets, a clap of thunder
rolled across the hot summer sky, drawing our attention to the storm
clouds massed on the western horizon. My companion remarked on this
timely reminder of the wrath of God.

A sense of capricious and unforgiving divine anger has shaped human behavior since before the beginnings of civilization. The chants of tribal
shamans in Ice Age caves interceded with the forces of the supernatural.
Revered ancestors stood watch over family land and harvests at Jericho and
Çätälhöyük. Divine kings served as land agents for the gods at Ur. The lords
of Maya Tikal and of Tiwanaku by Lake Titicaca used their supernatural
powers to communicate with the unknown. Before the days of climatology

and scientific records, changes of climate within the narrow span of human memory were thought to be the work of the gods. The only human recourse was propitiation through prayer, sacrifice, and temple building.

༄༅༈

Seven weeks after Easter in A.D. 1315, sheets of rain spread across a sodden Europe, turning freshly plowed fields into lakes and quagmires. The deluge continued through June and July, and then August and September. Hay lay flat in the fields; wheat and barley rotted unharvested. The anonymous author of the *Chronicle of Malmesbury* wondered if divine vengeance had come upon the land: "Therefore is the anger of the Lord kindled against his people, and he hath stretched out his hand against them, and hath smitten them."[1] Most close-knit farming communities endured the shortages of 1315 and hoped for a better harvest the following year. But heavy spring rains in 1316 prevented proper sowing. Intense gales battered the English Channel and North Sea; flocks and herds withered, crops failed, prices rose, and people again contemplated the wrath of God. By the time the barrage of rains subsided in 1321, over a million-and-a-half people, villagers and city folk alike, had perished from hunger and famine-related epidemics. Gilles de Muisit, abbot of Saint-Martin de Tournai in modern-day Belgium, wrote, "Men and women from among the powerful, the middling, and the lowly, old and young, rich and poor, perished daily in such numbers that the air was fetid with the stench."[2] People everywhere despaired. Guilds and religious orders moved through the streets, the people naked, carrying the bodies of saints and other sacred relics. After generations of good, they believed that divine retribution had come to punish a Europe divided by war and petty strife.

The great rains of 1315 marked the beginning of what climatologists call the Little Ice Age, a period of six centuries of constant climatic shifts that may or may not be still in progress.[3] The term itself is a misnomer, although there were indeed memorably cold winters when the Baltic Sea froze, winter markets stood for months on the frozen Thames, and glaciers advanced to overwhelm villages in the Alps. The new climatology tells us that the Little Ice Age was a zigzag of climatic shifts, few lasting more than a quarter century. Many scientists believe that these shifts ended in about 1860, when the present warming trend began.

Climatic stress, when it does not bring complete collapse, often acts as a spur to social reorganization and technological innovation. In the fourteenth century, Europe was a rural continent with only the most rudimentary infrastructure of roads, harbors, and local mills. Kings and queens reigned over kingdoms and crowded cities haunted by the constant threat of insufficient food. Nine of every ten workers were engaged in growing food, and still the entire continent lived only from year to year. But the exigencies of the Little Ice Age helped bring about an agricultural revolution, which began during the fifteenth and sixteenth centuries in the Low Countries, then spread to England a hundred years later. Many English landowners embraced the new agriculture as larger, enclosed farms changed the landscape. Innovative crops like turnips and clover provided insurance for herds and people against winter hunger. Britain, Flanders, and the Netherlands were self-sufficient in grain and livestock by the onset of the Industrial Revolution in the late eighteenth century. A new scale of agricultural production, combined with an ever-more efficient infrastructure, fed burgeoning cities and rising rural and urban populations. In western Europe, only France remained agriculturally backward in an era when deteriorating climate made bad harvests more frequent. As it has done throughout the Holocene, increasing hunger led to social dissolution and a loss of legitimacy for society's rulers. In this case, civil chaos joined with a philosophical enlightenment to produce the French Revolution, which in turn influenced the American ideal of democracy and the rise of the United States as an economic and industrial power.

The climatic shifts of the Little Ice Age continued into the 1840s. Mount Tambora's cataclysmic eruption in Southeast Asia in 1815 brought the famous "year without a summer" in 1816. The 1820s and 1830s saw warmer springs and autumns, with 1826 the hottest summer between 1676 and 1976. August 1829 was exceptionally cold and wet. Floods washed out bridges, ruined crops, and changed river courses. In the same year, Lake Constance in Switzerland froze over for the first time since 1740; it would not do so again until the exceptional cold of 1963. The winter of 1837/8 was so harsh in Scandinavia that ice linked southern

Norway with the port of Skagen at the northern tip of Denmark and extended out of sight of land to the west. The same unpredictable swings continued through the 1840s, with several cold winters and cool summers. But after 1850 the climate warmed slowly and almost continually, and has continued to do so until today. Thanks to modern instrumentation and vast computer databases, we know that global mean surface temperatures have risen between 0.4 and 0.8°C since 1860, and 0.2 and 0.3°C since 1900 in some parts of the world. Summer temperatures are now equal to the mean readings of the Medieval Warm Period. Many people believe this is the consequence of fossil fuels and other human pollutants, and not part of the natural gyrations of climate change. They are probably correct. For instance, in computer climate simulations, the surface temperature warming that resulted from known fluctuations in solar radiation between 1600 and the present amounts to only 0.45°C. Less than 0.25°C can be attributed to the period 1900 to 1990, when surface temperatures rose 0.6°C. Changes in solar radiation appear to account for less than half of twentieth-century warming, considerably less than in earlier centuries.

⚬⚬⚬

Ultimately, the cause of the warming is only a side debate. We live within the capsule of a global economy, seemingly oblivious to climatic events with the potential to kill thousands, in a time when human populations have exploded and cities are the dominant form of human settlement. With the Industrial Revolution, we took a giant stride into an era in which we are frighteningly exposed to potential cataclysm, enhanced by our own seeming ability to warm the earth and increase the probability of extreme climatic events. The potential scale of disaster is almost unrecognizable in historical terms. At least twenty million people died of hunger and famine-related epidemics resulting from ENSOs and droughts during the nineteenth century. Today, over 200 million people live on agriculturally marginal lands in northeastern Brazil, the Saharan Sahel, Ethiopia, and many parts of Asia. Deforestation, to the tune of about the acreage of Arizona annually, strips the earth bare. Millions of us dwell in high-rise buildings, in suburban housing and slums in heavily industrialized cities that are extremely vulnerable to the violent storm surges of hurricanes. Unlike the Cro-Magnons, the Chumash, or even the Maya, we do not have the option to move elsewhere. Today, the neighboring lands are filled with our neighbors.

What would happen, for example, if the Greenland ice sheet were to release so much meltwater into the North Atlantic that the Gulf Stream abruptly shut down, just as it did in the Younger Dryas? Would Europe be plunged into near-arctic conditions within a generation or less? Where would the present inhabitants of Scandinavia, Germany, France, the Netherlands, Poland, the Baltic states, and Russia go, and what would they eat? There are scientists who believe such a climatic switch is entirely possible.

Optimism assumes that we will adapt to this new, more vulnerable world. We humans do indeed have a striking ability to adapt to changing environmental circumstances. Yet optimism fades in the face of demographic reality. Of the six billion of us who now inhabit the earth, hundreds of millions still subsist from harvest to harvest, from rainy season to rainy season, just as Stone Age and Bronze Age farmers did in Europe five thousand years ago. Famine is a remote danger in Europe and North America, with their industrial-scale agriculture and elaborate infrastructures for moving food over long distances. Subsistence farmers and city dwellers on other continents, however, still live under the constant threat of hunger.

Every year, the media carry stories of famine and flood, of thousands perishing quietly in northeast Africa or Bangladesh while the world remains oblivious. The numbers are hard for us to assimilate in the prosperous, seemingly invulnerable West. They will become harder still to comprehend if global temperatures rise far above present levels, rising seas inundate densely populated coastal plains and force millions of people to resettle inland, or far more severe droughts settle over the Sahel and less well watered parts of the world. We can only imagine the death toll in a future era when climatic swings may be faster, more extreme, and completely unpredictable because of human interference with the atmosphere. The millions who died in the Irish potato famine of the 1840s, or the tens of millions who died from the Indian monsoon failures of the late nineteenth century, will pale to insignificance.

❦

Climate has helped shape civilization, but not by being benign. The unpredictable whims of the Holocene stressed human societies and forced them to either adapt or perish. This book has surveyed examples of successful adaptation, such as the switchover to farming during the Younger Dryas in southwestern Asia in about 10,000 B.C. and the demise of states like Tiwanaku, both in times of drought. The collapses often came as a complete surprise to rulers and elites who believed in royal infallibility and espoused rigid ideologies of power.

There is no reason to assume that we've somehow escaped this shaping process. Agriculture is less visible to us now—the number of people growing food has shrunk from 90 percent of the labor force in Europe five hundred years ago to less than 3 percent in the United States today—but we still need to eat. And now our vulnerability extends far beyond just growing food: our crowded coastlines with densely packed high-rises and apartment buildings, our communication and transport systems, our abstract worlds of finance and scholarship and entertainment, are beholden to the world's climate in ways both obvious and hidden. Like many civilizations before us, we've simply traded up in scale, accepting vulnerability to the big, rare disaster in exchange for a better ability to handle the smaller, more common stresses such as short-term droughts and exceptionally rainy years.

But if we've become a supertanker among human societies, it's an oddly inattentive one. Only a tiny fraction of the people on board are engaged with tending the engines. The rest are buying and selling goods among themselves, entertaining each other or studying the sky or the hydrodynamics of the hull. Those on the bridge have no charts or weather forecasts and cannot even agree that they are needed; indeed, the most powerful among them subscribe to a theory that says storms don't exist, or if they do, their effects are entirely benign, and the steepening swells and fleeing albatrosses can only be taken as a sign of divine favor. Few of those in command believe the gathering clouds have any relation to their fate or are concerned that there are lifeboats for only one in ten passengers. And no one dares to whisper in the helmsman's ear that he might consider turning the wheel.

NOTES

CHAPTER 1: THE THRESHOLD OF VULNERABILITY

1. Leonard Woolley described Ur in numerous popular books. His *Ur of the Chaldees: A Record of Seven Years of Excavation* (1929; New York: Norton, 1965), is good account for a general audience. Samuel Kramer, *The Sumerians* (Chicago: University of Chicago Press, 1963) is an excellent popular account of Sumerian civilization.

2. Woolley, *Ur of the Chaldees,* p. 14.

3. The archaeology of Mesopotamia is summarized by Susan Pollock, *Ancient Mesopotamia* (Cambridge: Cambridge University Press, 2000).

4. Jay McCorriston and Frank Hole, "The Ecology of Seasonal Stress and the Origins of Agriculture in the Near East," *American Anthropologist* 93 (1991): 46–69.

5. Harvey Weiss, "Beyond the Younger Dryas: Collapse as Adaptation to Abrupt Climate Change in Ancient West Asia and the Eastern Mediterranean," in Garth Bawdon and Richard Martin Reycraft, eds., *Environmental Disaster and the Archaeology of Human Response* (Albuquerque: Maxwell Museum of Anthropology, 2000), pp. 63–74.

6. This passage is based on John A. McPhee's *The Control of Nature* (New York: Farrar, Straus, Giraux, 1989), an elegant account of efforts to control the waters of the Big Muddy.

7. Ibid., p. 5.

8. John M. Barry, *The Great Mississippi Flood of 1927 and How It Changed America* (New York: Simon and Schuster, 1997).

CHAPTER 2: THE LATE ICE AGE ORCHESTRA

1. Ted Goebel, "The 'microblade adaptation' and recolonization of Siberia during the late Upper Pleistocene," in *Thinking Small: Global Perspectives on Microlithization,* ed. R. G. Elston and S. L. Kuhn, pp. 117–131 (Arlington: American Anthropological Association, 2002).

2. David Lewis-Williams, *The Mind in the Cave: Consciousness and the Origins of Art* (London and New York: Thames and Hudson, 2002), gives a useful general description. See also Paul Bahn and Jean Vertut, *Images of the Ice Age* (New York: Viking, 1988).

3. The late Ice Age environment of Europe is described in a vast specialist literature. The Cro-Magnons, the late Ice Age inhabitants of central and western Europe,

c. 45,000 to 15,000 years ago, are named after the Cro-Magnon rock shelter near Les Eyzies in southwestern France. Workers digging a cutting for a railroad in 1868 found a series of late Ice Age burials in the cave. So the site provided a generic name for the first modern humans in Europe. Clive Gamble, *The Palaeolithic Societies of Europe* (Cambridge: Cambridge University Press, 1999), offers an excellent guide to the Cro-Magnons and their complex archaeology.

4. John Hoffecker, *Desolate Landscapes* (New Brunswick, NJ: Rutgers University Press, 2002), gives a general description of late Ice Age environments in Eurasia, which also applies here.

5. Richard Klein, *The Human Career*, 2nd ed. (Chicago: University of Chicago Press, 1999). See also Christopher B. Stringer and R. McKie, *African Exodus* (New York: Henry Holt, 1996), and Richard Klein and Blake Edgar, *The Dawn of Human Culture* (New York: John Wiley, 2002).

6. Popular accounts of the Neanderthals abound. The best known is Chistopher Stringer and Clive Gamble, *In Search of the Neanderthals* (London and New York: Thames and Hudson, 1993).

7. Lewis-Williams, *Mind in the Cave,* gives a description.

8. See Lewis-Williams, *Mind in the Cave,* for a discussion of the shaman controversy, with references. This is a much-debated issue in the literature.

9. Useful accounts of paleoclimatology and post–Ice Age climate change include Raymond S. Bradley, *Paleoclimatology: Reconstructing Climates of the Quaternary*, 2nd ed. (New York: Academic Press, 1999), and Neil Roberts, *The Holocene: An Environmental History*, 2nd ed. (Oxford: Blackwell, 1998).

10. Richard Alley, *The Two Mile Time Machine* (Princeton, NJ: Princeton University Press, 2000).

11. J. R. Petit et al., "Climate and atmospheric history of the past 420,000 years from the Vostok ice core, Antarctica," *Nature* 399 (1999): 429–436.

12. The term "Holocene" comes from the Greek word *holos*, meaning "recent," and conventionally refers to the ten millennia since the end of the Ice Age. The technical boundary between what is called the Late Glacial and the Holocene is marked on ancient pollen diagrams and by a split in certain Scandinavian ice sheets, of interest only to the most arcane specialists. But for nonspecialists, the Holocene means two words: global warming.

13. Hoffecker, *Desolate Landscapes,* chap. 2, has an excellent description.

14. Björn Kurtén, *Pleistocene Mammals in Europe* (Chicago: Aldine, 1968), is authoritative. See also Adrian Lister, Jean Auel, and Paul Bahn, *Mammoths* (New York: Hungry Minds, 1994).

15. The needle is well attested in archaeological sites occupied 25,000 years ago, but may have been in use as early as 30,000 years before present (John Hoffecker, personal communication).

16. An engrossing account of Eskimo clothing will be found in Richard K. Nelson, *Hunters of the Northern Ice* (Chicago: University of Chicago Press, 1969), chap. 7.

17. This section is based on Hoffecker,*Desolate Landscapes,* chap. 6.

18. Ably described by Olga Soffer, *The Upper Palaeolithic of the Central Russian Plains* (New York: Academic Press, 1985). Also Hoffecker, *Desolate Landscapes,* chap. 6.

19. Recent years have witnessed a profileration of archaeological research in extreme northeastern Siberia and an accompanying literature explosion. For example, see Ted Goebel, "Pleistocene human colonization of Siberia and peopling of the Americas: An ecological approach," *Evolutionary Anthropology* 8(6) (1999): 208–227. Also John Hoffecker and Scott A. Elias, "Environment and archaeology in Beringia," *Evolutionary Anthropology* 12(1) (2003): 34–49. I am grateful to John Hoffecker for much stimulating discussion of these issues.

20. Accelerator mass spectrometry dating and the tree-ring calibration of radiocarbon dates are described in all basic method and theory textbooks. See, for example, Colin Renfrew and Paul Bahn, *Archaeology,* 3rd ed. (London and New York: Thames and Hudson, 2000), and Brian Fagan and Christopher DeCorse, *In the Beginning,* 11th ed. (Upper Saddle River, NJ: Prentice Hall, 2004).

21. The best starting point for this literature is John Hoffecker and Scott Elias, op. cit. (2003).

CHAPTER 3: THE VIRGIN CONTINENT

1. The Bering land bridge is well summarized by the essays in David A. Hopkins, ed., *The Paleoecology of Beringia* (New York: Academic Press, 1992), although, of course, there has been much periodical literature since.

2. The controversies are summarized in a growing popular literature, which offers a guide to the technical references. For example: James Adovasio with Jake Page, *The First Americans* (New York: Random House, 2002), and Tom Dillehay, *The Settlement of the Americas* (New York: Basic Books, 2001).

3. The genetic and linguistic evidence is the subject of much debate. For genetics, see Jason A. Eshleman, Ripan S. Malhi, and David Glenn Smith, "Mitochrondrial DNA studies of Native Americans: Conceptions and misconceptions of the population prehistory of the Americas." *Evolutionary Anthropology* 12(1)(2003): 7–18. For languages, see Terrence Kaufman and Victor Golla, "Language groupings in the New World: Their reliability and usability in cross-disciplinary studies," in Colin Renfrew, ed., *America Past, America Present: Genes and Languages in the Americas and Beyond* (Cambridge: McDonald Institute for Archaeological Research), pp. 57–67.

4. Richard Morlan, *Taphonomy and Archaeology in the Upper Pleistocene of the Northern Yukon Territory: A Glimpse into the Peopling of the New World* (Ottawa: National Museum of Man, 1979), p. 3.

5. Brian M. Fagan, *The Great Journey* (London and New York: Thames and Hudson, 1987).

6. Paul S. Martin and Henry Wright, eds., *Pleistocene Extinctions: Search for a Cause* (New Haven, CT: Yale University Press), 1967. See also Paul S. Martin and

Richard Klein, eds, *A Pleistocene Revolution* (Tucson: University of Arizona Press, 1974). The literature still proliferates on this thorny issue.

7. Ethnographic accounts of ancient rabbit hunts abound. See, for example, Robert F. Heizer, ed, *Handbook of North American Indians, Volume 8: California* (Washington, DC: Smithsonian Institution, 1978).

8. Hoffecker and Elias, "Environment and archaeology in Beringia."

9. Nancy H. Bigelow and Mary E. Edwards, "A 14,000-year paleoenvironmental record from Windmill Lake, Central Alaska: Evidence for high frequency climatic and vegetation variation," *Quaternary Science Reviews* 20 (2001): 203–215.

10. The early archaeology of Alaska: David R. Yesner. "Human dispersal into interior Alaska: Antecedent conditions, mode of colonization, and adaptations," *Quaternary Science Reviews* 20 (2001): 310–327.

11. Richard Alley, *The Two Mile Time Machine* (Princeton, NJ: Princeton University Press, 2000), p. 126; on Heinrich events, see pp. 153–155. Also Wallace S. Broecker, "Massive iceberg discharges as triggers for global climatic changes," *Nature* 372 (1993): 421.

12. Thomas Canby, "The search for the first Americans," *National Geographic Magazine* 156 (1979): 330–363.

13. The whole issue of coastal settlement of the Americas is bedeviled by a lack of archaeological evidence. Dillehay, *Settlement of the Americas*, pp. 66–71, has a discussion. For the Little Ice Age and doggers, see Brian Fagan, *The Little Ice Age* (New York: Basic Books, 2001), pp. 74–76.

14. Evidence for this settlement is summarized in Brian Fagan. *People of the Earth,* 11th ed. (Upper Saddle River, NJ: Prentice Hall, 2004), chap. 6.

15. Richard B. Lee, *The !Kung San* (Cambridge: Cambridge University Press, 1979).

16. Adovasio, *First Americans,* pp. 146–188, describes Meadowcroft and its controversies.

17. Adovasio, *First Americans,* p. 267.

18. Thomas Dillehay, *Monte Verde: A Late Pleistocene Settlement in Chile*, 2 vols. (Washington, DC: Smithsonian Institution Press, 1997).

19. Hoffecker, *Desolate Landscapes,* p. 51.

20. For a useful summary, see Donald Grayson, "The archaeological record of human impact on animals," *Journal of World Prehistory* 15(1) (2001): 1–68.

CHAPTER 4: EUROPE DURING THE GREAT WARMING

1. A series of articles by Wallace Broecker are invaluable. "Chaotic climate," *Scientific American* (November 1995): 62–68, surveys the Great Ocean Conveyor Belt; "What drives climatic cycles?" *Scientific American* (January 1990): 49–56, discusses links between the ocean, the atmosphere, and Ice Age climatic changes. George Philander, *Is the Temperature Rising?* (Princeton, NJ: Princeton University Press, 1998), offers a summary.

2. Jean Lynch-Stieglitz, William B. Currey, and Niall Slowey, "Weaker Gulf Stream in the Florida Straits during the last glacial maximum," *Nature* 402 (1999): 644–648.

3. See the references in note 1. Also: W. S. Broecker et al., "Routing of meltwater from the Laurentide ice sheet during the Younger Dryas," *Nature* 341 (1989): 318–21. See also J. T. Teller et al., "Meltwater and precipitation runoff to the North Atlantic, Arctic, and Gulf of Mexico from the Laurentide ice sheet and adjacent regions during the Younger Dryas," *Paleoceanography* 5 (1990) 897–905.

4. Lawrence Guy Strauss, "The archaeology of the Pleistocene-Holocene transition in southwest Europe," in Lawrence Strauss, Berit Eriksen, John M. Erlandson, and David Yesner, eds., *Humans at the End of the Ice Age* (New York: Plenum, 1996), pp. 83–100. See also Martin Street et al., "Final Paleolithic and Mesolithic research in reunified Germany," *Journal of World Prehistory* 15(4) (2001): 365–453.

5. For a general description, see David Lewis-Williams, *The Mind in the Cave: Consciousness and the Origins of Art* (London and New York: Thames and Hudson, 2002).

6. Neil Roberts, *The Holocene: An Environmental History,* 2nd ed. (Oxford: Blackwell, 1998), chaps. 3 and 4.

7. M. C. Burkitt, "A Maglemose harpoon dredged up from the North Sea," *Man* 238 (1932): 99.

8. Roberts, *The Holocene,* pp. 68ff.

9. For an excellent summary with these examples, see Roberts, *The Holocene,* chaps. 2 and 4.

10. Michael Williams, *Deforesting the Earth* (Chicago: University of Chicago Press, 2002), makes this important point.

11. Roberts, *The Holocene,* pp. 81ff, summarizes.

12. Roberts, *The Holocene,* p. 110.

13. Berit Valentin Eriksen, "Resource exploitation, subsistence strategies, and adaptiveness in late Pleistocene–early Holocene northwest Europe," in Lawrence Strauss, Berit Eriksen, John M. Erlandson, and David Yesner, eds., *Humans at the End of the Ice Age* (New York: Plenum, 1996), pp. 79–100.

14. John Speth, *Bison Kills and Bone Counts* (Chicago: University of Chicago Press, 1983), offers a fascinating analysis of fat, meat yields, and bison hunting in North America that has great relevance here.

15. A vast literature surrounds the bow and arrow. J.-G. Rozey, "The revolution of the bowmen in Europe," in Clive Bonsall, ed., *The Mesolithic in Europe* (Edinburgh: John Donald, 1989), pp. 13–28, offers an excellent summary for the purposes of this chapter.

16. Saxon T. Pope, *Hunting with the Bow and Arrow* (Berkeley: University of California Press, 1923), is a classic work based on Pope's experiences with Ishi, a California Indian.

17. An excellent summary of the Ahrensburg sites can be found in Klaus Breest and Stephan Veil, "Some new thoughts on old data on humans and reindeer in the Ahrensburgian Tunnel Valley in Schleswig-Holstein, Germany," in N. Barton, A. D.

Roberts, and D. A. Roe., eds., *The Late Glacial in North-west Europe* (London: Council for British Archaeology, 1991), pp. 1–6.

18. Bodil Bratlund, "A study of hunting lesions containing flint fragments on reindeer bones at Stellmoor, Schleswig-Holstein, Germany," In N. Barton, A. D. Roberts, and D. A. Roe, eds., *The Late Glacial in North-west Europe* (London: Council for British Archaeology, 1991), pp. 193–207.

CHAPTER 5: THE THOUSAND-YEAR DROUGHT

1. A good summary is Ofer Bar-Yosef, "The Impact of late Pleistocene–early Holocene climate changes on humans in Southwest Asia," in Lawrence Guy Straus et al., eds., *Humans at the End of the Ice Age* (New York: Plenum Press, 1996), pp. 61–78.

2. Dorothy Garrod is one of the unsung heroes of Stone Age archaeology. She was the first woman to be appointed a professor of prehistoric archaeology anywhere and, at that, to the prestigious Disney Chair at Cambridge University. She is principally remembered for her work at Mount Carmel in the late 1920s and 1930s, which revealed Neanderthal burials. For an excellent account of the Kebarans and their successors, see Donald O. Henry, *From Foraging to Agriculture* (Philadelphia: University of Pennsylvania Press, 1989).

3. Bar-Yosef, "Impact of late Pleistocene–early Holocene climate changes," p. 75.

4. Ofer Bar-Yosef and François R. Valla, eds., *The Natufian Culture in the Levant* (Ann Arber, MI: International Monographs in Prehistory, Archaeological Series 1, 1991).

5. For a basic summary on acorns, see Sarah Mason, "Acornutopia? Determining the role of acorns in past human subsistence," in John Wilkins, David Harvey, and Mike Dobson, eds., *Food in Antiquity* (Exeter: University of Exeter Press, 1995), pp. 7–13. See also the overview in Brian Fagan, *Before California: An Archaeologist Looks at Our Earliest Ancestors* (Walnut Creek, CA: AltaMira Press, 2003), chap. 6.

6. Walter Goldschmidt, "Nomlaki ethnography," *University of California Publications in American Archaeology and Ethnology* 42(4) (1951): 303–433.

7. Bar-Yosef and Valla, *Natufian Culture in the Levant*, pp. 27ff.

8. Andrew M. T. Moore, *Village on the Euphrates: From foraging to Farming at Abu Hureyra* (New York: Oxford University Press, 2000). This exemplary monograph and its accompanying specialist reports by the botanist Gordon Hillman and others are the basis for the descriptions of Abu Hureyra in this chapter.

9. This account of Lake Agassiz is based on S. W. Hostetler et al., "Simulated influences of Lake Agassiz on the climate of central north America 11,000 years ago," *Nature* 405 (2000): 334–337.

10. W. S. Broecker et al., "Routing of meltwater from the Laurentide ice sheet during the Younger Dryas," *Nature* 341 (1989): 318–21. See also J. T. Teller et al., "Meltwater and precipitation runoff to the North Atlantic, Arctic, and Gulf of Mexico from the Laurentide ice sheet and adjacent regions during the Younger Dryas," *Paleoceanography* 5 (1990) 897–905. For the Antarctic controversy, see Andrew J.

Weaver et al., "Meltwater Pulse 1A from Antarctica as a trigger of the Bolling-Allerod Warming," *Science* 299 (2003): 1709–1713.

11. H. Renssen, "The climate in the Netherlands during the Younger Dryas and Preboreal: Means and extremes obtained with an atmospheric general circulation model," *Netherlands Journal of Geosciences* 80(2) (2001): 19–30. See also Dan Hammarlund et al., "Climate and environment during the Younger Dryas (GS–1) as reflected by composite stable isotope records of lacustrine carbonates at Torreberga, southern Sweden," *Journal of Quaternary Sciences* 14(1) (1999): 17–28.

12. This section is based on Moore, chap. 12.

13. J. R. Harlan, "A wild wheat harvest in Turkey," *Archaeology* 19(3) (1967): 197–201.

14. M. R. Heun et al., "Site of einkorn wheat domestication identified by DNA fingerprinting," *Science* 278 (1997): 1312–14.

15. Gordon Hillman and M. S. Davis, "Measured domestication rates in wild wheats and barley under primitive conditions, and their archaeological implications," *Journal of World Prehistory* 4(2) (1990): 157–222.

16. Theya Molleson, "The eloquent bones of Abu Hureyra," *Scientific American* 271(2) (1994): 70–75.

CHAPTER 6: THE CATACLYSM

1. R. J. Braidwood and L. S. Braidwood, eds., *Prehistoric Archaeology Along the Zagros Flanks* (Chicago: University of Chicago Press, 1983), chap. 1.

2. Melinda A. Zeder et al., *Documenting Domestication: New Genetic and Archaeological Paradigms* (Washington, DC: Smithsonian Institution Press, 2002).

3. Kathleen Kenyon. 1981. *Excavations at Jericho, Vol. 3.* (Jerusalem: British School of Archaeology). See also Henry, op. cit. (1989).

4. Discussed at greater length in Brian Fagan, *From Black Land to Fifth Sun* (Reading, MA: Helix Books, 1998), pp. 81–83.

5. Obsidian now commands an extensive literature. The first publication on the topic was Colin Renfrew, J. F. Dixon, and J. R. Cann. "Obsidian and Early Cultural Contact in the Near East," *Proceedings of the Prehistoric Society* 32 (1966): 1–29. See also the discussion in Fagan, *From Black Land to Fifth Sun*, chap. 7.

6. James Mellaart, *Çatal Hüyük* (New York: McGraw Hill, 1967); Ian Hodder, *On the Surface: Çatalhöyük 1993–95* (Cambridge, England: McDonald Institute for Archaeological Research, 1996). The spelling for the site in the Hodder reference is the most widely used today.

7. Hostetler et al., "Simulated influences of Lake Agassiz on the climate of central north America 11,000 years ago," *Nature* 405 (2000): 334–337.

8. The description of Euxine Lake and the resulting cataclysm is based on William Ryan and Walter Pitman, *Noah's Flood: The New Scientific Discoveries About the Event That Changed History* (New York: Simon & Schuster, 1999).

9. Alisdair Whittle, "The First Farmers," in Barry Cunliffe, ed., *Prehistoric Europe: An Illustrated History* (Oxford: Oxford University Press, 1994), pp.136–168.

10. Whittle, "First Farmers."

11. This description is based on Ryan and Pitman, *Noah's Flood*, chap. 8.

12. Whittle, "First Farmers." See also Andrew Sherratt, *Economy and Society in Prehistoric Europe: Changing Perspectives* (Princeton, NJ: Princeton University Press, 1997), chap. 11.

13. Whittle, "First Farmers." Also Sherratt, *Economy and Society in Prehistoric Europe*, pp. 339ff.

14. A lyrical description can be found in Simon Schama, *Landscape and Memory* (New York: Knopf, 1995), p. 115.

15. For the effects of fire see Michael Williams, *Deforesting the Earth* (Chicago: University of Chicago Press, 2002), and Stephen J. Pyne. *Vestal Fire: An Environmental History Told Through Fire, of Europe and Europe's Encounter with the World* (Seattle: University of Washington Press, 1997).

16. Whittle, "First Farmers," has a summary of the literature.

17. For this research, see R. Alexander Bentley, Chikhi Lounes, and T. Douglas Price, "The Neolithic transition in Europe: Comparing broad scale genetic and local scale isotopic evidence," *Antiquity* 77(295) (2003): 112–117. Also T. Douglas Price et al., "Prehistoric human migration in the *Linearbankeramik* of Central Europe," *Antiquity* 75(289) (2001): 593–603.

18. Williams, "First Farmers," has a definitive analysis.

19. Whittle, "First Farmers."

20. Sherratt, *Economy and Society in Prehistoric Europe*, chap. 13.

21. Caroline Malone, *Avebury* (London: English Heritage, 1989), is the best popular account. See also Alisdair Whittle, "The Neolithic of the Avebury area: Sequence, environment, settlement, and monuments," *Oxford Journal of Archaeology* 12(1) (1993): 29–53.

22. Stuart Piggott, *The West Kennet Long Barrow Excavations 1955–6* (London: Her Majesty's Stationary Office, 1963).

CHAPTER 7: DROUGHTS AND CITIES

1. Literature on southern Mesopotamia is abundant. Charles K. Maisels, *The Near East: Archaeology in the "Cradle of Civilization"* (London: Routledge, 1993). See also the same author's *The Emergence of Civilization* (London: Routledge, 1999).

2. Nicholas Postgate, *Early Mesopotamia: Economy and Society at the Dawn of History* (London: Kegan Paul, 1993).

3. Leonard Woolley wrote reams on Ur. His *Excavations at Ur* (New York: Scribners, 1930), is a widely read popular account. See also Brian Fagan. *Return to Babylon* (Boston: Little Brown, 1979), for the general historical background.

4. Samuel Kramer, *The Sumerians.* (Chicago: University of Chicago Press, 1963), remains the best popular source on Sumerian literature. Quote from p. 56.

5. Harvey Weiss, "Beyond the Younger Dryas: Collapse as adaptation to abrupt climate change in ancient west Asia and the eastern Mediterranean," in Garth Bawdon and Richard Martin Reycraft, eds. *Environmental Disaster and the Archaeology of Human Response* (Albuquerque: Maxwell Museum of Anthropology, 2000), pp. 63–74.

6. Weiss, "Beyond the Younger Dryas."

7. Weiss, "Beyond the Younger Dryas."

8. First identified by Leonard Woolley. See Susan Pollock, *Ancient Mesopotamia: The Eden That Never Was* (Cambridge: Cambridge University Press, 1999), chap. 3.

9. Frank Hole, "Environmental instabilities and urban origins," in Gil Stein and M. S. Rothman, eds., *Chiefdoms and Early States in the Near East: The Organizational Dynamics of Complexity* (Madison, WI: Prehistory Press, 1994), pp. 121–143. See also McCorriston and Hole, op. cit. 1991.

10. Joy McCorriston and Frank Hole, "The Ecology of Seasonal Stress and the Origins of Agriculture in the Near East," *American Anthropologist* 93 (1991): 46–69.

11. Mike Davis, *Late Victorian Holocausts* (New York: Verso, 2001), part 1, offers a remarkable analysis of Victorian famine that is truly frightening in its implications for our times.

12. McCorriston and Hole, "Ecology of Seasonal Stress," p. 51.

13. McCorriston and Hole, "Ecology of Seasonal Stress," p. 52.

14. Hole, "Environmental instabilities."

15. Pollock, *Ancient Mesopotamia.* For a good summary of Sumerian religion, see Kramer, *The Sumerians,* chap. 5.

16. Kramer, *The Sumerians,* p. 77.

17. Kramer, *The Sumerians,* p.78.

18. Robert McC. Adams, *Heartland of Cities* (Chicago: University of Chicago Press, 1981).

19. This incident was described by J. S. Cooper, *Reconstructing History from Ancient Inscriptions: The Lagash-Umma Border Dispute* (Malibu, CA: Undena Publications, 1983).

20. Guillermo Algaze, "The Uruk expansion," *Current Anthropology* 30(5) (1989): 571–608.

21. Fagan, *Return to Babylon,* chaps. 9 and 10.

22. Key references on the Akkadians are Mario Liverani, ed., *Akkad: The First World Empire* (Padua: Sargon, 1993). See also Hans J. Nissen, "Settlement patterns and material culture of the Akkadian period: Continuity and discontinuity," in Mario Liverani, ed., *Akkad: The First World Empire* (Padua: Sargon, 1993), pp. 91–106. Also Piotr Steinkeller, "Early political development in Mesopotamia and the origins of the Sargonic empire," in Liverani, ed., *Akkad,* pp. 107–130.

23. This section is based on Harvey Weiss and Marie-Agnès Courty, "The genesis and collapse of the Akkadian empire: The accidental refraction of historical law," in Mario Liverani, ed., *Akkad: The First World Empire* (Padua: Sargon, 1993), pp. 131–156. Also on Weiss, "Beyond the Younger Dryas." See also Harvey Weiss et al.,

"The genesis and collapse of third millennium north Mesopotamian civilization," *Science* 261 (1993): 995–1004.

24. Summarized by Barbara Bell, "The Dark Ages in ancient history, I. The first Dark Age in Egypt," *American Journal of Archaeology* 75 (1971): 1–26.

CHAPTER 8: GIFTS OF THE DESERT

1. Neil Roberts, *The Holocene: An Environmental History*, 2nd ed. (Oxford: Blackwell, 1998), pp. 115–120.

2. The notion of a Saharan pump comes from Neil Roberts, "Pleistocene environments in time and space," in Robert Foley, ed., *Community Ecology and Human Adaptation in the Pleistocene* (London: Academic Press, 1984), pp. 25–53.

3. Andrew R. Smith, *Pastoralism in Africa* (London: Hurst, 1992).

4. Roberts, *The Holocene,* p. 116.

5. Descriptions of Saharan rock art abound. A recent and admirable summary is Alfred Muzzolini, "Saharan Africa," in David Whitley, ed., *Handbook of Rock Art Research* (Walnut Creek, CA: AltaMira Press), pp. 605–636. A comprehensive bibliography accompanies the article.

6. Fred Wendorf, Romauld Schild, and Angela Close, *Loaves and Fishes: The Prehistory of Wadi Kubbaniya* (Dallas: Southern Methodist University Press, 1986), summarizes this important site.

7. J. Desmond Clark, "A Re-examination of the evidence for agricultural origins in the Nile Valley," *Proceedings of the Prehistoric Society* 37(2) (1971): 34–79.

8. Rudolph Kuper, ed., *Forschungen zur Umweltgeschichte der Ostsahara* (Koln: Heinrich Barth Institut, 1989).

9. Stefan Kröpelan, "Untersuchungen zum Sedimentationsmilieu von Playas im Gilf Kebir (Südwest Ägypten)," in Kuper, ed., *Forschungen*, pp. 183–306; Katharina Neumann, "Vegetationsgeschichte der Ostsahara im Holozän Holzkohlen aus prähistorischen Fundstellen," in Kuper, ed., *Forschungen,* pp. 13–182. Also: Compton J. Tucker, Harold E. Dregne, and Wilbur W. Newcomb, "Expansion and contraction of the Sahara Desert from 1980 to 1990," *Science* 253 (1991): 299–301; Wim Van Neer and Hans-Peter Uerpmann, "Palaeoecological significance of the Holocene faunal remains of the B.O.S. missions," in Kuper, ed., *Forschungen,* p. 307–341.

10. Smith, *Pastoralism in Africa,* (1992).

11. Described in Kuper, ed., *Forschungen*.

12. *War Commentaries of Julius Caesar,* trans. Rex Warner (New York: New American Library, 1963), p. 222.

13. Research quoted in Smith, *Pastoralism in Africa,* chap. 7.

14. Smith, *Pastoralism in Africa,* chap. 7.

15. Fred Wendorf et al., eds., *Cattle Keepers of the Eastern Sahara: The Neolithic of Bir Kiseiba* (Dallas: Southern Methodist University Press, 1984).

16. A good summary of Saharan domestication evidence appears in Fiona Marshall and Elizabeth Hildebrand, "Cattle before crops: The beginnings of food production in

Africa," *Journal of World Prehistory* 16(2) (2002): 99–143. See also the essays in Fekri Hassan, ed., *Droughts, Food, and Culture* (New York: Plenum/Kluwer, 2002); Karim Sadr, "Ancient pastoralists in the Sudan and in South Africa," in *Tides of the Desert: Contributions to the Archaeology and Environmental History of Africa in Honour of Rudolph Kuper*, ed. Jennerstrasse 8 (Köln: Heinrich-Barth-Institut, 2002), pp. 471–484.

17. Marshall and Hildebrand, "Cattle before crops."

18. Marshall and Hildebrand, "Cattle before crops."

19. The Predynastic cultures of Egypt have been described by many authors. Fekri Hassan's "The Pre-Dynastic of Egypt," *Journal of World Prehistory* 2 (2) (1988): 135–186, is an excellent starting point.

20. An account of the Badarian culture that controversially places greater emphasis on their cattle-herding activities will be found in Toby Wilkinson, *Genesis of the Pharaohs* (London and New York: Thames and Hudson, 2003).

21. Wilkinson, *Genesis of the Pharaohs,* presents this dating and the controversial arguments that follow.

22. Described by Barry Kemp, *Ancient Egypt: The Anatomy of a Civilization* (London: Routledge, 1989), arguably the best analysis of Ancient Egypt ever written.

23. Described by Hassan, "The Pre-Dynastic of Egypt."

24. William Willcocks, *Sixty Years in the East* (London: Blackwell, 1935).

25. Analyzed by Kemp, *Ancient Egypt*. Also Michael A. Hoffman et al., *The Predynastic of Hierakonopolis* (Cairo: Egyptian Studies Association, 1982).

CHAPTER 9: THE DANCE OF AIR AND OCEAN

1. The history of El Niño is described in César N. Caviedes, *El Niño in History: Storming Through the Ages* (Gainesville: University Press of Florida, 2001). See also Brian Fagan, *Floods, Famines, and Emperors: El Niño and the Collapse of Civilizations* (New York: Basic Books, 1999).

2. George Philander, *Is the Temperature Rising?* (Princeton, NJ: Princeton University Press, 1998).

3. Michael Glantz, *Currents of Change: Impacts of El Niño and La Niña on Climate and Society*, 2nd ed. (Cambridge: Cambridge University Press, 2001), is a wonderful basic source on ENSO.

4. Jay S. Fein and Pamela L., Stephens, eds., *Monsoons* (New York: John Wiley, 1987), is a good starting point on this subject.

5. Mike Davis, *Late Victorian Holocausts* (New York: Verso, 2001).

6. Barry Kemp, *Ancient Egypt: The Anatomy of a Civilization* (London: Routledge, 1989), p. 43, where an admirable essay on Egyptian kingship can be found.

7. Fekri Hassan, "Nile floods and political disorder in early Egypt," In H. Nüzhet Dalfes, George Kulka, and Harvey Weiss, eds., *Third Millennium B.C. Climate Change and Old World Collapse* (Berlin: Springer-Verlag, 1994), pp. 1–24.

8. This section is based on Barbara Bell, "The Dark Ages in ancient history, I. The first Dark Age in Egypt," *American Journal of Archaeology* 75 (1971): 1–26; and

her "Climate and the history of Egypt: The Middle Kingdom," *American Journal of Archaeology* 79 (1975): 223–269.

9. Bell, "Dark Ages in ancient history," where quote citations will be found.

10. *The Admonitions of Ipuwer* (Papyrus Leiden 334) are published in Miriam Lichtheim, *Ancient Egyptian Literature: A Book of Readings*, 3 vols. (Berkeley: University of California Press, 1973–1980).

11. Harvey Weiss, "Beyond the Younger Dryas: Collapse as adaptation to abrupt climate change in ancient west Asia and the eastern Mediterranean," in Garth Bawdon and Richard Martin Reycraft, eds. *Environmental Disaster and the Archaeology of Human Response* (Albuquerque: Maxwell Museum of Anthropology, 2000), pp. 63–74.

12. The Uluburun shipwreck is described in many articles. For a popular account, see Brian Fagan, *Time Detectives* (New York: Simon & Schuster, 1995), chap. 9.

13. Amarna letters: Raymond Cohen and Raymond Westbrook, eds., *Amarna Diplomacy: The Beginnings of International Relations* (Baltimore: Johns Hopkins University Press, 2000), p. 112.

14. Trevor Bryce, *The Kingdom of the Hittites* (Oxford: Clarendon Press, 1998), offers an excellent general description of Hittite civilization. See also O. R. Gurney, *The Hittites* (London and New York: Thames and Hudson, 1990).

15. Rhys Carpenter, *Discontinuity in Greek Civilization* (Cambridge: Cambridge University Press, 1966).

16. Reid A. Bryson, Hubert H. Lamb, and D. L. Donley, "Drought and the decline of Mycenae," *Antiquity* 467 (1974): 46–50.

17. Barry Weiss, "The decline of Bronze Age civilization as a possible response to climatic change," *Climatic Change* 4(2) (1982): 173–198.

18. Robert Fagles, op. cit. Book 18, (1990), p. 485.

19. William Taylour, *The Mycenaeans*, 2nd ed. (London and New York: Thames and Hudson, 1990), gives a good general description of Mycenaean civilization.

20. Thucydides, *History of the Pelopponesian War*, trans. Charles Foster Smith (Cambridge, MA: Harvard University Press, 1935), p. 3.

21. Michael C. Astour, "New evidence on the last days of Ugarit," *American Journal of Archaeology* 69 (1965): 253–258.

22. Brian Fagan, *Egypt of the Pharaohs* (Washington, DC: National Geographic Society, 2000), pp. 249–252.

CHAPTER 10: CELTS AND ROMANS

1. Ammianus Marcellinus (A.D. 330–395) was the last great Latin historian of the Roman empire. Quote from *Ammianus Marcellinus*, trans. John C. Rolfe (Cambridge, MA: Harvard University Press, 1958–63), vol. 3, p. 111.

2. Carole E. Crumley and William H. Marquandt, eds., *Regional Dynamics: Burgundian Landscapes in Historical Perspective* (San Diego: Academic Press, 1987).

Crumley's chapter, "Celtic Settlement Before the Conquest: The Dialectics of Landscape and Power," pp. 237–264, is relevant for this section.

3. Anthony Harding, "Reformation in Barbarian Europe, 1300–60 B.C.," in Barry Cunliffe, ed., *Prehistoric Europe: An Illustrated History* (Oxford: Oxford University Press, 1994), pp. 304–335.

4. Bent Aaby, "Cyclical climatic variations in climate over the past 5500 years reflected in raised bogs," *Nature* 263 (1976): 281–284.

5. Quoted in Sigurdur Thorarinsson, *The Eruption of Hekla, 1947–1948* (Reykjavik: H. F. Leiftur, 1967), p. 6.

6. For Hekla, see Zelle Zeilinga de Boer and Donald Theodore Sanders, *Volcanoes in Human History: The Far-reaching Effects of Major Eruptions* (Princeton, NJ: Princeton University Press, 2002), chap. 5.

7. Franklin's weather observations were the subject of his "Meteorological imaginations and conjectures," which can be found in John Bigelow, ed., *The Complete Works of Benjamin Franklin* (New York: G. P. Putnam, 1888), p. 488.

8. The Mt. Tambora eruption is described in Brian Fagan, *The Little Ice Age* (New York: Basic Books, 2001), chap. 10.

9. Jane Dunn, *Moon in Eclipse: A Life of Mary Shelley* (London: Weidenfeld and Nicholson, 1978), p. 271.

10. Johann Huizinga, *The Autumn of the Middle Ages* (Chicago: University of Chicago Press), pp. 1–2.

11. A somewhat outdated description of the Ice Man appears in Konrad Spindler, *The Man in the Ice* (New York: Crown, 1994). More recent revelations are in specialist literature.

12. Andrew Fleming, "The prehistoric landscape of Dartmoor. Part I: South Dartmoor," *Proceedings of the Prehistoric Society* 44 (1978): 97–123. Also, the same author's "The prehistoric landscape of Dartmoor. Part 2: North and East Dartmoor," *Proceedings of the Prehistoric Society* 49 (1983): 195–242. Discussed, also, by Neil Roberts, *The Holocene: An Environmental History*, 2nd ed. (Oxford: Blackwell, 1998), pp. 198–199.

13. Discussed by Bas van Geel et al., "The role of solar forcing upon climate change," *Quaternary Science Review* 18 (1999): 331–338. Maunder Minimum is discussed in Fagan, *The Little Ice Age*, pp. 120–123.

14. Bas van Geel and Bjorn E. Berglund, "A causal link between a climatic deterioration around 850 cal BC and a subsequent rise in human population density in NW-Europe?" *Terra Nostra* 7 (2000): 126–130.

15. Caius Julius Caesar, *Seven Commentaries on the Gallic War*, trans. Carolyn Hammond (New York: Oxford University Press), Commentary 5:2. Roberts, *The Holocene*, p. 201.

16. Barry Cunliffe, *The Ancient Celts* (London: Penguin Books, 1999), is the standard account of Celtic life and includes a comprehensive guide to further reading.

17. A summary of Biskupin will be found in Peter S. Wells, *Farms, Villages and Cities: Commerce and Urban Origins in Late Prehistoric Europe* (Ithaca, NY: Cornell University Press, 1984), chap. 5.

18. Timothy Taylor. 1994. "Thracians, Scythians, and Sacians, 800 B.C. to A.D. 300," In Cunliffe, ed., *Prehistoric Europe*, pp. 373–410.

19. Posidonius (c. 135–c. 51 B.C.) was a Stoic philosopher, scientist, and historian, who traveled in southern Gaul in the 90s B.C. Quotes from Cunliffe, *Ancient Celts*, pp. 105–106.

20. This section draws from Cunliffe, *Ancient Celts*, chaps. 3 and 4. Livy, *History*, bk. 5:34, quoted in Cunliffe, *Ancient Celts*, pp. 68–9. See also the fundamental source on the migrations, H. D. Rankin, *Celts and the Classical World* (Portland, OR: Aeropagitica Press, 1987).

21. A well-known passage from Strabo's *Geography*, bk. 4(4):2. Quoted in Cunliffe, *Ancient Celts*, p. 93.

22. Crumley, "Celtic Settlement Before the Conquest."

23. Movements of the zones chronicled in Crumley, "Celtic Settlement Before the Conquest." For information on the changes in agriculture, see Helena Hamerow, *Early Medieval Settlements: The Archaeology of Rural Communities in North-West Europe 400–900* (Oxford: Oxford University Press, 2002), chap. 5.

24. Summarized by Peter Wells, *The Barbarians Speak* (Princeton, NJ: Princeton University Press, 1999), chap. 5.

25. Crumley, "Celtic Settlement Before the Conquest."

26. Hamerow, *Early Medieval Settlements,* chap. 5.

27. This section is based on a diversity of sources, synthesized by David Keys, *Catastrophe* (London: Century Books, 1999).

28. Procopius, *History of the Wars*, trans. H. B. Dewing (Cambridge, MA: Harvard University Press, 1914), bk. IV, xiv, 36, 39–42.

29. A controversial interpretation of ancient climates appears in M. G. L. Baillie. *Exodus to Arthur: Catastrophic Encounters with Comets* (London: Batsford, 1999). This section is based on Keys, *Catastrophe,* Pt. IX.

30. On the Avars, see Keys, *Catastrophe*, Pt. III.

31. Quoted in Keys, *Catastrophe*, p. 49.

32. Her Majesty's Stationary Office, *A Meteorological Chronology Up to 1450*, quoted in Keys, *Catastrophe*, p. 114.

33. R. White and P. Barker, *Wroxeter: The Life and Death of a Roman City* (Stroud, Eng.: Tempus, 1998).

CHAPTER 11: THE GREAT DROUGHTS

1. Norman Davies, *Europe: A History* (New York: Oxford University Press, 1996), p. 356.

2. Douglas J. Kennett and James P. Kennett, "Competitive and cooperative responses to climatic instability in coastal southern California," *American Antiquity* 65 (2000): 379–95.

3. Another important summary of the impact of the Medieval Warm Period on the southern California coast is L. Mark Raab and Daniel O. Larson, "Medieval climatic anomaly and punctuated cultural evolution in coastal southern California," *American Antiquity* 62 (1997): 319–36.

4. Quoted from Rose Marie Beebe and Robert M. Senkewicz, eds., *Lands of Promise and Despair: Chronicles of Early California, 1535–1846* (Berkeley, CA: Heyday Books, 2002). p. 33.

5. Harold E. Bolton, ed., *Fray Juan Crespi: Missionary Explorer on the Pacific Coast 1769–1774* (Berkeley, CA: University of California Press, 1927), p. 37.

6. A summary of Chumash culture may be found in Brian Fagan, *Before California: An Archaeologist Looks at Our Earliest Ancestors* (Walnut Creek, CA: AltaMira Press, 2003), chap. 14.

7. A complex literature on California acorns is summarized in Fagan, *Before California*, chap. 6.

8. This section is based on Jeanne Arnold, ed., *Origins of a Pacific Coast Chiefdom* (Salt Lake City, UT: University of Utah Press, 2001), chap. 14.

9. This section is based on Patricia M. Lambert and Phillip L. Walker, "Physical enthropological evidence for the evolution of social complexity in coastal southern California," *American Antiquity* 65 (1991): 963–73, and Patricia M. Lambert, "Health in prehistoric populations of the Santa Barbara Channel Islands," *American Antiquity* 68 (1993): 509–22.

10. Phillip L. Walker, "Cranial injuries as evidence of violence in prehistoric California," *American Journal of Physical Anthropology* 80 (1989): 51–61.

11. Arnold, *Origins of a Pacific Coast Chiefdom,* chap. 14, has an extended discussion.

12. The archaeology of the Southwest and of the Ancestral Pueblo is well summarized by Linda Cordell, *Prehistory of the Southwest,* 2nd ed. (New York: Academic Press, 1997). See also Stephen Plog, *Ancient Peoples of the American Southwest,* (London and New York: Thames and Hudson, 1997).

13. Travis Hudson and Frank Underhay, *Crystals in the Sky* (Banning, CA: Malki Museum Press, 1978.

14. Quoted from Tesse Naranjo, "Thoughts on migration by Santa Clara Pueblo," *Journal of Anthropological Archaeology* 14 (1995): 249–250.

15. Cordell, *Prehistory of the Southwest*, chaps. 8ff.

16. Chaco Canyon's archaeology is diffuse and published in many books and journals. Gwinn Vivian and Bruce Hilpert, *The Chaco Handbook* (Salt Lake City, UT: University of Utah Press, 2002), summarizes all aspects of the canyon and will lead the reader into the more specialized literature.

17. Carla van West, "Agricultural potential and carrying capacity in southwestern Colorado, A.D. 901–1300," in Michael A. Adler, ed., *The Prehistoric Pueblo World, A.D. 1150–1350* (Tucson, AZ: University of Arizona Press, 1996), pp. 214–227.

18. Again, there is a profuse literature on the Ancestral Pueblo. For the purposes of this chapter, see Jeffrey Dean's essay "A model of Anasazi behavioral adaptation," in George Gumerman, ed., *The Anasazi in a Changing Environment* (Cambridge: Cambridge University Press, 1988), pp. 25–44. See also Jeffrey S. Dean and Garey S. Funkhauser, "Dendroclimatic reconstructions for the southern Colorado Plateau," in W. J. Waugh, ed., *Climate Change in the Four Corners and Adjacent Regions* (Grand Junction, CO: Mesa State College, 1994), pp. 85–104.

19. Linda Cordell, "Aftermath of chaos in the Pueblo Southwest," In Garth Bawdon and Richard Martin Reycraft, eds., *Environmental Disaster and the Archaeology of Human Response* (Albuquerque: Maxwell Museum of Anthropology, 2000), pp. 179–193.

20. Cordell, "Aftermath," and *Prehistory of the Southwest,* chap. 11.

21. A. E. Rautman, "Resource variability, risk, and the structures of social networks: An example from the prehistoric Southwest," *American Antiquity* 58 (1993): 403–424.

22. John R. Roney, "Mesa Verde manifestations south of the San Juan River," *Journal of Anthropological Archaeology* 14 (1995): 170–183.

23. Naranjo, "Thoughts on migration by Santa Clara Pueblo," p. 250.

CHAPTER 12: MAGNIFICENT RUINS

1. John Lloyd Stephens, *Incidents of Travel in Central America, Chiapas and Yucatan* (New York: Harpers, 1841), pp. 175–176.

2. Michael Coe, *Breaking the Maya Code* (London and New York: Thames and Hudson, 1992), offers an excellent popular account of decipherment.

3. General accounts of Maya civilization abound. The most widely available is Michael Coe, *The Maya*, 6th ed. (London and New York: Thames and Hudson, 1999).

4. Linda Schele and David Freidel, *A Forest of Kings* (New York: William Morrow, 1990), is a widely quoted, if sometimes controversial, journey through the Maya world as revealed by glyphs. Linda Schele, David Freidel, and Joy Parker, *Maya Cosmos* (New York: William Morrow, 1993), is a sequel about the Maya cosmic perspective.

5. Scott Fedick, ed., *The Managed Mosaic* (Salt Lake City: University of Utah Press, 1996), is the source for this summary.

6. Vernon L. Scarborough, "Resilience, resource use, and socioeconomic organization: A Mesoamerican pathway," in Garth Bawdon and Richard Martin Reycraft, eds., *Environmental Disaster and the Archaeology of Human Response* (Albuquerque: Maxwell Museum of Anthropology, 2000), pp. 195–212.

7. David Webster, *The Fall of the Ancient Maya* (London and New York: Thames and Hudson, 2002), is an excellent up-to-date account. Also T. Patrick Culbert, "The collapse of classic Maya civilization," in Norman Yoffee and George Cowgill, eds., *The Collapse of Ancient States and Civilizations* (Tucson: University of Arizona

Press, 1988), pp. 212–234. See also the same author's edited *The Classic Maya Collapse* (Albuquerque: University of New Mexico Press, 1973).

8. David A. Hodell, Jason H. Curtis, and Mark Brenner, "Possible role of climate in the collapse of classic Maya civilization," *Nature* 375 (1995): 341–347. See also David A. Hodell et al., "Solar forcing of drought frequency in the Maya lowlands," *Science* 292 (2001): 1367–1370.

9. Gerald Haug et al., "Climate and the collapse of Maya civilization." *Science* 299 (2003): 1731–1735. I am grateful to Gerald Haug for stimulating discussion on these findings.

10. Richardson Benedict Gill, *The Great Maya Droughts: Water, Life, and Death* (Albuquerque: University of New Mexico Press, 2000), is a gold mine of information.

11. Pedro Cieza de León (1518–1554) is a major source on the conquest of Peru and on the Andean region at Spanish contact. The quote is from his *Discovery and Conquest of Peru: Chronicles of the New World Encounter*, trans. Alexandra Parma Cook and David Noble Cook (Durham: Unniversity of North Carolina Press, 1998), p. 125.

12. Alan Kolata, *Tiwanaku* (Oxford: Blackwell, 1993), is a useful summary of the city and state.

13. This section is based on Alan Kolata, "The agricultural foundations of the Tiwanaku state: A view from the heartland," *American Antiquity* 51(4) (1986): 748–62. See also Alan Kolata and Charles Ortloff, "Thermal analysis of Tiwanaku raised field systems in the Lake Titicaca Basin of Bolivia," *Journal of Archaeological Sciencc* 16(3) (1989): 233–63.

14. See Alan Kolata, "Environmental thresholds and the "natural history" of an Andean civilization," in Bawdon and Reycraft, *Environmental Disaster,* pp. 163–178.

15. L. Thompson et al., "A 1,500-year tropical ice core record of climate: Potential relations to man in the Andes," *Science* 234 (1986): 361–364.

16. Kolata, "Environmental thresholds," p. 173.

EPILOGUE

1. Isaiah 5:25.

2. Quoted in William Chester Jordan, *The Great Famine* (Princeton, NJ: Princeton University Press, 1996), p. 147. Jordan's book is a magnificent study of this catastrophe. See also Henri Lemaître, ed., *Chronique et Annales de Gilles le Muisit, Abbé de Saint-Martin de Tournai (1272–1352)* (Paris: Ancon, 1912).

3. The Little Ice Age is described for a general audience in Fagan, *The Little Ice Age* (New York: Basic Books, 2001).

ACKNOWLEDGMENTS

The Long Summer developed out of two previous books about climate change in the past. In *Floods, Famines, and Emperors* I examined the role of El Niños and related phenomena on ancient societies. *The Little Ice Age* described the volatile and ever-changing climate of A.D. 1300 to 1860, from Medieval times in Europe to the Industrial Revolution. The current volume paints a longer climatic canvas, from the late Ice Age to the end of the Medieval Warm Period. It is in many respects a sequel to the earlier books and involved complex interviewing, as well as research—in laboratories and libraries, and in the field—into a bewildering array of subjects. These included deep-sea cores, the properties of simple bows, Danish eels, acorns, Maya iconography, and Assyrian writings on drought.

Inevitably, a book of this broad scope drew on the expertise of many scholars, too many to thank individually. One of the joys of writing a work like this is what you learn from people, often outside your own discipline. My e-mail correspondence became deliciously esoteric at times, and I am grateful to the many colleagues and friends who sent me on my cyberway toward the right experts. I owe a particular debt to Richard Alley, David Anderson, David Brown, William Calvin, Barry Cunliffe, Jeffrey Dean, Karen Greer, Donn Grenda, Gerald Haug, John Hoffecker, Doug Kennett, Sturt Manning, George Michaels, Andrew Moore, Patrick Nunn, Neil Roberts, Alison Rautman, Andrew Robinson, Peter Rowly-Conwy, Yvonne Salis, Chris Scarre, and Stuart Smith. If I have omitted your name, my apologies and my heartfelt thanks for your help.

Only those who have had the privilege of working with a caring and expert editor can know how much Bill Frucht of Basic Books has contributed to this book. His black pen is perceptive, his insights and encouragement are beyond rubies. I value our long-term association and friendship more than I can say. The same goes for Shelly Lowenkopf, who has been at my side throughout the gestation of *The Long Summer*. His enthusiasm is boundless, his insights are priceless, his companionship and friendship much valued. My agent, Susan Rabiner, has been a tower of strength from the beginning. Thanks, too, to the production staff at Perseus, who have made a beautiful book out of my arabesques.

Lastly, my thanks and love to Lesley and Ana, who have tolerated my writing for many years, and to the cat Copernicus, who invariably gets in the way. No wonder they (cat and humans alike) *never* read my books!

Funding for some travel in connection with this book came from Academic Senate Funds of the University of California, Santa Barbara.

Brian Fagan

INDEX